I have found the book that I wish I had wr
sidered and reread, *In Search of Education*
Embrace the Uncertain is the most refreshi
field that I have read for some time. At the outset it is a thorough,
ing, provocative and scholarly work that presses the reader to account for
their own educational thinking and practices. Rix offers absorbing narratives to lead us into very accessible explanations of the assumptions we
hold that direct our thinking about and practices in education. Using the
metaphor of "embrace" we are invited to explore and analyse our own
beliefs and sets of relationships, conceptual and practical, with education
and schooling. Drawing on Dewey, amongst many others (I did say this is
a meticulously scholarly book), we are presented with education as a
means for applying certitude in an increasingly uncertain world.

Jonathan Rix lithely exposes obviously ridiculous foundations of the
way we have gone about the business of educating and schooling while
reassuring the reader that we can, by "embracing the uncertain" do it
another way. In doing so, we will untether ourselves from the misadven-
ture of schooling in its present form and create opportunities for children
and young people free from the very thin identities we have bestowed
upon them that hinder learning. Those around me will certainly be urged
to procure and read this thought-changing book.

Roger Slee, *PhD, Professor in Disability and Inclusion,*
University of Leeds, Founder and Editor-in-Chief,
International Journal of Inclusive Education

I found this book absorbing, funny, moving and thought provoking. As
educationalists, the book challenges us to stop wanting, needing, planning
for and expecting certainty, and it calls on us to resist fixedness in our
pursuit of a "better" way. I have learned to question my own dependence
on certainty because as Jonathan Rix explains so eloquently, we can keep
education open to possibilities if we go where uncertainty leads us. In this
book we also learn that uncertainty (rather than certainty) is the substrate
for developing more inclusive and participative ways of being through
education. The author employs anecdote, theory, philosophy, drawings,
diagrams, models and polemic to support and entertain us in our journey
toward relinquishing certainty in favour of more fluid ways of being. Most
of all, the book reminds us that singular, monolithic, authoritarian and
fixed positions on what education is and how it should unfold, are useless.
Please read the book. It will inspire you!

Deborah Robinson, *EdD (SFHEA), Professor of Special Educational*
Needs and Inclusion, Institute of Education, University of Derby

At a time when educational outcomes are the tail wagging the dog, when research gurus promote off-the-shelf solutions and top-down approaches to solve educational inequities, when curriculum means follow a textbook, and when research fetishize certainty through experimental designs and big data analysis, Jonathan Rix challenges the reader to do the opposite: Embrace uncertainty. *In Search of Education, Participation and Inclusion* offers a fresh look at educational exclusion and its possible solutions. This book, filled with intimate stories and thoughtful reflections, argues that uncertainty can lead us on an unimagined path that can be more expansive and inclusive than those we imagine in the first place. Those looking for easy (certain) solutions to complex educational exclusions search elsewhere; those who have the courage to embrace the uncertain and serpentine path towards a more just and inclusive education, look no further.

Federico R. Waitoller, *PhD, Associate Professor,*
Department of Special Education at The University of Illinois at
Chicago, Associate Editor, Review of Educational Research

In Search of Education, Participation and Inclusion provides the reader with an excellent critical overview of current theories and practices concerning inclusive education. It looks at this relevant subject from multiple perspectives. It navigates the complex and often conflictual debate about inclusive education by developing an exciting dialogue with other disciplines that helps review and expand our frame of reference regarding this topic. In addition, it goes straight to the point in addressing some of the most pressing questions that researchers and practitioners usually struggle with when they aim to secure all children more equal and fair opportunities for education. Finally, the author effectively supports reflection on educational research and practices with powerful examples taken from his wide professional and personal experience. Accordingly, while the book helps the reader achieve a thorough understanding of the complex problems inclusive education faces today, it also provides an authoritative guide to those working in this crucial field.

Fabio Dovigo, *PhD, Professor, Educational Psychology Department,*
Danish School of Education, Aarhus University,
Founding Editor, European Journal of Inclusive Education

IN SEARCH OF EDUCATION, PARTICIPATION AND INCLUSION

In Search of Education, Participation and Inclusion offers an original, coherent and inspiring approach to the delivery of education for all. **Jonathan Rix**, backed by extensive research, builds upon his wide-ranging professional and personal experiences to explore three conceptual innovations – models of certainty and uncertainty, the *while* of participation and communities of provision. Through these innovations, the reader examines the challenges faced by school systems in delivering inclusive and participatory experiences of learning.

Topics explored include:

- theories of education, participation and inclusion.
- the constraints on our education systems as they struggle to deliver certainty in a world of uncertainty.
- how the challenges of our systems collaborate with inequality to produce marginalised experiences of participation.
- the exclusionary nature of our communities of provision.
- how we can understand and enhance moments of participation.
- how embracing uncertainty can lead to more meaningful participation and towards more inclusive communities.
- policies and practices that enhance the possibility of education for all.

This is a crucial read for any educator, educational leader or researcher with an interest in the development of innovative theory and practice in the fields of inclusive education and participatory practice.

Jonathan Rix is a professor of Participation & Learning Support at The Open University and Inland Norway University of Applied Sciences, having taught for many years in schools and other community settings. His award-winning research has included groundbreaking participatory projects involving disabled people, multi-national studies of special education, explorations of effective pedagogy in mainstream schools and parental experiences of services. Among his numerous publications is *Must Inclusion be Special?*, also published by Routledge.

IN SEARCH OF EDUCATION, PARTICIPATION AND INCLUSION

Embrace the Uncertain

Jonathan Rix

Routledge
Taylor & Francis Group

LONDON AND NEW YORK

Designed cover image: @carolinerix_pix

First published 2024
by Routledge
4 Park Square, Milton Park, Abingdon, Oxon OX14 4RN

and by Routledge
605 Third Avenue, New York, NY 10158

Routledge is an imprint of the Taylor & Francis Group, an informa business

British Library Cataloguing-in-Publication Data
A catalogue record for this book is available from the British Library

ISBN: 978-1-032-25071-7 (hbk)
ISBN: 978-1-032-25072-4 (pbk)
ISBN: 978-1-003-28140-5 (ebk)

DOI: 10.4324/9781003281405

Typeset in Sabon
by SPi Technologies India Pvt Ltd (Straive)

I am not sure who to dedicate this to. Obviously, it would be a good idea to dedicate it to Caroline, but then again the two young(ish) people who share our lives deserve a look in, Isabel and Robbie. But what about the rest of my family, Jamie, Helen, Louisa, Richard and all their children and grandchildren? What about my friends? I ought to thank Rune and John in particular. And what about Simon, he's put up with me for years. But if I start down that line, where do I stop? Should I mention Ryan, Bazzer, Greg and Jane? What about my parents, Caroline's parents, our parent's friends, the people I have taught, colleagues in so many places of work, the people who have supported me and my family over the years and those people I have read or listened to? They have all played their part. And now I start to think about it, there are quite a lot of others I could thank, living, dead, human and non-human. I mean I loved our dog Wally, and I still feel guilt about the five gerbils I killed when I was supposed to be looking after them for the school. And I am very grateful for having lived in some exceedingly friendly houses and to have spent many, many hours meandering through all kinds of bewitching landscapes. I love looking at birds too. And swimming, walking … Whilst the gerbil-guilt brings back so many people and places I should be apologising to, for the things I have said and done that were so out of place. If I start where do I stop? What about my history? My future? My known and unknown pasts and possibles? And what about you?

I dedicate this book to the unknown reader

CONTENTS

1

WHAT DOES IT TAKE TO EMBRACE? PART 1 – BEING APART

In the beginning...

Nearly six decades have passed since I learned how to spell 'blood'. I had just suggested the spelling was 'blud', and the teacher wanted to make it very clear I was wrong. She did this by spelling out her correct version whilst hitting me across the back of my knees with two fingers: 'B – thwack – L – thwack – O – thwack – O – thwack – D – thwack'. I can still spell blood as she wished. I recall she spelt it on my left leg. I still remember her name. About ten years after that, I had another teacher who thought they could get me to learn verb forms by twisting my ear. Perhaps unsurprisingly, the approach had by now lost its potency. I can remember his name and the ear he twisted but not the verb forms he cared so much about. My strongest memory is the sense of victory I had over him as my classmates looked on at my belligerent silence.

Education is a physical and social experience. It is emotional, sensory, cognitive, functional and ongoing. It is always in a relationship with the past, present and future. It is a relationship of environments, structures, peoples and being. Not surprisingly, therefore, our learning emerges and stays with us in ways that are hard to predict. This means that when we engage in any process of teaching (or the organisation of teaching and learning contexts), we are entering into a constantly contested space. This contestation is between and within all these relationships and their experiences of being. Upon entering this space, it makes sense to adopt a position, to have a guiding vision for the way in which we are going to manage ourselves (and hopefully others). This is not a radical suggestion of course.

DOI: 10.4324/9781003281405-1

The first question most people want answered when they arrive on their first teaching training/education course is something along the lines of 'How do I get them to behave/listen to me?'.

The view of most of my teachers – not uncommon in England when I was a lad and still believed by many people across the world – was that learning can be forced (or beaten) into the learner. It is based upon a banking notion of knowledge – that this predetermined information/skill/understanding/practice can be transferred into each (individual) learner. It is a short step from here to a presumption that resistance simply has to be overcome or broken down and that each (individual) learner will behave/listen if you show them that you mean business.

So, what relevance has this to the notion of an embrace? Isn't an embrace a thing of love and fellowship? Isn't it defined as clasping with affection, seizing eagerly and accepting cordially? Isn't it more akin to the kind of practice evident in this classroom experience, described by a primary teacher in Scotland she begins with the children:

> We'll look at a topic and I say what sort of things are you interested in. And I always explain to them it's pointless me planning a topic of work for you if you've done it already or you're not interested. I say because it's your learning that will be affected.
>
> *(Spratt, 2016, p. 235)*

She understands that they are in a relationship:

> So they're actually very happy to come out with an idea of telling me what they've learnt already, what they already know, so we can sort of do a little recap on that but then build on their interests.
>
> *(Spratt, 2016, p. 235)*

This practice probably seems far more constructive and engaging than using force. It is clearly situated in a completely different view of learning, in which the child is an active agent in the meaning making. It seems underpinned by friendliness, enthusiasm and cordiality. It is possible to suggest that the teacher sees knowledge as emerging from the context in which an issue is explored and arises through personal and collective experiences and expectations. In this second narrative, the child seems to be viewed with respect and regard, unlike in the tales from my youth where the respect and regard seemed to be lacking (or presumed to be in one direction only?).

But this is a huge over-simplification (of course). I feel sure that the teachers who were inflicting physical pain upon me thought they were doing the right thing. They believed in their model of learning and teaching. They would have regarded being a teacher as a moral and honourable occupation too. They may not have used the phrase, but they would have seen themselves as being socially just people delivering socially just goals, just as much as any teacher today. And (of course?) not all of my teachers thought that beating me was the best way to proceed (even if they wished to); some of them, for instance, focused on building relationships of trust.

A fundamental challenge for any advocate of educational change is the variety of beliefs and practices which any practitioner can (theoretically) choose to embrace with; for example, consider a study exploring the understandings of social justice among educators concerned with social justice (Thomas et al., 2019). Even though the educators had a seemingly unified goal, conflicting and contradictory understandings emerged. These included practitioners who didn't want to support activism to those who wanted to create agents of change. It included practitioners who saw social justice as being about changing learners and those who saw it as being about changing institutions. It included some practitioners who thought social justice was constrained by assessment or feared a checklist approach to difference or felt that the simple act of focusing upon the idea of social justice would alienate people from the outset. The practitioners might have presumed that in seeking social justice they were embracing the same idea, but actually they were all embracing something slightly different. As these differences emerged across this social justice project, the practitioners recognised that they needed to explore concepts and language, as well as who was served by practices and why and what the practices (can/could) look(ed) like. Thomas et al. suggested that these diverse perspectives and views could be seen as being in tension, requiring deeper understanding. For them, a way forward involved 'embracing the questions' (p. 31) posed by the tensions.

The idea of embracing such differences (perhaps of seeking common ground or coming to understand other people's points of view) has had many advocates over the years. But what might such an embrace entail?

Embrace – the metaphor?

Let's imagine a simple embrace for a moment. Imagine something you might wrap your arms around. A person, a creature, an animate or inanimate being; a parent, child, lover, cushion, tree or lamp-post. You choose. You embrace.

> Is this a one-off embrace or have you done this before? How long is (does) this embrace (feel)? Who/what can stop it? Is it public or private or is that immaterial? What motivates this embrace? Does it feel like a choice or an obligation or simply what you do? Do you feel safe in this embrace or does this feel like stepping into the unknown? Are you both embraced?

Are you both embracing? Are you both consciously engaged? Could you involve others? What/who else have you/they/it embraced before? Do you like to embrace/be embraced/be embracing?

There must be other questions that could be asked; there always are. But let's go back to the last question posed above. Can you see/feel a difference between those three states?

- Embrace
- Embraced
- Embracing

There are moments in an embrace when you are very aware of your own physical/emotional/conscious engagement. You see yourself and feel yourself in this moment; this can be infused with memories or thoughts of other possibilities, or you can be lost in it, wrapped up in its individuality. And you may wonder: is this 'you embracing them' or 'them embracing you'? There are moments where you are intensely aware of the response of the other; you can feel how they are reacting to you, you sense the shape they are taking and you may be aware of choices they are making and of their feelings in this moment. And then there can also be moments when you sense a point of togetherness, a oneness beyond me/I and you/it. This can be for the briefest moment. It can feel like a flash of epiphany. It can take your breath away. The embrace both holds and releases. You are beyond being others. And you can never quite know (unless the other can convince you?) that you shared that moment or whether it was all part of your own embrace and your responses to being embraced.

Now consider embracing something which is intangible: a belief, a practice, an understanding or an identity. How do you embrace a belief? How does a belief embrace you? Is there a moment of embracing where the belief and you are one? Let's go back to my 'blud'. The teacher had a belief about spelling, its importance and her role in getting pupils (we were definitely pupils) to spell correctly; she had a belief about who I was and how to get me to remember this package of information; she had beliefs that were enamoured by a particular pedagogy, through a particular curriculum. In the moment of my misspelling, she was in the embrace of these ideas; she held to them and they wrapped around her. They gave her the solution: 'B – thwack – L – thwack – O – thwack – O – thwack – D – thwack'. She (was) embrace/d/ ing by the belief, the understanding, the practice, an identity. And this drew me (and all the other witnesses to that spelling lesson) into this embrace, into a belief about school and learning and our place in it.

A key part of any embrace is that it is a process of enclosing and enfolding as well as being enclosed and enfolded. But the nature of the enclosure and enfoldment is not predetermined. An embrace can be a way to influence and include (or to be influenced and included), but its essence can vary hugely. An embrace is fundamentally an intimate relationship, one that is deeply felt. Its impact, influence, nature, essence and character can be positive or negative or both or neither. That is a matter of perspective. It is a process that can be momentary, repeated or ongoing, singular or collective. And it can be all of these things at the same time. After all, where did that embrace with blud/ blood begin – where will it end? An embrace is constantly situating itself. It is always in context, enacted in a time and a space. It is of the past, in the present and for the future. And in the human world, it will be social and cultural because it will always involve us.

Whose embrace is it anyway?

We (are) all embrace/d/ing.

≅ Some moments are small and fleeting.
≅ Some are lifelong and to our core.
≅ Some come, some go, some come back again.

Importantly (for this book at least), our embrace/d/ing can be both collectively and personally situated, and not always of our choosing. It is oh so easy to be drawn into an embrace and to then find it oh so hard to step away again.
But (and this may be a big but):

≅ for an embrace to begin, you must come into contact with it.
≅ for an embrace to end, you have to recognise that you are within it and you have to envision a place beyond.

[This last bullet point is (probably) a large part of what this book is trying to achieve. It aims to explore the complex interplay of embraces within the worlds of education and where they could possibly lead.]
So, what about me? When I engage in a moment of teaching, I am held by beliefs far closer to the Scottish teacher cited above (who saw that the child is an active agent in meaning making), rather than to the teachers who believe they should/can fill the child with knowledge. I am a fan of creativity in the learning space, of open learning opportunities and building upon our shared knowledge. I want to focus upon social relationships, responding to diverse access preferences and finding ways to represent people as they can be (rather than via boxes we can squeeze them into). I am enthused by the political message of the social model and of inclusion. I am one of those who sees social justice as being about transforming our systems and processes.

I see equitable provision as a matter of collective action, not something delivered individual by individual (Rix, 2015).

This very brief summary might be the kind of starting point needed if we embrace the questions as Thomas et al. suggested; a pencil portrait of the embrace where *I am*, to help you situate me. In many places (countries), such views are widely shared and in many others, they seem deeply unrealistic (and probably naive). But part of the embrace *I am* within is that we have to begin from where people are – not from where we think they should be. Learning (at any age and in any context) starts with what we know and what makes sense to us. To move ourselves to a different way of being – to *there*, we have to understand the embrace of others, not just because we have to take their views into consideration but because we have no choice. The 'I' and 'Us' are always 'Them'; we are always in relationships with each other. It may be way down our list of priorities, but my/your/our/their embrace is always mine/yours/ours/theirs too.

The asymmetry in an embrace?

Being in an ongoing relationship with each other's moments of embrace means these moments are subject to the power which exists within relationships, in the give and take between us (Foucault, 1980, 1982). And there will frequently be asymmetry in those moments.

If we accept that we are in the embrace of all ideas and practices associated with teaching, then we are all in an embrace with the dominant political, economic, cultural and environmental traditions that motivate and define our everyday experiences of learning. As part of the dominant education system, we acquiesce in these embraces. We are enwrapped by policies, structures and processes that govern what we can or cannot do, even if we do not want to be. These policies, structures and processes have asymmetric power, which embraces us. These policies, structures and processes will struggle to be responsive to the alternative embraces in which *I am/we/they are*.

One might conclude from this asymmetry, that if we wish to make a change, all that is required is political power to enforce a change in the education landscape. However, it never quite works like this; the power is always multi-directional, even if one feels powerless in the face of another's embrace.

Let's consider some 'dominant' ideas from recent years, to see how embraces can overlap and shift as institutional, collective and personal experiences merge and dissipate. Here are four examples that have (been) embraced (us) on a fairly global scale: comprehensive education, information communication technology, multicultural education and labels of special educational needs.

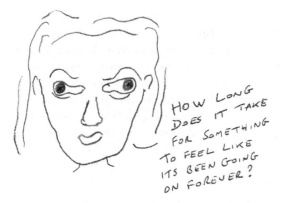

FIGURE 1.1 Embracing tradition.

1. A comprehensive embrace?

Comprehensive schooling began to (be) embrace/d/ing from the 1960s onwards. It was based upon a simple principle – that all children of a given age are educated together, in a single educational institution, in non-selective classes. Sass (2015) suggests that if we wish to understand the success or failure of comprehensive systems, we need to consider five concepts from Huber and Stephens (2001):

≅ the capacity of political institutions to veto key moves in a policy.
≅ the tendency to continue with policies that parties do not believe in but are popular.
≅ the need for key societal actors to find a policy attractive.
≅ the legacies of previous policies.
≅ the ideological hegemony within classes or movements.

Ironically, perhaps, these help us to see both how the comprehensive ideal was never fully embraced in many countries and how it has come to hold later policies in its own embrace.

The degree of comprehensiveness adopted by countries varied between national systems, as well as between primary, secondary and post-secondary levels of schooling (Sass, 2015). In Sweden and Finland, for example, a comprehensive system had been fully implemented by the start of the 1970s (West, 2016). A similar policy was being adopted in England but by 'request' to local authorities rather than by requirement. Here you could see all five concepts holding the process of change within their embrace, in ways that constrained its acceptance. Consequently, in England the number of comprehensives only ever peaked at about 80% of state schools (including rebranded secondary moderns which were part of a non-comprehensive, selective local authority systems) (Martin, 2020). Hardly surprisingly the comprehensive goals of social mobility were not delivered (Van de Werfhorst, 2018). The English policy was introduced too, without any generally agreed set of aims or purposes, with no attempt made to reorganise the private sector and little extra money to assist in the refurbishment and redevelopment of the schools. This created clear social and geographical variations between areas, which encouraged opposition and the search for alternatives (McCulloch, 2016).

The first alternative was the introduction of parent choice. This idea (was) embraced (in) both England and Sweden, resulting in the fragmenting of both the systems, even though they had developed differently. This change in policy however did not eradicate the language of comprehensive education. Even in systems where surreptitious and/or explicit selection was widely in practice (e.g. in England with its grammar schools, city-technology colleges, grant-maintained schools, specialist schools, private schools and academies), the discourse was still around providing education accessible to all, with entry to schools not being based upon selection. It would seem that the fundamental idea at the root of comprehensiveness felt/feels fair to a majority of people. The comprehensive idea has taken a firm hold in a collective embrace, even if the comprehensive means by which it is delivered has not.

2. A technological embrace?

Human history has been a constant flow of technological innovation. Since the 1970s, there has been a particular focus on information communication technology, with online and mobile hardware and software more recently coming to the fore. There has been huge investment in these technologies within schools. They have clearly been embraced with great commitment by policy makers at global, national and local levels. However, there has long been an evident lack of return on this investment (Twining, 2008). For example, they have been held up as an opportunity to engage with disabled people, but there is clearly still a digital divide for disabled learners (Seale, 2020); and for other populations too there is limited access to technology, as well as a lack of expertise among teachers (Onesmus, 2020). Where studies have explored schools' use of technologies that the children use at home, it is clear they don't align and children feel that their out-of-school digital practices are only relevant when doing homework (out of school) (Twining et al., 2017).

Many teachers would seem to be in the embrace of other ideas. They are constrained by the everyday operation of their schools; they are struggling to access the knowledge they need to use the technologies; they want for the support and time to develop their ideas (Wilson & McKinney, 2012). Even when they have been involved in a project that should build these capabilities, developing their confidence remains a challenge, as does finding meaningful ways for them to apply them in learning situations (Cornelius &

Shanks, 2017). It seems likely that their capacity to engage in new ways is being constrained by the embrace of the 'traditional grammars' of schooling, those regular structures and rules that have organised the work of instruction, such as single teachers, subjects, classes, lessons, age-grades and testing (Tyack & Tobin, 1994). This was brought home to me in Norway. A friend's daughter was doing her Mathematics homework on the tablet provided by the school .... except she wasn't. The questions were online, but she had to answer them in her maths book, then take a photo of the work and upload it onto the school system for the teacher to mark.

As a parent, I have always found this refusal to engage with technology incredibly frustrating. My son, Robbie, is marginalised by many of our dominant communication forms. The spoken word is a particular barrier. He does, however, know how to search the internet, use cameras, PowerPoint, speech recognition, subtitles and phone applications. As a family, WhatsApp is an endless source of delight and surprise. We have shared videos and still pictures of our lives for years. But can we get schools and colleges to do it? No. They are in the embrace of so much that constrains them:

- Policies about privacy, use of mobile phones, Wi-Fi and YouTube.
- Concerns about equitable access to equipment, lack of training, damage to expensive technology.

The reasons have been wide, varied and ongoing. Even after staff have invited me in to talk about how we do things as a family, even after they have gone on training courses and even after we have provided the equipment ... nothing happens. In the end, we just had to conclude that the dozens of practitioners in his life did not have the creative space to (allow themselves to) embrace technology as a tool for communication.

3. A multicultural embrace?

Multicultural education came to prominence in the 1980s and 1990s having grown out of the Civil Rights Movement, which brought educational justice to the fore in the early 1970s. From the outset, multicultural education challenged the curriculum to reflect the race, ethnicity, native language and social class of all students, not just those from the majority group. It also challenged *how and why* education was done and *who* benefited. From the outset, it faced a backlash (Nieto, 2017). At its heart was an emphasis upon ensuring students' experiences were reflected in the content and were engaged in knowledge creation; it had a focus upon developing positive racial attitudes, differentiating the curriculum and using school cultures and structures to empower all learners (Banks & Banks, 2009). However, the breadth of these aims led to numerous recommendations and approaches; it also ran up against an idea which embraced people from all backgrounds – that 'minority' cultural groups should seek to assimilate and be accepted by the dominant society (Alghamdi, 2017).

Approaches associated with a multicultural embrace within schools have also been characterised by the lack of their critical and transformational dimensions. They have tended to downplay intersectional perspectives, issues around hierarchy and power structures, and to have been represented through English language publications (Cuéllar et al., 2020). This reflects my experience of half-hearted multiculturalist educational approaches in the UK. These have mostly seemed to consist of surface changes, such as welcome signs in different languages, adding a bit more diversity to the reading list in the English Literature curriculum, mentioning a few famous people who are not white in other subjects and briefly considering slavery in history. It is hardly surprising therefore that as part of the Black Lives Matters movement, there were still extensive calls for a decolonisation of the curriculum.

In the UK, there was also a focus upon citizenship courses and the development of 'British values', which despite the diversity of the context can be seen as primarily monocultural (Ashcroft & Bevir, 2018). This focus on values reflected another major challenge for multicultural education. Its political nature divides/d people over its application; its challenge can/could feel deeply personal. It can call for people to tolerate behaviours that are not part of the majority identity while at the same time revealing how some majority practices have to change to be equitable for the minority.

It is perhaps not surprising that such policies became entangled with people's views about the value of any costs and their benefits. But as a consequence, such views encouraged a lack of meaningful funding and a narrative that it was an idea in retreat (Watters, 2011). However, that did not mean the idea of multiculturalism went away. Even though very different political parties came to power and even though it was widely criticised by people who had the power to overturn them, broadly speaking multicultural policies continued on the statute books in many countries, (Bloemraad & Wright, 2014; Mathieu, 2018). This perhaps reflects the reality of an embrace that could not be ignored: the increasing multicultural nature of many societies (Watters, 2011). It also underlines the competing and ongoing nature of the embraces in which we find our selves and how these inform the nature of our aspirations (and how such aspirational embraces maintain their hold).

4. A label to embrace?

The tendency for the prior embrace to maintain its hold is also evident in the use of labels within education. It has long been known that there is huge variability in countries' understandings of special educational needs. The variability in their definitions, for example, means they cannot be categorised for comparison without creating a deceptive sense of commonality

(Riddell et al., 2006) and consequently can only be listed as a tool for reflection (see OECD, 2012). In a study I undertook with colleagues looking at special education in 50 countries, once all the obvious similarities were grouped together there were 60 different categories (Rix et al. 2013).

At the core of this approach is an idea which has both been embraced by and embraces vast swathes of the education establishment. A belief in finding observable phenomena as evidence of behaviours or characteristics. This is despite robust evidence about the unreliability of the processes and categories involved. There are, for example, contested boundaries in relation to dyslexia (Elliott & Gibbs, 2008), moderate learning difficulties (Norwich et al., 2014) and autism (Timimi, 2021). It is argued that they are not really categories at all, because of 'consistently inconsistent findings' (Timimi, p. 19) and decades of research bedevilled by 'replicability crises'.

This embrace of unreliable categories is evident in the variability in diagnosis, too. For example, in 2020, in one English local authority, 3.4% of diagnosed children had been diagnosed with an autistic spectrum disorder, but in another local authority it was 25%. In every one of the 12 reported categories (covering sensory, intellectual, functional and behavioural difficulties or impairment), there were these kinds of discrepancies. If you took the top-ten and bottom-ten English local authorities (to iron out the extremes) embracing any label, you were more than four times likely to have a particular diagnosis in a top-ten embracing authority than in the bottom ten. This even applied for what might seem like a highly evident sensory-related category such as a hearing impairment. The only exceptions where the ratio fell slightly below 3:1 were around issues of behaviour and communication, which are usually identified by the teacher (DfE, 2020).

At the heart of the problem are the theoretical constructs (embraces?) underpinning the diagnoses and assessments that govern the world of special education. Their lack of conceptual clarity is recognised as 'a widespread and fundamental problem in psychology' (Bringmann et al., 2022). This creates huge tensions between different people's interpretations and priorities. Their openness to (re-/mis-) interpretation is why the Society for Humanistic Psychology, Division 32 of the American Psychological Association, in February 2020, called for us to move beyond the limits of individual diagnosis. They concluded that the impact of social and structural determinants was already supported by robust scientific evidence. In contrast, the search for in-person factors – which is at the heart of diagnosis and assessment – continues to 'elude scientists'. They suggested that these experts were merely holding onto hope for 'the next taxonomic revolution'.

Given the chaotic nature of this embrace, it is not perhaps surprising that so many teachers feel unprepared to work with children who have been embraced by it. Perhaps unsurprisingly, this is something we will return to in later chapters.

FIGURE 1.2   An average cartoon?

Embrace the metaphor!

In looking across these four examples, we can see how our ideas may be:

≅ never really embraced because of a commitment to a prior embrace.
≅ claimed to be being embraced but they are not (well, not really).
≅ embraced in ways people did not expect and despite the refusal of many people to embrace.
≅ criticised as being failed embraces despite not really being embraced (or only partially at best) in the first place.
≅ embracing us despite clear evidence that we are embracing with an illusion and many people want to stop.

The embrace is a metaphor, of course. As Lakoff and Johnson (1980) recognised, metaphors bring about associations that both structure and focus our thinking on particular aspects of experience. They can be the means by which we coherently understand an experience, how we think and act. Through their associations, they can help explain our past and present, as well as guide our future actions. By making experience coherent, hiding some features and highlighting others, metaphors can function in a self-fulfilling cycle, creating 'truth'.

Applying the notion of the embrace to comprehensive education, technology, multiculturalism and labelling may not provide a deeper insight into each of these issues, but it can help us to understand the ways in which we engage with ideas, new and old, developing and developing, emerged and emerging. Looking across these examples, we can see how our mechanistic responses and reliance upon established embraces corrupt our intentions and work against our notions of social justice.

An embrace has a connection to love, it has a connection to holding one another, it has a connection to being constrained, but it also has a use in a legal context. It is used to talk about a person or process that is entwined with bribery or other corrupting practices within the legal system. The value of the embrace as a metaphor is that it speaks to the fundamental nature of the social and physical interaction at the heart of our lived experience. It connects us to the relational nature of education and all learning. It helps us to consider how we are both holding and held by our political, economic, cultural and environmental traditions. It provides a frame to explore the tensions that exist between what is intended and what is delivered, between what is aspired to and what is accepted, between our beliefs and our practices.

An embrace can both provide security and/or togetherness, but it can also trap us, throttle the life out of something or hold us apart.

This then is the subject of this book. It is about resolving a dichotomy between our embraces. It confronts how our search for security and togetherness so often traps us in ways that work against these goals, leaving us less secure and less together. It explores our *being* apart, and how this makes our search for education, participation and inclusion so much harder. It offers a way forward by identifying how we can (counterintuitively?) come together through our separation, by our embrace with our individual and collective insecurity.

References

Alghamdi, Y. (2017). Multicultural education in the US: Current issues and suggestions for practical implementations. *International Journal of Education*, 9(2), 44–52.

Ashcroft, R., & Bevir, M. (2018). Multiculturalism in contemporary Britain: Policy, law and theory, *Critical Review of International Social and Political Philosophy*, 21(1), 1–21.

Banks, J., & Banks, C. (2009). *Multicultural education: Issues and perspectives*. John Wiley & Sons, Inc.

Bloemraad, I., & Wright, M. (2014). Utter failure or unity out of diversity. Debating and evaluating policies of multicuturalism. *International Migration Review*, 48(1), 292–334.

Bringmann, L., Elmer, T., & Eronen, M. (2022). Back to basics: The importance of conceptual clarification in psychological science. *Current Directions in Psychological Science*, 31(4), 340–346.

Cornelius, S., & Shanks, R. (2017). Expectations and challenges: The implementation of mobile devices in a Scottish primary school. *Technology, Pedagogy and Education*, 26(1), 19–31.

Cuéllar, C., Queupil, J., Cuenca, C., & Ravest, J. (2020). A systematic review on multiculturalism and educational leadership: Similarities and contrasts in knowledge production across societies. *Multicultural Education Review*, 12(4), 235–249.

Department for Education. (2020). *Special educational needs in England: January 2020*, London.

Elliott, J., & Gibbs, S. (2008). Does dyslexia exist? *Journal of Philosophy of Education*, 42(3–4), 475–491.

Foucault, M. (1980). *Power/Knowledge: Selected interviews and other writings, 1972–1977*, edited by Gordon, C. (p. 16). Pantheon.

Foucault, M. (1982). The subject and power (Afterword). In H. L. Dreyfus & P. Rabinow (Eds.), *Michel Foucault: Beyond structuralism and hermeneutics*. Harvester Press.

Huber, E., & Stephens, J. (2001). *Development and crisis of the welfare state. Parties and policies in global markets*. The University of Chicago Press.

Lakoff, G., & Johnson, M. (1980). Conceptual metaphor in everyday language. *Journal of Philosophy*, 77, 453–486.

Martin, J. (2020). Telling stories about comprehensive education. Hidden histories of politics, policy and practice in post-war England. *British Journal of Educational Studies*, 68(5), 649–669.

Mathieu, F. (2018). The failure of state multiculturalism in the UK? An analysis of the UK's multicultural policy for 2000–2015. *Ethnicities*, 18(1), 43–69.

McCulloch, G. (2016). British Labour Party education policy and comprehensive education: From Learning to Live to Circular 10/65. *History of Education*, 45(2), 225–245.

Nieto, S. (2017). Re-imagining multicultural education: New visions, new possibilities. *Multicultural Education Review*, 9(1), 1–10.

Norwich, B., Ylonen, A., & Gwernan-Jones, R. (2014). Moderate learning difficulties: Searching for clarity and understanding. *Research Papers in Education*, 29(1), 1–19.

OECD. (2012). CX3.1 special educational needs (SEN). Retrieved February 16, 2013, from http://www.oecd.org/social/family/50325299.pdf

Onesmus, G. (2020). Hindrance to technologically guided education in Kenya secondary schools: A case study of Embakasi girls' school. *Journal of Learning for Development*, 7(3), 423–432.

Riddell, S., Tisdall, K., Kane, J., & Mulderrig, J. (2006). *Literature review of pupils with additional support needs*. Final Report to the Scottish Executive Education Department Centre for Research in Education Inclusion and Diversity (CREID).

Rix, J. (2015). *Must inclusion be special? Rethinking educational support within a community of provision*. Routledge.

Rix, J., Sheehy, K., Fletcher-Campbell, F., Crisp, M., & Harper, A. (2013). Exploring provision for children identified with special educational needs: An international review of policy and practice. *European Journal of Special Needs Education*, 28(4), 375–391.

Sass, K. (2015). Understanding comprehensive school reforms: Insights from comparative-historical sociology and power resources theory. *European Educational Research Journal*, 14(3–4), 240–256.

Seale, J. (2020). Were we right? A re-evaluation of the perceived potential of technology to transform the educational opportunities and outcomes of learners with special educational needs. *History of Education*, 49(2), 247–264.

Spratt, J., (2016). Childhood wellbeing: What role for education? *British Educational Research Journal*, 42(2), 223–239.

Thomas, M., Clayton, C., Huang, S., & Garcia, R. (2019). Being in tension: Faculty explorations of the meaning of social justice in teacher education. *Excelsior: Leadership in Teaching and Learning, 12*(1), 17–36.

Timimi, S. (2021). The social cultural construction of autism, trends in SEN identification: Contexts, causes and consequences, SEN policy research forum, *Journal of Research in Special Educational Needs, 21*(1), 28–32.

Twining, P. (2008). Framing IT use to enhance educational impact on a school-wide basis. In J. Voogt & G. Knezek (Eds.), *International handbook of information technology in primary and secondary education* (Vol. 20, pp. 555–577). Springer Science & Business Media.

Twining, P., Browne, N., Murphy, P., Hempel-Jorgensen, A., Harrison, S., & Parmar, N. (2017). *NP3–new purposes, new practices, new pedagogy: Meta-analysis report.* Society for Educational Studies.

Tyack, D. & Tobin, W. (1994). The "grammar" of schooling: Why has it been so hard to change? *American Educational Research Journal, 31*(3), 453–479.

Van de Werfhorst, H. (2018). Early tracking and socioeconomic inequality in academic achievement: Studying reforms in nine countries. *Research in Social Stratification and Mobility, 58*, 22–32.

Watters, C. (2011). Education, migration and the 'failure' of multiculturalism, *British Journal of Sociology of Education, 32*(2), 319–327.

West, A. (2016). A (short) history of comprehensive education in England. *"Reclaiming Education" Alliance Conference 2016*, November 12th, 2016, London.

Wilson, A., & McKinney, S. (2012). Glow or Glimmer? A case study of ICT innovation in a Scottish secondary school. *Scottish Educational Review, 44*(1), 57–69.

2

THE EMBRACE OF CERTAINTY

Trapped?

I was caught cheating by my history teacher once. He looked down at the 14-year-old me, sat at the back of the classroom in my black and white school uniform, copying from the textbook and asked: 'Are you trying to make a fool out of me, boy?' I looked back up at him, open book on my lap, and smiled 'Yes, I am, Sir'. It seemed like the honest thing to say, but perhaps unsurprisingly it only made matters worse. The point of this story however is not the extensive series of detentions which resulted but why it mattered in the first place.

The textbook in question had been written by the aforesaid History teacher. I cannot remember the name of the book or its topic, but I do remember that he used to sit there and read out extensive sections of the book and we were supposed to make notes about it. I soon came to realise there was no point in making real notes. I just got the book from the library (or 'borrowed' the notes from my brother who had dutifully copied them out a couple of years before) and then in the lessons I could pretend to scrawl and listen to him ramble on instead. It was very dull stuff. Spoken or read. But the key thing was, it was a textbook. It was truth. You could be tested on it. Here was history, confined and defined, in a way that suited the curriculum and exams of the day. If you went by the book (his book), you could be an A student. [Needless to say, I was not an A student. In the end I think I was a C student for History. Not bad for a cheat. Appropriate, even?]

Here then were some of the essential confines of my/our scholastic certainty:

The subject; the pupil, the teacher; the classroom; the uniform
the text; the test; the grade; the pedagogy; the curriculum.

DOI: 10.4324/9781003281405-2

These boundaried schooling notions exemplify what Dewey called our 'quest for certitude'; a quest that has determined the principles underpinning core human concepts related to being and knowing. As he put it:

> The objects of knowledge form the standards of measures of the reality of all other objects of experience. Are the objects of the affections, of desire, effort, choice, that is to say everything to which we attach value, real? Yes, if they can be warranted by knowledge; if we can *know objects* having these value properties, we are justified in thinking them real. But as objects of desire and purpose they have no place in being until they are approached and validated through knowledge. The idea is so familiar that we overlook the unexpressed premise upon which it rests, namely that only the completely fixed and unchanging can be real. The quest for certitude has determined our basic metaphysics.
>
> *(Dewey, 1930, pp. 24–25)*

This quest is a response to living in what Dewey called 'a world of hazards'. The reality of endless change means that we live in circumstances that lack a 'true or complete being'. This need to accept the dominance of doubt is profoundly troubling for many people. The state of never knowing can easily generate a sense of futility and purposelessness within our lives. Our exploration of its existence has been at the root of millennia of philosophical and religious reflection, informing the faith and beliefs of large swathes of humanity. But it also creates a fundamental practical problem. The buildings we build crumble, the people within our systems perish, our systems mutate, decline and collapse. We respond by rebuilding, by replacing, by redesigning and restructuring, but it is always working against the tide. We need to be willing to undertake these tasks to feel that what we are doing will stand the test of time, resisting the tide as our ancestors did; and to encourage ourselves to do this, we tell ourselves that we are progressing, that the future is better, will be better, that our systems will enable us to find more meaning among the futility and purposelessness.

In order to achieve this semblance of certainty, we respond in a manner akin to the first law of thermodynamics. This law has been frequently (ironically?) revised, but it can be reasonably equated with the concept that within a closed system energy is conserved, its form can change but not its quantity. The key factor in achieving consistency is the nature of the system which is created. The system must be closed; its boundaries must be defined. This is also the basis on which we create our education systems, legal and scientific systems and various other institutionalised structures we understand to be socially essential. Each system is closed. All those within them have their position and function prescribed by the system or the creators of the system.

FIGURE 2.1 Know your place.

One cannot enter without having a position and function prescribed. Every action undertaken (in theory) has a purpose which fits within predetermined aims, goals and ways of working.

And of course, the reason we define each system and the parameters of our roles and actions is in order to make it (feel) controllable.

'Take a detention, boy'.

Where does our certainty begin?

(Accepting my own fallibility in this matter), certainty begins in an ideological belief that certitude can exist. But...

HOW IS THIS IDEOLOGICAL BELIEF REIFIED
BY OUR EDUCATION SYSTEM(S)?

I am tempted to suggest that certainty (within the educational context of children and young people) comes into existence through/by/with the traditional grammars of schooling. As is evident in my history lesson, this means certainty comes into existence through/by/with such things as the subject, the pupil, the teacher, the classroom, the uniform, the text, the test, the grade, the pedagogy; the curriculum. But in many ways, this is just too obvious. I need to give you a richer description than that. If I am to be fair to certainty, I must demonstrate educational certitude on its/their own terms. I will therefore make an attempt to pull out some strands (or things I am framing to be strands) to demonstrate this technology of certainty in operation.

Over the next few pages, I am going to present collections of ideas that seem to me to embrace our education systems. I will explore how we are schooled in certainty under six headings:

➤ Certain purposes
➤ Certain knowledge
➤ Certain behaviour
➤ Certain abilities
➤ Certain tests
➤ Certain comparisons

The examples I share are intended to show how ideas of certainty effect day-to-day experiences in schools, local and national policies, as well as issues around pedagogy, the visible and hidden curricula, assessment and so forth.

Five things to bear in mind as I go about this:

- Firstly, I am not going to share with you academic literature associated with these issues. I could quite easily demonstrate the points using published research alongside national and international policy documents. However, my intention is to show the very everydayness of certainty. I want to show how it permeates so many people's thinking about schooling.
- Secondly, I will not attempt to provide a detailed analysis of the many areas I will touch upon. I am cherry-picking the online world. I am looking for readily available non-controversial examples, which will demonstrate the prevalence of certainty as a commonplace (generally unquestioned) presumption that underpins schooling all around the world. My sources are websites for schools, governments (and their agencies), newspapers, bloggers, educationalists and training providers.
- Thirdly, I am going to SHOUT at you through the medium of font, to exemplify the kinds of terms that I reckon can be associated with our search for certainty. I appreciate that this may not be a pleasant experience, but I hope it is transparent. [I also appreciate that the underlying nature of language is about the creation of boundaries of meaning, which are themselves a nod to a belief in certainty, but I hope you will appreciate (or enjoy reflecting upon) why I have not capitalised the whole document.]
- Fourthly, I have not just presented you with a list or collection of lists, since a list of things is never an answer. A list is an attempt to control. But it is undermined by both the fallibility of words and the experience of living. This experience of living comes from the relationship within and between the listed things; it is the pupil studying the subject with the teacher in the classroom, both (perhaps) wearing uniforms, following a curriculum which includes selected texts and predetermined tests and a view about what learning is. Through this dynamic socio-cultural, environmental, inter and

intrapersonal interplay each listed thing creates/created/recreates/recreated the notions and experiences of each other listed thing. And, of course, that does not include endless qualities, biases and dimensions at play in any of these ongoing interactions. In writing up these ideas, I have therefore tried to point towards these interactions.

- Fifthly, I am aware that in answering a question about the reification of the idea of certainty, I am playing along with the ideological belief that certitude can exist. Even if I temper my response with all kinds of provisos and acknowledgement of variables at play, I am going to create notions of truth that are from some perspectives not true. It would be nice to have a neat metaphor for this. Is understanding the process of reification, perhaps, like a chicken and egg situation involving all the birds ever born? Or is it, perhaps closer to the issue of whether a thing observed has only happened if it is observed? Either way, we can come up with an answer, but its truth will require us to make some compromises; Truth is (after all) a human compromise with Being.

Certain purposes

Let us begin with an EDUCATION AND SCHOOLS MINISTER in England. Many would agree with what he has to say:

> Education is the engine of our economy, it is the foundation of our culture, and it's an essential preparation for adult life.
>
> *(Nick Gibb, 2015)*

Gibb went on to lay out a range of characteristics of Education in the three arenas identified in his quote. For example, in relation to the economy, people have to have knowledge and skills to succeed. Importantly, he can point to what the REQUIRED KNOWLEDGE and SKILLS are (including NUMERACY and LITERACY). He can also QUANTIFY England's effectiveness in delivering them and recommend PROGRAMMES which will effectively enable them. He then recognises the centrality of social justice to an education system and its foundational role in England's CULTURE. But in doing this, he warns that we must not divide culture from knowledge and that it is through SUBJECTS that people become creative, engaged CITIZENS. He can list a range of subjects. Similarly, in preparing CHILDREN to be ADULTS, he refers to evidence of school practices that increase ACHIEVE-MENT and SPECIFIC CHARACTER TRAITS associated with this achievement. Such achievement can only be delivered by ACADEMIC RIGOUR of the HIGHEST STANDARDS. It is also worth noting that it is through the VALUES he has laid out that each child in England can reach their POTENTIAL.

These certain purposes are going to keep on popping up too. But going with the flow, let's have a look at those SUBJECTS mentioned by Gibb. The online world is full of opinions about these.

Certain knowledge

Echoing Gibb, the TutorHunt website (2022) suggests that to 'better ourselves' and 'realise our potential', we need to ensure we have particular TYPES OF KNOWLEDGE, which will open doors to PROFESSIONS and will enable us to mix socially. They suggest that we experience the world differently through knowledge gathered in education and, in particular, if we study A BROAD RANGE of subjects. There are various subject categories on the site, but they specifically list up front: MATHS, ENGLISH, BIO-LOGY, CHEMISTRY, PHYSICS, GENERAL SCIENCE, FRENCH, GERMAN and SPANISH. The subjects don't just define the learners either; they also play a key role in both how we understand our system and the way in which we manage it. For example, campaigners for SCHOOL CHOICE in the United States (Rees, 2016) explain its value by pointing to the additional time spent on MATHS and READING in Charter schools, while Simply Learning Tuition (2022) states that greater choice is ensured in Sweden because to enter SENIOR HIGH SCHOOL you need to have at least 12 SUBJECT PASSES, but to enter a vocational programme you only need passes in eight subjects (including SWEDISH).

Elsewhere, the nature of these subjects is not above criticism, but the underlying notion of the prescribed area of knowledge is more robust. For example, Michelle Liew (2018) who blogs on children, psychology and education recognises that the dominant subjects may not be enough to live successfully in the world as we find it and therefore we need a range of additional LIFE SKILLS. But, central to her argument is that these should be delivered through 12 new school subjects (such as MONEY MANAGEMENT, CAREER MANAGEMENT, MENTAL HEALTH and STRESS MANAGEMENT, as well as THE ENVIRONMENT). She explains the need for these with a range of categorical statements and the occasional use of QUANTITATIVE DATA; these are intended to demonstrate how a TYPE OF KNOWLEDGE or the skills associated with it are essential to a WELL-ROUNDED ADULT. Similar concerns have led to calls for a COMPETENCE-BASED CURRICULUM (Stamou et al., 2019), which has been recommended as an approach across the European Union since 2006, and is evident in other countries, such as Turkey, where there is a focus upon VALUES EDUCATION, in particular NATIONAL VALUES.

The focus of practitioners is invariably directed by the requirements of the system around them. For example, in an English CURRICULUM with a focus upon students studying prescribed areas of knowledge to a suitable

STANDARD, teachers feel the need to have EXPERTISE within those areas of knowledge. For example, a primary school teacher, John Brunskill (2015), talks about BEING ABLE TO ANSWER CHILDREN'S QUESTIONS so you do not act as a ceiling to their learning. This requires deep knowledge, which is only possible if you are a SUBJECT SPECIALIST. This specialism means the teaching is superior, with the children learning from MASTERS who have TECHNICAL KNOWLEDGE. This enables the teacher to be responsive to learners, from BEGINNER learners to those who are EXPERT. His suggestion is that TEACHER TRAINING should be changed. This reflects a global requirement for teachers to be formally QUALIFIED and to engage in ONGOING PROFESSIONAL DEVELOPMENT. It also reflects a belief, for example, in Singapore (Stewart, 2022) that the cornerstone of a successful system is training, professional development, career development and REGULAR APPRAISAL. As part of his call for a change to training in England, Brunskill suggests that Teachers should learn about PLANNING, QUESTIONING, ASSESSMENT and BEHAVIOUR MANAGEMENT; they should have training in some CORE SUBJECTS, and then they should SPECIALISE. All of this would be FORMALLY ASSESSED and ACCREDITED.

This expectation that teachers will have particular knowledge and behave in particular ways is neatly mirrored by the similar expectations our schools place on the children and young people with whom they work. The nature of who the learner should be and how that can be achieved is a popular topic globally.

Certain behaviour

The Classroom Management Expert blog (Yussif, 2021), for instance, focuses on the importance of MANAGING BEHAVIOUR. He notes that the best days in teaching are those with no surprises. This depends upon schools having enough ROUTINES and PROCEDURES, as without them things cannot run smoothly for teachers. For example, at lunchtime, people need to know when and where to sit, and when they are allowed to move. He writes that routines keep children ON TASK and give teachers CONTROL. These produce a sense of belonging, so children can explore within the boundaries and STANDARDS that have been set. Time and energy are NOT WASTED and the teacher feels like a MASTER OF THEIR JOB. As an example, he suggests that by PREPARING, teachers can PREDICT the behaviour of talkative students and put in place STEPS to MANAGE THEM so more time is spent on CLASS ACTIVITIES.

The purpose of this approach is to TRAIN STUDENTS as LEADERS and RESPONSIBLE CITIZENS, teaching prescribed VALUES such as 'CARE AND COMPASSION, DOING ONE'S BEST, FAIRNESS, FREEDOM, HONESTY and TRUSTWORTHINESS, INTEGRITY, RESPECT,

RESPONSIBILITY, UNDERSTANDING, TOLERANCE, and INCLU-SION'. It also engenders trust in parents, creates EFFECTIVE SCHOOL ADMINISTRATION and IMPROVES student achievements. The Staff Writer on Reference (2021) would largely agree with Yussif. For them, a key component of managing behaviour, encouraging learning and assessing progress is the LESSON PLAN. This breaks the lesson into INSTRUCTIONAL STEPS, which both ensure all LEARNING OBJECTIVES are met and increase the SAFETY of everyone involved in the process.

Similar values and effects are attributed to a variety of other in-school factors. The Sanskriti School (2019), for example, points to the importance of UNIFORM. They believe this encourages EQUALITY, a focus on learning, instilling DISCIPLINE and GOOD BEHAVIOUR; this saves TIME, REDUCES ABSENTEEISM and promotes pride and motivation. Students often agree with this too. Chloe Spencer (2013) writes about uniform being a 'BADGE of pride' that 'creates an identity for a school'. She sees it as an important part of being a school student. She quotes a head teacher who suggests wearing a uniform with pride means you are half-way to being RESPECTFUL.

The importance of these kinds of values is also frequently associated with EXAMS. Youth Employment UK (2021) believes that exams enable a person to develop SPECIFIC CHARACTERISTICS to live the kind of life they want to live; in particular, SELF-MANAGEMENT, INITIATIVE, ORGANI-SATION and SELF-BELIEF SKILLS (such as resilience and maintaining positive attitude). *The Times of India* would seem to concur. Abdul Kalam (2021), writing in their lifestyle section, notes that exams are a means of developing the individual, ensuring A SET OF VALUES, while enabling particular TYPES OF THINKING and SELF-ASSESSMENT. Through them, people learn to OVERCOME FAILURE and are encouraged to be BETTER LEARNERS. He suggests that exams are like the roots of the educational tree and that 'A TREE IS NOTHING WITHOUT ITS ROOTS'.

An underlying challenge in delivering the kinds of behaviours identified above is how we explain to ourselves when things go wrong (or why they go right?). A useful technology of certainty in this regard is the notion of the limited individual. The online world is heaving with views about this.

Certain abilities

Kalam (2021), for instance, notes the relevance of EXAMS to the teacher, and how they can enable them to understand the INTELLECTUAL CAPACITIES of children and young people and to create opportunities to rectify shortcomings in those capacities. Although he does not say this, it seems fair to presume that this kind of insight is valued by others too, such as the employers mentioned by Youth Employment UK. They suggest that QUALIFICATIONS frequently associated with exams are valuable because employers understand their meaning. Together they make LIFE SKILLS visible, demonstrating that someone is LITERATE and that they can develop KNOWLEDGE and SKILLS in a SPECIALIST SUBJECT AREA.

The function of QUALIFICATIONS and EXAMS as a means to explain a person's INTELLECTUAL CAPACITY is relevant to other terms associated with the notion of *what a person can be*. For example, earlier I mentioned 'POTENTIAL'. The learner is defined by this thing – capacity or potential. This suggests some form of a boundary, which the person must either surpass or reach the outer limits of. Another comparable, popular (and perhaps interchangeable) word is 'ABILITY'.

Globally, there are numerous terms used by school systems which utilise such concepts to define where a person will learn, what they will learn and how they will learn (e.g. in English-speaking contexts: TRACKING, EDUCATIONAL STRATIFICATION, ABILITY GROUPING, SORTING, STREAMING, SETTING, BANDING or DIFFERENTIATION). Lydia Atieno (2022) writing from a Rwandan context in the *New Times* suggests ability grouping can be used in both REGULAR and SPECIAL EDUCATION SYSTEMS. She alludes to our systemic capacity to identify SIMILAR ACADEMIC ABILITY, so that we can place SIMILAR LEARNERS TOGETHER. The teachers she quotes in her article all explain their use of this approach in terms of control. They talk about KNOWING SKILL LEVELS, enabling EFFICIENT PLANNING, TARGETING INSTRUCTION, MEETING NEEDS, TAILORING INSTRUCTION to specific needs, DELIVERING EFFECTIVE STRATEGIES and learning at a COMFORTABLE PACE.

The MASTERS FOR ARTS in Teaching programme (2022) involving a number of US universities also uses the technologies of certainty in outlining the benefits of Ability Grouping in the Classroom. They infer that CLASSROOM ACTIVITIES ARE CLOSED by nature when they state that children become bored when they have finished work and others have not, while those not finishing are made to feel inferior. The TRADITIONAL CLASS, they suggest, focuses upon AVERAGE LEARNING ABILITY, and this leaves a third under-challenged and a third over-challenged. They recognise that ability grouping provides time to INCREASE KNOWLEDGE, to DEVELOP ABILITY, to LEARN A SUBJECT MORE FULLY and for students to REACH 'THEIR OWN POTENTIALS'. It also allows for the ALLOCATION of students to different groups for different subjects or for different aspects or topics of different subjects.

An interesting addendum comes in an article from an Indian English Language paper, the *Deccan Herald* (2013), which is not a fan of ability grouping. In addition to many of the points raised above, they suggest teachers and administrators feel ability grouping is advantageous because the group is homogenous and pupils can advance at their own speed with people of COMPARABLE ACHIEVEMENT. An article about mixed-age teaching

(Sullivan, 2022) raises another issue, the necessity of CAREFUL PLANNING for a homogenous group so that all pupils can learn in the SAME SEQUENCE as their peers. Sullivan notes that a wide range of academic abilities serves as a barrier to this, as it makes it difficult to PLAN. She presumes the use of TEXTBOOKS with grade-based content to reflect CURRICULUM STANDARDS and LEVELS associated with STANDARDISED LEARNING OBJECTIVES and TESTING. In this context, with multiple abilities, there is a need for multiple GRADING EVALUATION SYSTEMS. This all means teachers need SPECIALISED TRAINING in INSTRUCTIONAL STRATEGIES and CURRICULUM. This links us back to issues of ACCREDITATION, as well as to issues raised earlier about qualifications and subject knowledge.

A NOTE

When I was re-reading this chapter, at this point I tried to recall how many more examples I had given of the technologies of certainty. On that basis, I presume that some readers may be wondering something similar. Adopting a very popular technology of certainty – the essay length – I would like to confirm that you are just half-way through this examination (of the issue). It is remarkable how many there are.
    Do you think it is useful to have some certainty at this point?

Clearly a challenge for a system that believes in the notion of the limited individual is the certainty by which those limitations are defined. As suggested above, exams are one way, but ensuring the rigour of any assessment is definitely something which troubles many writing in the online world, frequently drawing upon ideas which we have already met in our consideration of certain purposes, knowledge, behaviour and abilities.

Certain tests

To support teachers and their institutions to identify STUDENT ABILITIES, there are numerous STANDARDISED TESTS available. International Student (2022), for example, lists three assessments for undergraduate admission in the United States (1. SCHOLASTIC ASSESSMENT TEST (SAT), 2. TEST OF ENGLISH AS A FOREIGN LANGUAGE (TOEFL) and 3. AMERICAN COLLEGE TESTING (ACT)) and at least eight others for graduate and professional admissions, recognising that they can't list them all. Another popular set of tests are COGNITIVE ABILITIES TESTS. In England, for instance, these are used with children at the start of secondary school, to

ASSESS THEIR VERBAL, NON-VERBAL, QUANTITATIVE and SPATIAL REASONING. This supplements the FORMAL TESTING AT THE END OF PRIMARY SCHOOL and is used to 'identify a student's ACADEMIC ABILITIES' as opposed to knowledge (Pretest Plus, 2022), so they are 'PLACED in a class that's SUITED to their LEARNING PACE'.

Glenn Fahey (2020) writing for the Centre for Independent Studies blog in Australia suggests that ASSESSMENTS such as these offer OBJECTIVE and COMPARABLE TOOLS for MONITORING PROGRESS, INFORMING PRACTICE and MEASURING TEACHER and SCHOOL PERFORMANCE. He acknowledges, for example, that the NATIONAL LITERACY and NUMERACY TESTS in Australia may need improving, but the solution is for them to be more RIGOROUS and BETTER ALIGNED to the CURRICULUM. END-OF-SCHOOL EXAMS are also a means of MEASURING both the individual learner's ACHIEVEMENT and NATIONAL STANDARDS. As noted by the Local Schools Network (2013), the nature of these varies hugely between nations but the standards are generally framed around subjects deemed relevant by that country, allowing for some COMPARISON across nations.

This notion of curricula certainty is a central function of predetermined GRADE LEVELS such as the English KEY STAGES. These define a certain range of SCHOOL YEARS and lead to progressive, STANDARDISED EXAMS during a child's education. They are evident too in links to DEVELOPMENTAL MILESTONES, particularly in the Early Years, variations of which exist in many different countries. The Centers for Disease Control and Prevention (2022) in the United States defines these as how 75% OR MORE of children play, learn, speak, act and move by a certain age, while the Health Service Executive in Ireland (2022) provides CHECKLISTS which allow you to JUDGE a child in COMPARISON to AVERAGES for COMMU-NICATION, HEARING, SOCIAL and EMOTIONAL BEHAVIOUR, PROBLEM-SOLVING, LEARNING and UNDERSTANDING.

Closely allied to these notions of ability and average development are notions associated with NEEDS, such as SPECIAL or ADDITIONAL. So, for example, Kathy Sellgren (2017) reports on the views from the head of education at the Policy Exchange thinktank. He firstly believes there are KEY CONCEPTS and CURRICULUM to be learned; secondly, if children need additional support to understand them, it is sensible to GROUP THEM TOGETHER to ENSURE they learn them. Evaluating whether a person has these needs involves a raft of RULES, PROCEDURES, ROLES and TIME-LINES. For example, in Scotland, the COORDINATED SUPPORT PLAN (CSP) begins with a REQUEST IN WRITING for an ASSESSMENT, and an EXPECTATION that the local authority should comply unless one was done recently. The process requires formal and informal PROFESSIONAL EVALUATIONS, alongside FORMAL MEDIATION or INDEPENDENT ADJUDICATION PROCESSES. Charities such as the National Deaf Children's Society (2022) offer guidance about the kinds of AREAS that will be identified (such as RECEPTIVE SKILLS, EXPRESSIVE LANGUAGE, CONCENTRATION AND ATTENTION, SELF-HELP, MOTOR SKILLS, RESPONSIBILITY, SOCIAL SKILLS, CONFIDENCE and SELF-ESTEEM). A similar process is followed in England, if a child is to be identified as having special educational needs and/or disabilities. Here too there is a focus upon gathering EVIDENCE from health and educational professionals, with a protocol and legal STRUCTURE to be adhered to. Both systems are littered with conceptual JARGON often encapsulated in ACRONYMS. So, for example, in England a CHYP with SEND can go through A STATUTORY ASSESSMENT PROCESS, leading to an EHC plan. [A child or young person with special educational needs and disabilities can have a legal assessment leading to an EDUCATION HEALTH AND CARE PLAN (Gov.Uk, 2022).]

In many parts of the world, this educational evaluation will include a specific MEASUREMENT of INTELLIGENCE, organised by paediatricians or psychologists, to provide a formal DIAGNOSIS of INTELLECTUAL IMPAIRMENT. Andrew Flores (2022), a LICENSED therapist in the field of psychology, who uses EVIDENCE-BASED practices, states that PERFORMANCE-BASED TESTS and STANDARDISED TESTS given by paediatricians or psychologists can MEASURE GENERAL COGNITIVE ABILITY in children over the age of eight, providing a score relative to other people. He assures readers that a person with an INTELLIGENCE QUOTIENT (IQ) of 70 could learn two words after hearing them spoken once, while someone with an IQ of 130 would remember three. He talks too about the many different TYPES OF INTELLECTUAL DISABILITIES and the need for COMPREHENSIVE ASSESSMENTS by TRAINED professionals in addition to measuring IQ. As above he is able to provide a long list of the kinds of things to be assessed. The capacity of these assessments to provide certitude is a key benefit for MentalHelp.net (2022) too. They recognise that a thorough review of MEDICAL HISTORY will identify physical or medical CAUSES of troubling symptoms, which can then be followed by A COMPREHENSIVE MEDICAL EXAM, including possible GENETIC AND NEUROLOGICAL TESTING, EVALUATION OF SOCIAL AND FAMILIAL HISTORY, EDUCATIONAL HISTORY, PSYCHOLOGICAL TESTING TO ASSESS INTELLECTUAL FUNCTIONING, ADAPTIVE FUNCTIONING, SOCIAL AND BEHAVIOURAL OBSERVATIONS, alongside interviews with caregivers and teachers.

Of course, the notion of the limited individual does not just apply to children and young people but also to all the other component 'parts' of the education system; the teachers, schools, local authorities, national systems and so forth. Standardisation and testing can just as well be applied here.

Certain comparisons

The idea of COMPARABILITY is not just relevant to individual students. It is also a key way of thinking about the school within school systems. For example, the PROGRAMME FOR INTERNATIONAL STUDENT ASSESSMENT (PISA) was developed at the end of the 20th century to provide comparative data on 15-year-olds' performance in reading, mathematics and science across nations. The PISA tests are undertaken by ACCREDITED National Service Providers (NSPs) in each country. It is intended to deliver school-level results to enable school improvement and allow schools to BENCHMARK their performance with national education systems. This ability to COMPARE is, according to the Organisation for Economic Co-operation and Development (OECD, 2022), more important than ever in a global, KNOWLEDGE–BASED ECONOMY, in which there is growing interest in seeing how prepared students are for participating in a globalised society. They also see it as a means to set educational TARGETS. A key adviser to the programme, Andreas Schleicher, identified that simply relying on NATIONAL EXAMS is not enough, because comparing against people in your own country is potentially dishonest and not a reflection of the global marketplace in which the student will have to operate (Coughlan, 2013).

National and international tools for SCHOOL COMPARISON are widely seen as a means of driving change and improvement in schools. Lemos and Van Reenen (2014) maintain that basic modern MANAGEMENT TECHNIQUES are a means of improving schools; in particular, RIGOROUS COLLECTION OF DATA on lessons, SYSTEMATIC FEEDBACK, supporting staff who struggle and rewarding 'GREAT TEACHERS'. They conclude that success can be equated to an INCREASE in NATIONAL EXAM SCORES. They suggest too that MEASURING MANAGEMENT is the clearest way to ensure school improvement. This is because all other variables will rise in the process. Such thinking can also be seen to have influenced policy development (e.g. Gibb, 2016) and in turn been linked to the development of TRAINING, such as the NATIONAL PROFESSIONAL QUALIFICATIONS for practising and aspiring school leaders. The UK Health and Safety Executive (2022) states that this managerial approach requires school leaders to follow employer's POLICIES, PROCEDURES and STANDARDS, ensuring appropriate staff training and COMPETENCIES, with a focus upon CONTROLLING the REAL RISKS so that things can be done in SAFETY.

The administrative team of a school (and local authority) are also part of the technology of certainty. Vincent Paget (2019), Operations Manager for a New Zealand educational data management company, suggests administrators are often responsible for RECORDING, CHECKING and ANALYSING STUDENT DATA. This opens channels of communication with parents and enables TAILORED TEACHING STRATEGIES, allowing students to be involved in LEARNING STRATEGY and GOAL SETTING. Setting up and managing REPORTING PROCEDURES provides PEACE OF MIND, REASSURING PEOPLE that SAFETY, WELL-BEING, ACADEMIC and PERSONAL DEVELOPMENT are being TAKEN CARE OF. It also supports the VISION and decision-making of school leaders, allowing them to know where the school's STRENGTHS and WEAKNESSES lie. It can enable them to understand the knowledge and skills that children NEED and at what STAGE in their education. All of this promotes ORGANISATIONAL ACCOUNTABILITY.

For many, accountability (through such mechanisms as the LITERACY and NUMERACY TESTS discussed above – e.g. Fahey, 2020) is the means to strengthen education outcomes. In reporting on the Swedish education systems, the OECD (2015) concludes that it is the lack of ACCOUNTABILITY at various LEVELS of the system which forms the key challenge for improving student performance and 'DRIVING THE SYSTEM FORWARD'. This is set alongside the barriers created by unclear education PRIORITIES and piecemeal reform that hinders ALIGNMENT and COHERENCE. They suggest this will be improved by the SCHOOLS INSPECTORATE being able to issue tougher SANCTIONS. However, they also note that practitioners feel a need to DOCUMENT DECISIONS to protect themselves from potential future SCRUTINY. This they suggest reflects less trust within the system and increasing BUREAUCRATISATION. Even though the practitioners felt that this increase in bureaucratic control reduced certainty, the OECD concluded that to overcome these challenges and increase certainty, the system requires PRINCIPLES that are stable and a tighter relationship between practice and RESEARCH.

This link between practice and research is also evident across nations and policy domains, in the call for EVIDENCE-BASED PRACTICES and TEACHING STRATEGIES. Leaders in this field (Coe and Kime, 2019) point to the need for RANDOMISED CONTROL TRIALS. They call for EVERYONE who plays a part in the education of learners to push this agenda. They see MEASUREMENT as the means to operationalise and define the constructs we test. We need to generate and TEST HYPOTHESES, seek RIGOROUS and relevant EVIDENCE and recognise this as the 'FINAL ARBITER' on how to improve systems, schools and classrooms.

Echoing this call, Vukovic (2021), in the *Teacher Magazine*, suggests that outstanding Australian schools, according to the NATIONAL SCHOOL IMPROVEMENT TOOL, are those where all teachers give high priority to such EVIDENCE-BASED STRATEGIES. This allows them to establish where students are DEVELOPMENTALLY and ACADEMICALLY, decide appropriate INTERVENTIONS and MONITOR progress and effectiveness. It enables teachers to identify a STARTING POINT for further teaching and to pitch learning at an APPROPRIATE level. It means they can SET REALISTIC GOALS and TARGETS to address INDIVIDUAL NEEDS.

FIGURE 2.2 Overflowing with knowledge and ability?

Similarly, Reading Rockets (2022) in the United States point to the LEGAL REQUIREMENT for schools to use SCIENTIFICALLY BASED RESEARCH whenever possible. They maintain RESEARCH-BASED PRACTICES should be MATCHED with the student's knowledge and skills. These should also be reflected in the development of INDIVIDUALISED EDUCATION PROGRAMS (IEP). By RECORDING WHAT WORKS, the teacher has EVIDENCE across time to offer insights into the teaching and learning of 'STUDENTS WITH DISABILITIES'. It also means that parents can demand EVIDENCE for the use of any 'academic, social and behavioural practices or INTERVENTIONS'.

> **You can breathe now. I am done with the online world of certainty**.

Where certainty leads

Over the last few pages, I have tried to map out some patterns of certainty embracing/embraced-by our education systems, patterns which inform how our schools function. I am bound to have missed plenty, but I hope I have shown that certainty is what school systems currently seek and are encouraged to seek and that this is evident in widely held beliefs by all kinds of people. I have endeavoured to show key ideas within systems constructed by policy and national drives for accountability. I have shown how it is played out in presumptions about teaching practices, normalised behaviours and support processes. I have explored its appearance within mechanisms of assessment, qualifications, research and the comparison of people and systems. I have made links across to the constraints of the curriculum and by implication upon the focus for our pedagogy.

For all the talk of Dewey and Vygotsky, communities of practice and learning communities to which many are introduced in teacher training/education/development, our education systems are still premised upon rewarding those who have answers; we build qualifications, assessments and curricula around these boundaries of certainty. This means we match our pedagogy to suit these, relying upon set texts and the recall of information (including rote learning). But this is hardly surprising; we still replicate practices which build upon the traditional roots, and our historical focus upon types of knowledge and school behaviours.

So, let's consider the process that is followed when people approach an issue from a position of certainty. Having looked across the broad range of examples above, it would seem to me that a pattern emerges. (A certain pattern, perhaps?) Accepting the limitations of any model and that its main value is as a tool for reflection, I will present this pattern as a model of certainty (Rix, 2020). I will then outline how this might be playing out in relation to three of the ideas which I touched on above: school quality, areas of knowledge and the identification of a need for additional support.

A model of certainty (see Figure 2.3)

We begin with certainty (a); perhaps we are seeking it or wanting it or perhaps we believe in it or think with it (b). Our search for certainty may lead us to think in scientific, institutionalised or legal ways, seeing personal or physical realities in a fixed way, drawing on conceptual frameworks and cultural traditions (c). To build on our certainty, we will need to seek causal connections, between objects and subjects, and to observe, measure, discuss and prove these connections (d). Exploring these causal connections will provide us with knowledge to apply within our fields or within our lives, which will both be informed by and inform the certainties with which we began (e). This will lead to a fixed position, an absolute, something which can be tested and judged against the processes of certainty, and this will create our parameters of the whole or part of the whole (f). We will be positioned with this absolute as a fact or a law, a rule or recognised truth; it will provide us with definitions or boundaries or norms, an evidence-base for our future (g); and it will

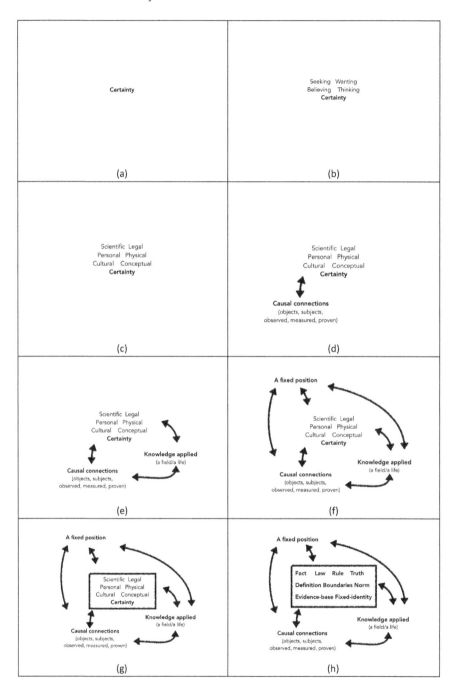

FIGURE 2.3 A model of certainty.

enable us to create a determinate function, identity or practice, one from which an individually framed being, concept or system can emerge (H).

Certain example 1 – School quality (see Figure 2.4)

We begin with an acceptance that there is a space for learning and that the quality of this space can be understood. This space is defined in legal and institutional terms, by its established routines and structures, as a school. This means it will follow a curriculum, adopt systems of assessment, include academic and non-academic activities and be populated by teachers, students, administrators and so forth. In order to explore the quality of this space, we will look for evidential connections between these routines and structures and we will presume that there can be a causal link which demonstrates the nature of the quality. We will therefore seek to make connections between such things as the spaces, documentation, resources, practices and personnel and learners. In order to understand these links, we will explore the objects and we will find ways to evaluate or measure them and the possible connections between them. We might choose to use, for example, exam scores, student attendance and teacher training as three points of measurement. We will propose hypotheses about these objects and their relationships and treat these as routes to knowledge. The measurements or evaluations will reify the objects further; so, perhaps, teacher training becomes to be seen as a route for knowledge development to teachers, student attendance comes to be seen as

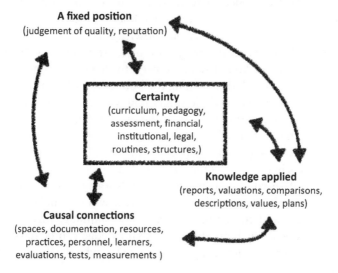

FIGURE 2.4 A model of certainty – Applied to the notion of school quality.

something which is positive for all concerned, while high exam scores equate to successful learning. (Each of these could themselves be points of investigation, involving the identification of key component parts and the causal connections between them.)

The links we are identifying now form themselves as knowledge (perhaps as a report or a school development plan or a league table) which we value and which in turn underline the relevance of the legal, scientific and cultural constructs which defined the process in the first place. By finding links, we confirm the relative truth of what we are seeking and how we are thinking about the nature of quality and how it is to be understood. Consequently, our focus is upon the established school practices and processes, and we accept our interpretation of their effect upon quality. We now have a view on the quality of the space and the constructs to demonstrate this quality. And the more we do this, the more we are held in a self-validating loop, where our ideas are constrained by the boundaries of quality which we have focused upon. The process itself would be iterative, shifting between our ideas about possible connections and the application of the knowledge which emerges, but our position becomes fixed, both in terms of what we value as quality and how we come to understand that quality.

Certain example 2 – Areas of knowledge (see Figure 2.5)

We begin with an acceptance that knowledge can be encapsulated within a boundaried conceptual structure. The language which is used to frame that knowledge is by its essence in turn framed by the understanding of that knowledge. So, a word will have a meaning, but that meaning will be dependent upon the context of the established knowledge frame. For example, *triangle* has potentially different meanings in music, art and maths. In coming to understand the area of knowledge, we need to define the constructs out of which it is made; this includes defining the boundaries of what is and what is not included. To be able to include something, we need to be able to demonstrate its connection to other aspects of the overall. So, picking up the triangle once more, in music it will have meaning when it is being used alongside other instruments (itself a particular construct), while it will have a different meaning if it is being measured for 'area' with a 'ruler' in maths, and a different role again if serving as a 'template' for 'spray painting' in art. These connections between the triangle and its context will inform how our understanding emerges and the nature of that understanding; this will create a framework through which an individual's knowledge can be developed and evaluated (a framework of the area of knowledge which defined itself in the first place).

An individual or a collective interaction with the triangle will confirm or construct the item as a specific item within the area of knowledge and the nature of that area too. The capacity of the individual to utilise it within the

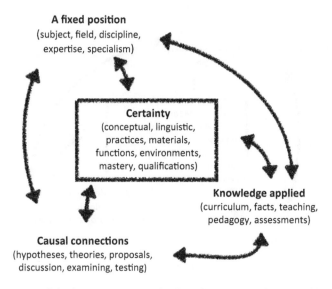

FIGURE 2.5 A model of certainty – Applied to the notion of areas of knowledge.

context as framed by that context will also serve as the fixed moment, a point of reference about a person's understanding of that area of knowledge. The capacity to show that understanding can be tested. Of course, once you have entered this framework and accepted the function of the triangle within this area of knowledge, the capacity of the triangle to be something else is constrained by that knowledge area. It is boundaried by a fixed identity. Using the understandings of the triangle from the other areas of knowledge will not hold sway in any other area in which you are operating. This is why it is so difficult for a biologist to transform the area of knowledge associated with physics or it is unlikely that a course on citizenship will develop significant knowledge of Latin.

Certain example 3 – Evaluating additional support (see Figure 2.6)

We begin with an understanding that learners can struggle within education systems. In evaluating the parameters of the struggle, the dominant conceptual frameworks and cultural traditions focus us upon a learner as an individual. We therefore seek to explore causal connections between the struggles and some aspect of that individual. To frame the individual and that struggle, we identify a characteristic (or characteristics) which gives us a reference point for our focus in seeking the causal basis. This characteristic will also reflect the areas of certainty out of which the understanding of the evaluation began, drawing upon established conceptual frameworks and cultural traditions. As such, it is likely to be situated biologically, culturally and/or environmentally.

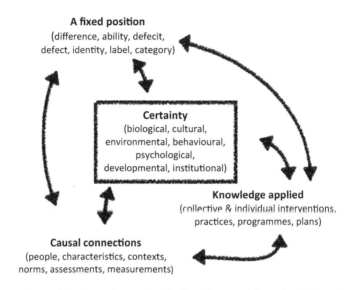

FIGURE 2.6 A model of certainty – Applied to the provision of additional support.

The relational nature of the school context and the norm-based references associated with this field require the characteristic to be considered in relation to other people. In order to situate and evidence this characteristic and its causal connections, the contexts and characteristics will be observed, discussed and measured. This will allow for a degree of proof. This emergent understanding will of itself be applied both collectively and individually. This response will of itself reinforce the understanding of the individual through the application of the knowledge associated with the established conceptual framework which defined that understanding at the outset. This will further increase the focus upon the understanding of the characteristics associated with that individual and increase the focus upon a singular core identifier. Since the focus is on an individual struggling in the system, its relational nature will be understood as some sort of difference, ability, defect, deficit or difficulty associated with that individual.

(some) Certain reflections

A fundamental conundrum which arises when we apply the model of certainty is that we have to oversimplify the complexity to make it manageable; in creating boundaries, we inevitably restrict the problem to individual or constrained points of reference and therefore limit our areas of influence. Consequently, insights and commonalities from other defined areas cannot be drawn upon; and the shared or less obvious are missed. For example:

- In the context of school quality, the model of certainty animates a focus upon the 'types' and 'outcomes' of learning which that system prioritises. It ensures an aim towards the 'sorts' of values the system recognises and rewards as the right ones. It understands itself through the behaviours and achievements which it seeks and/or encourages. This means that schools are only judged on their own terms, and the quality is unlikely to be linked to things which are not seen as schooling priorities. For instance, the school's impact upon relationships between families or siblings, the development of friendships or the political views of children. These would not typically be focused upon or measured in evaluating quality, but schools will undoubtedly have an impact in these areas. (Of course, if we chose to make them parameters for certainty, then they could be a focus, but in so doing it would leave less room for other established points of reference and would create pre-defined constraints around how we understand relationships, friendships and/or political views).
- In the context of areas of knowledge, the need to stay within the defined area(s) means that the world is seen through the subject focus. If you need to see the world differently, then you need to use a different subject or change the subject from within the subject or come up with a new area of knowledge. This is why people are always calling for new topics that need to be studied (or which need to be taught); for example, the numerous calls for 21st-century curricula or a focus upon 21st-century skills. However, the area of knowledge does not have a place until it has been formally constructed. In the school context, responses to this call are affected both by institutional and policy priorities, and also by the practicalities of what can be achieved in the available time. As a result, calls for change frequently lead to a focus upon cross-curricula activities or thematic areas of study. However, even if the aim is to make people break across the boundaries of the areas of knowledge, these cross-curricular or new fields are themselves also boundaried, in order to be argued for, explained and/or assessed. Similarly, arguments about curricula see topics being added and topics being removed but not a fundamental shift in the underlying paradigm of the subjects.
- In the context of the evaluation of additional support, the oversimplification leads to the individualisation of the problem, both in terms of who can evaluate the problem, who is defined by it and who can support, manage and fund the solutions that emerge. The certainty breaks down the whole into increasingly smaller parts trying to conjoin them as best they can and track their progress. The numbers of people involved within the overall system make this an impossible task to roll out across the system for all, and so it becomes a rationed approach, allocated to a few, who are as likely to be trapped as they are supported. The process of individualisation fixes people in a moment or identity that the system has created. It also constrains understanding and practices, encouraging a focus upon what

was identified in the past and a conviction that individualised support is the solution to individual needs. The system is discouraged from seeing the problem as being beyond the individual experience and discouraged from seeking collective or broader structural solutions.

Another fundamental conundrum which emerges from oversimplification is the need to define the roles of the people within the structure, so that people (and the systems) know what is expected of them. Prescribing roles within the structure constrains the individual's voice and limits their influence to their prescribed role. This makes it much harder to draw upon the collective experience of the context. It also makes it harder for people to work across boundaries (both internal boundaries within an institution and boundaries between institutions). A (disappointing) consequence of this, for instance, is the ongoing struggle to deliver the kinds of collaborative practice which policy makers have been calling for over many years. It also limits the capacity of our schools to take advantage of the skills, understandings and past histories of numerous others who may have useful things to contribute. This exacerbates our tendency to reinvent institutionalised patterns of behaviour and to resist potential bottom-up or emergent solutions that have not come through the 'right' channels. We will return to these challenges later.

An end of certainty

People within systems are aware of the problems that our embrace with the technologies of certainty can create (of course). In order to compensate for them, the defining of the parameters of the problem and evaluation of responses may be undertaken by multiple people within the situation or across a period of time. Conflicting or confirming fixed positions may be identified and used to demonstrate the complexity of the situation. The need to re-evaluate and to re-visit may well be part of the systemic response to the challenges which it is facing. For example, in the context of additional support, they may create continua of provision and processes into which they can allocate people in an attempt to match systemic notions of need with systemic notions of appropriate support. More generally, they may produce policies of the sort which we have identified above, exhorting people to move beyond professional boundaries, or which provide targeted funding for types of problems and areas of need, and so forth.

And, of course, the idea of certainty is reassuring. (Some readers, for example, will have found it useful to know they were half-way through a section on the technologies of certainty). Many people within our school systems will see the application of the model of certainty as a highly effective way to organise and evaluate our ways of working (and being) within the system, as well as the quality of the learning that takes place within it.

They may feel that (their) responses based on the technologies of certainty are what is required in the face of a complex world. They may highly value these processes and their outputs, recognising that they play a fundamental role in how we understand and deliver education and make use of our available resources. The problem for them is that certainty, and its underpinning good sense, is undermined by the reality of the everyday, which is always eroding and reconfiguring. They (we) are constantly confronted by the uncertainty which is at the heart of all human experience. After all, as suggested at the start of this chapter, the fundamental barrier in any search for certainty is the uncertainty we are trying to keep at bay.

This then is where we will next head. The everyday uncertainty at the heart of schooling and the theory behind inclusion. (All things being equal).

References

Atieno, L. (2022). The importance of 'ability grouping' for learners. Retrieved June 9, 2022 from https://www.newtimes.co.rw/lifestyle/importance-ability-grouping-learners

Brunskill, J. (2015). We need subject specialists. Retrieved June 9, 2022 from https://www.teachprimary.com/learning_resources/view/we-need-subject-specialists

Centers for Disease Control and Prevention. (2022). CDCs developmental milestones. Retrieved June 14, 2022 from https://www.cdc.gov/ncbddd/actearly/milestones/index.html

Coe, R., & Kime, S. (2019). *A (new) manifesto for evidence-based education: Twenty years on.* Evidence Based Education: Sunderland, UK.

Coughlan, S. (2013). How Pisa became the world's most important exam. November 27. Retrieved June 14, 2022 from https://www.bbc.co.uk/news/business-24988343

Dewey, J. (1930). *The quest for certainty.* Unwin Brothers.

Fahey, G. (2020). Don't expel school accountability. Retrieved June 15, 2022 from https://www.cis.org.au/commentary/opinion/dont-expel-school-accountability/

Flores, A. (2022). Who can assess intellectual disability Retrieved June 14, 2022, from https://escorpionatl.com/who-can-assess-intellectual-disability

Gibb, N. (2015). The purpose of education. The Department for Education. Retrieved June 9, 2022 from https://www.gov.uk/government/speeches/the-purpose-of-education

Gibb, N. (2016). The importance of school leadership. Retrieved June 14, 2022 from https://www.gov.uk/government/speeches/the-importance-of-school-leadership

Gov.UK. (2022). Children with special educational needs and disabilities (SEND). Retrieved June 14, 2022 from https://www.gov.uk/children-with-special-educational-needs/print

Health and Safety Executive. (2022). The role of school leaders – Who does what. Retrieved June 14, 2022, from https://www.hse.gov.uk/services/education/sensible-leadership/school-leaders.htm

Health Service Executive in Ireland. (2022). Your baby's developmental milestones from 3 to 5 years Retrieved June 14, 2022, from https://www2.hse.ie/wellbeing/babies-and-children/checks-milestones/developmental-milestones/3-5-years/

International Student. (2022). Standardized tests. Retrieved June 14, 2022 from https://www.internationalstudent.com/study_usa/application-process/standardized-tests/overview/

Kalam, A. (2021). Why exams are important. Retrieved June 9, 2022 from https://timesofindia.indiatimes.com/readersblog/vinoth9487/why-exams-are-important-33513/

Lemos, R., & Van Reenen, J. (2014). Why school management matters even more than we thought. Retrieved June 14, 2022 from https://www.theguardian.com/teacher-network/teacher-blog/2014/may/20/good-school-management-matters

Liew, M. (2018). 12 school subjects that should be introduced today to change the world tomorrow. Retrieved June 9, 2022 from https://www.learning-mind.com/school-subjects/

Local Schools Network. (2013). What are the examination systems in other countries? Retrieved June 17, 2022 from https://localschoolsnetwork.org.uk/faq/what-are-examination-systems-other-countries

Master for Arts in Teaching. (2022). 5 benefits of ability grouping in the classroom. Retrieved June 14, 2022 from https://www.masterofartsinteaching.net/lists/5-benefits-of-ability-grouping-in-the-classroom/

MentalHelp.net. (2022). The diagnosis of intellectual disabilities. Retrieved June 14, 2022 from https://www.mentalhelp.net/intellectual-disabilities/diagnosis/

National Deaf Children's Society. (2022). How are additional support needs identified and assessed? Retrieved June 14, 2022 from https://www.ndcs.org.uk/information-and-support/education-and-learning/getting-additional-support/getting-additional-support-scotland/how-are-additional-support-needs-identified-and-assessed/

OECD. (2015). Accountability - Improving schools in Sweden: An OECD perspective. Retrieved June 15, 2022 from https://www.oecd.org/education/school/Improving-Schools-in-Sweden.pdf

OECD (2022). PISA for schools. Retrieved June 14, 2022 from https://www.oecd.org/pisa/aboutpisa/pisa-based-test-for-schools-faq.htm

Paget, V. (2019). 3 reasons why school administration is important for student education. Retrieved June 15, 2022 from https://www.orah.com/blog/3-reasons-why-school-administration-is-important-for-student-education

Pretest Plus (2022). Year 7 CATs: Everything parents need to know. Retrieved June 14, 2022 from https://pretestplus.co.uk/year-7-cats-everything-parents-need-to-know/

Reading Rockets (2022). Evidence-based practices at school: A guide for parents. Retrieved June 15, 2022 from https://www.readingrockets.org/article/evidence-based-practices-school-guide-parents

Rees, N. (2016). 5 reasons why school choice is important right now. Retrieved June 16, 2022 from https://www.educationnext.org/5-reasons-why-school-choice-is-important-right-now-rees/

Reference (2021). What is the role of the teacher in the classroom? Retrieved June 16, 2022 from https://www.reference.com/business-finance/role-teacher-classroom-e7c23c7113b3e1a1

Rix, J. (2020). Our need for certainty in an uncertain world: The difference between special education and inclusion? *British Journal of Special Education*, 47(3), 283–307.

Sanskriti. (2019). Why students must wear school uniforms. Retrieved June 16, 2022 from https://www.sanskritischools.com/blog/students-must-wear-school-uniforms/

Sellgren, K. (2017). Should young children be grouped by ability? December 1, 2017. Retrieved June 14, 2022 from https://www.bbc.co.uk/news/education-42154013

Simply Learning Tuition. (2022). Everything you need to know about the Swedish education system. Retrieved June 16, 2022 from https://www.simplylearningtuition. co.uk/advice-for-parents/everything-you-need-to-know-about-the-swedish-education-system/

Spencer, C (2013). What's the point of school uniform? *The Guardian*. Retrieved June 16, 2022 from https://www.theguardian.com/education/mortarboard/2013/oct/03/ why-wear-school-uniform

Stamou, E., Fooks, G., Marmer, E., Zurabishvili, T., & Leaders, W. P. (2019). CHIEF (cultural heritage and identities of Europe's future) grant agreement no: 770464 WP: 1 theoretical design & policy review deliverable: 1.4 cross-national comparison of educational policies and curricula.

Stewart, V. (2022). How Singapore developed a high-quality teacher workforce. Retrieved June 16, 2022 from https://asiasociety.org/global-cities-education-network/ how-singapore-developed-high-quality-teacher-workforce

Sullivan, E. (2022). The disadvantages of mixed-age groupings. Retrieved June 14, 2022 from https://www.ehow.co.uk/info_8697965_disadvantages-mixedage-groupings.html

The Deccan Herald. (2013). Benefits of ability grouping. February 27. Retrieved June 14, 2022 from https://www.deccanherald.com/content/315371/benefits-ability-grouping.html

TutorHunt Website. (2022). What is the importance of academic subjects in everyday life? Retrieved June 9, 2022 from https://www.tutorhunt.com/importance-of-academic-subjects.asp

Vukovic, R. (2021). Evidence-based practice – What is it and why is it important? Retrieved June 15, 2022 from https://www.teachermagazine.com/au_en/articles/ evidence-based-practice-what-is-it-and-why-is-it-important

Youth Employment UK. (2021). How important are exams and qualifications? Retrieved June 9, 2022 from https://www.youthemployment.org.uk/how-important-are-exams-and-qualifications/

Yussif. (2021). Why is classroom management important? Retrieved June 16, 2022 from https://classroommanagementexpert.com/blog/what-is-the-importance-of-classroom-management/

3
WHERE UNCERTAINTY LEADS?

Free?

In the mid-1990s, while working at a secondary school in Hackney, North London, I was asked to cover for another teacher and teach their A-level Maths lesson. A-level maths is relatively 'advanced' and is (was) typically studied by 16–18-year-olds in England. My mathematical track record was not great from an academic point of view. At 15, I had got a B for Maths at the level 'below' (O-level), and my teacher had told my parents he was amazed I had even passed. My task was now to teach (or oversee?) quadratic equations for a double lesson (about 90 minutes).

In preparation, I had been told to instruct the students to 'get on with the exercises in the [text] book'. As soon as we sat down, a hand went up and a student asked a question. I did not understand a word they were talking about.

So, what do you do?

I decided to go with the flow.

As the hand lowered, I asked the young person what they understood about quadratic equations. Their reply had far more detail than I had gleaned from my quick perusal of the book, but it did not give me a clue about how I might help answer their question. My only hope was to rely upon all the other people in the room. So, I opened the issue to the floor. Was what we had just heard a full explanation?

And so it began. Collective quadratic equations among about 15 or so young people, all talking about the problems they had been set. Sometimes there was silence as they worked on something, sometimes there was a great

DOI: 10.4324/9781003281405-3

deal of chat, sometimes it was just one or two people in discussion. People came up and wrote things on the board, crossed to each other's tables to have a look at what they were doing or hung out listening to what someone else had to say. I learned loads. At the end, I would probably have been able to answer that first question I had been asked.

I cannot remember at which point I told them I was clueless. But I do recall having a tear in my eye when at the end of the lesson they all concurred that it was the best A-level maths lesson they had ever had. Of course, all I had done was not know anything about the topic we were learning about.

Now it could be suggested that this is just a romantic tale of an ageing pedagogue and that numerous aspects of it mean it is not relevant to a huge range of classroom situations. It could, for example, be suggested that the students are older and wiser, they have a pre-determined interest in the subject, they are all literate, verbal and academically capable. But I do think that would be missing the point. I think that a group of children, young people and adults anywhere can be brought together around a common point of interest and learn things, if we are open to it.

We just have to go where uncertainty leads us. As Biesta notes:

When we keep education open anything can happen, anything can arrive.

(p. 23)

The other limitation of this tale, though, is that it is primarily about pedagogic risk. In trying to resolve issues of education, participation and inclusion, the risks we are confronting are not just pedagogic (as important as they are). As was evident in the previous chapter, the range of areas in which people confront uncertainty with certainty is system wide.

So, let's consider the nature of that uncertainty, as it batters against the many defences we have shored up through our embrace with certainty. Let's consider how our best attempts at certitude turn out to be a chimera. [Please note: I mean something we seek that is an illusion, not a mythical creature with a lion's head, goat's body and serpent's tail].

In approaching this task, rather than give an example to set against each of those capitalised concepts set out in Chapter 2, I will seek to demonstrate the underlying contradictions and points of doubt within the arena in which those concepts sit. I will place these under five headings:

- Uncertain meanings
- Uncertain practices
- Uncertain grammars
- Uncertain standards
- Uncertain evidence

FIGURE 3.1 Properly prepared.

I am not going to follow the pattern of the last chapter either, by seeking everyday examples to demonstrate the existence of uncertainty. Whereas I was happy to cherry-pick the internet to show the prevalence of our embrace with certainty, it seems sensible to rely upon the research of others to explicate how this is undermined. Inevitably, I am still selecting my examples, but I could have given many more for each of the issues I touch upon, and I could have touched upon many other issues of certainty which have uncertainty at their heart. (I recognise too that I am relying upon research in a way that might be seen as using a technology of certainty; as I will explore later in the book, however, listening to understandings that arise from these technologies is not fundamentally problematic, it is succumbing to their overwhelming dominance.)

Uncertain meanings

Words are (always) an important starting point for uncertainty. For instance, there is a common call at the heart of an *education-for-all* policy discourse for 'collaboration'; yet there is confusion about what is meant by the term and little robust research into its effective delivery and impact. What research there is suggests that its implementation is inconsistent (Kennedy & Stewart, 2011) and at the heart of this failing is a need to establish shared understandings across professional boundaries which are both deep and entrenched (Edwards, 2012; Benevides et al., 2022). Similar discordances have been evident in relation to 'inclusion' (e.g. Amor et al., 2019), 'personalisation' (e.g. Courcier, 2007; Beach, 2017) and 'differentiation' (e.g. Hart, 1996; Gaitas & Martins, 2017).

Broader terms such as 'culture' and 'ethos' are also hazy and situated in contested spaces, even though they are a key part of how schools present and define themselves. For example, in Ireland there is much made of the drive for an inclusive ethos and culture; however, any changes are cosmetic and surface-level, with the long-established 'academic' focus still dominating (McKeon, 2020). Similarly, a doctoral study explored how two governing boards developed and implemented a 'vision' for children considered to have special educational needs (Walker, 2021), but their aspirations were undermined by having to respond to change and having to engage with other organisations.

At an even more fundamental level, our understandings of 'childhood' vary considerably too. A study looking at the attitudes of 75 university students at the National University of Sciences and Technology in Pakistan, for example, revealed their multidimensional conception of 'the child' (Qamar, 2021). Although the vast majority alluded to the innocence of childhood, there was more generally reference to childhood both as:

- vulnerability, deficit and becoming
  and
- socially situated, agentive and being.

This tension of *being* and *becoming* was evident in statements which positioned the child as both active and passive. Such complexity is also apparent to an academic arguing for a simplistic notion of childhood. Fowler (2020) recognises that the simple certainty of an age definition fails both to acknowledge a child's moral status or interests, and that physical and mental changes don't suddenly happen at a set point in time. He also accepts though that it is far harder to develop criteria based on a person's capacities and competence. This is because they are hidden and will be contested. He therefore calls for a simple age-based understanding because of the impossibility of defining childhood (and a child) more deeply.

> Developing institutions that have fine-grained knowledge to assess the capacity of each child might thus be impossible, given the depth of information this would require. At the very least it would be prohibitively costly.
>
> *(Fowler, 2020 p. 10)*

Which (of course) is exactly what our school systems are doing all the time. Such assessment is, for instance, at the heart of the continuum notion of special educational, the almost universal use of ability grouping and any number of norm-based processes. In view of Fowler's conclusion that assessment of a child's capacity is impossible, you may recall the variability I mentioned in Chapter 1. This related to countries' diverse understandings of special educational needs, the unreliability of the categories and processes we use to define capacity and ability, and the inconsistent ways in which we to allocate people to provision.

Agreeing the meaning for assessments involving labelled categories is clearly one of the major challenges for the seekers of certainty. Identifying and applying special and needs requires finding observable phenomena as evidence of behaviours or characteristics. The markers that experts search for have been selected as a focus because of their practical value in the diagnostic process. But consequently, they can also be seen as theoretical constructs in their own right, requiring us to unpack '*the constructs underlying [the] symptoms*' (Wilshire et al., 2021). This creates considerable space for disagreement. Perhaps, unsurprisingly, people propose different solutions. For instance:

- a concern with the use of traditional taxonomies has led some to develop a diagnostic system focused upon symptoms (Waszczuka et al., 2017).
- a recognition by the British and American Psychological Associations that functional and individual diagnosis are a flawed basis for evidence-based practice and non-clinical uses has led to an exploration of holistic solutions which take the issue of context into account (Rix, 2023).

This last bullet point is always one which makes me stop and ponder. Why do people carry on believing in approaches which are clearly inadequate? If the people who are placed at the heart of the technologies of certainty by policy makers and bureaucrats are saying something is wrong, why are they not listened to? Is this head-in-the-sand approach evident across a whole range of other practices too?

Uncertain practices

The difference in practices which emerge from these diverging understandings leads to huge variations in the provision that is available to people. In the UK, this process is often referred to as a postcode lottery. For example (to name but a few), in England there is a lottery in school behaviour management policies (Caslin, 2021), adolescent social care (Patel, 2022), children's palliative care (Tuckwell, 2017), school careers guidance (Holt-White et al., 2022), special educational needs and disability provision (OFSTED, 2021) and music education (Savage, 2021). Such lotteries are evident globally too. This can be between services and nations as well as within them, for example, in relation to diagnosis and additional support (Rix, 2015) and in relation to personal assistance schemes (Nally et al., 2022). It can also be seen as a consequence of systems which encourage local control to deliver national policies.

Local differences are also evident in everyday classroom practice. For instance, exploring the experiences of 49 learners on an English course, Huang (2021) was unable to fit the teaching practices under one theoretical position. Teachers were using diverse activities, tasks and exercises including seemingly contradictory communicative language and mechanical drill approaches. Similarly, Iskandar and Lusiana (2019) noted in a three-month observational case study of a single teacher how she used various strategies in order to accomplish the objective of the learning. In seeking to differentiate, she might modify activity format or output expectations, shift the focus, simplify the input or alter a challenge.

This (perfectly sensible) flexibility is also evident in the use of lesson plans. A survey of 289 trainee teachers in England (exploring the writing, use and evaluation of such plans) showed that these students used different methods. They also concluded that lesson plans may be being used for too many purposes. Only 8% of trainees said they had followed the plan as they had written it, with an equivalent percentage saying they did not refer to it at all (Capel et al., 2019). Similarly, a survey of 200 Afghan teachers (Behzad, 2013) suggested that over 80% produced the plans as required by regulations but not as they had been taught in teacher training, with nearly a third not following the plans they had produced.

This variability is not just evident in relation to plans teachers have produced themselves. Looking at the use of a scripted lesson plan related to sex education in 105 South African schools (Speizer et al., 2020), the researchers concluded it was probably a lack of teacher fidelity in implementing the plans, which meant the program did not have the intended results. This discordance can also play out at a very local level. For example, the Swedish individual development plan is a document that is meant to summarise each individual student's achievements in relation to subject objectives and standards and the support they require. However, the documents teachers produce typically lack information about what is to be learned; are nonsensical, vague, generalised; and make presumptions about the children (Korp et al. (2019). I recall being told by a Norwegian teacher about a similar document they had been expected to produce. She said that producing anything meaningful for every child in a class was impossible.

Variability and the impossibility of reliably individualising practice at scale is a challenge across institutions associated with education. It is also evident that the uncertainties outlined in this section are interwoven with the uncertainty of meanings in the section before. Of course, they are also entwined with the traditional structures that are supposed to create constancy, and which dominate the framing of education within schools. So, let's look towards some of those now.

Uncertain grammars

The processes that frame classroom practice are also less certain than intended. Let's begin with how people dress. A doctoral study in the United States explored the impact of dress codes on student behaviour and learning in four middle schools (Dulin, 2016). It concluded they were simply exchanging one set of problems for another. They were wasting time and having no significant effect on school safety, discipline, climate and attendance. While another doctoral study concluded that for older pupils it made a positive difference on attendance, discipline and academic achievement (Monroe, 2009), for younger pupils it created more problems, and all in all had both positive and negative impacts. A study in Turkey also identified how it could divide a community (Cinoglu, 2014). Students disagreed with parents, teachers and school administrators on all points that a uniform increased academic achievement, supported discipline, contributed to school safety and was more functional. The variability which comes with context was also evident in a study involving 462 students in Mongolia (Sabic-El-Rayess et al., 2019). Here they were more likely to influence poor students' negative perceptions of themselves and encourage school dropout. Issues arose as a result of:

- different qualities of uniform (from tailor-made to free handouts).
- numbers of people who wore them.
- preferential practices in handing out uniforms.
- biased funding practices within the system.
- shifting perceptions of poverty.
- how students viewed their and others' clothing.

The authors also noted studies where free uniforms had reduced attendance because parents used the additional money for uniforms to fund street selling and created a localised marketplace with suppliers controlling the prices.

It is part of the nature of uncertainty that it leads (unsurprisingly?) to surprises and exacerbates the widespread disagreement about so many core ideas. In Chapter 2, we talked about calls for new school subjects to deal with our changing life experiences. However, similar arguments take place in relation to the established curriculum and what is being taught. For example, Boaler (2008) suggests that schools teach an impoverished version of mathematics of little bearing on the mathematics of life, work or academia. She recognises that pupils would be shocked by the levels of uncertainty involved in the work of high-level mathematics. A similar failure is evident in music as part of the English National Curriculum. Bate (2020) concludes that music's value is not a set of skills or knowledge. It is about exploring its inherently destabilising nature arising from being in a continual temporal state of flux. (She also suggests that the curriculum's focus upon a fixed canon of music and musical skills works against the social justice goals which policy makers suggest is a key goal of the education system.)

The failure of fixed subjects to represent the complex, interweaving nature of knowledge is evident in the materials used to represent them too. For instance, when considering the curriculum, text books, educational software and teacher guides associated with six different subjects in the Greek system, Antoniou (2021) concluded that the connections between the subjects were rare, superficial and failed to enhance the integration of knowledge. Generally, integration was left to cross-thematic activities, tacked on as a parallel or complementary to the main curricula. Similarly, the fixed nature of subject exams constrains what is studied. Puttick (2015) explored the role of chief examiners in framing the knowledge associated with geography. He concluded that accreditation restricts the nature of the powerful knowledge taught in school. Students in their case study were told they had to study a topic because it was specified and would be on the exam. As a result, they expected and accepted this accreditation rationale, even though it limited their access to powerful knowledge.

In their discussion about the 'powerful knowledge' required, Gericke et al. (2018) demonstrate how it takes different forms. They recognised a subject-situated notion, with its focus upon content knowledge, but they also recognised that at a classroom level this content is variously understood by teachers and students. They suggest that powerful knowledge needs to be understood more flexibly, as something that can be described and identified at different levels of society, institutions and the classroom. An interesting example of this is evident in a study at university level (Steinberg & Waspe, 2016). This study concluded that students did not agree with lecturers about what academic rigour meant. Across the four aspects of rigour they identified, they noted that teachers and students disagreed about three of them, in relation to expectations, balance between breadth and depth and the integration of theory and practice. Ultimately, students were interested in the practicalities of study and the practical application of ideas, whereas the lectures were focused upon theory and practice alongside breadth and depth of knowledge.

This mismatch in the relevance of the curriculum is discussed in a New Zealand study (Kidman et al., 2011) exploring Maori children's experience of the science curriculum. They conclude it was not aligned with the children's cultural contexts. Evidently, the challenge for subjects is that they are not constructed locally but rely upon disciplinary structures. However, disciplinary-specific concepts and language will cause localised difficulties. For example, local understandings of what is meant by 'cultural' has been shown to mean very different things in different countries. The CHIEF study (Hrstić et al., 2019) looked at curriculum documents across a range of countries (including Georgia, Germany, Greece, Turkey, India and the UK) and noted a lack of basic definitions. It pointed towards a great variety of interpretations across the nations too and a need to understand the tensions which emerge from such contradictory positions.

As a final example of the lack of certainty at the heart of the grammars of schooling, let's consider examinations. As Williams and Wong (2009) noted in the context of universities, these continue to be dominated by traditional closed-book invigilated exams, even though our everyday social and business spaces are filled with technology and calls for knowledge economy skills. They also frequently experience grade inflation evident at different times across various levels of the system. This common experience leads to both their redesign and the creation of policies of containment, involving political responses which are not 'rationalist' (Kippin & Cairney, 2022). The process of examinations is clearly not meritocratic either, even though this would appear to be one of its appeals. For instance, the national examination in the Indonesian educational system uses centralised-designed testing that exacerbates rather than confronts inequalities. Sidik (2020) points to the differences in facilities, teacher distribution and infrastructure at the heart of this disjunction and suggests that the considerable exam expenditure would be better spent on confronting these differences.

The pressure which the exam process brings also works against notions that they are good for character building and the development of self-esteem. For instance, a systematic review of the stress experienced by people in their last years of school, looking at studies across 17 countries, identified that over 15% of young people reported very high or high levels of distress, with a strong connection to the examination experience (Wuthrich et al., 2020). More specifically, Vanner (2018) describes two schools where an emphasis on exam success creates a competitive relationship between peers. This resulted in increased victimisation of both high- and low-performing students. It also meant that other priorities, such as sexual violence experienced after school hours, were set aside, so students could stay longer and study in preparation for these exams.

It is also noticeable how grammars that frame practice have emerged and shifted over the years. For example, in the introduction we talked about a collective embrace of new ideas such as comprehensive schooling and multiculturalism. Could these now be considered grammars of education? Similarly, notions such as inclusion, collaboration and differentiation (mentioned in the section about uncertain meanings) have also come to be a key part of how schools understand themselves and frame (claims about?) their ways of doing things. Ideas can also be reinvented across the years and so take on new identities and characteristics while playing similar functions. A good example of this education's embrace of standards.

Uncertain standards

Competition between schools and between nations as mentioned above, and the way this can play into uncertainty within the examination process, are part of what Allodi (2017) calls the 'unrealistic expectation of perfection'. Wiliam (2010), for example, concludes that standardised tests are not a particularly good tool for holding districts, schools and teachers accountable, since differences between schools generally explain less than 10% of variance in student scores. Despite this, large-scale assessments can be seen to influence policy and curriculum reforms across the world (Mulongo, 2017). Wagner et al. (2012) suggest that while it is possible to agree on technical parameters for effective assessment (such as sample sizes, alpha coefficients, test–retest reliability and predictive validity), the nature of who gets tested, what gets tested, when they get tested, as well as how and why they are tested are all contested issues. Exemplifying this contestation, Bradbury et al. (2021) concluded that Standard Assessment Tests in English schools fulfil a biopolitical function that identifies children as failing/acceptable/ successful. They suggest that without tests, these divisions would be far more nuanced. Similarly, progress measures and school league tables are of limited value for making quantitative comparisons; for example, the differential effects of schools on different pupil groups. Consequently, many have argued that they are at best a tool for self-evaluation and as screening device for the start of further investigation (Leckie & Goldstein, 2017).

As with exams, the process of engaging with these quantitative measures can also work against the intended improvements. In a study involving Early Years Foundation Stage assessments in England, Hood and Mitchell (2017) noted that during the process children and practitioners act in ways that produce inequalities. They also noted how educators' perceptions of the children were not considered. Summative key stage tests have also been shown to lower self-esteem for low-achieving pupils, while encouraging transmission teaching and highly structured activities, as well as a focus upon summative assessment (Harlen & Deakin Crick, 2002). It is perhaps not surprising that this feeds into a negative student view of the classroom.

The drive to have these standardised assessment, tests and tables fits into a long tradition (in many systems) of not trusting unsupervised teachers (e.g. Coolahan & Donovan, 2009). However, the resulting search for accountability itself damages trust, while building suspicion, professional cynicism and low morale (Sahlberg, 2010). The issue of trust is also key part of the history of school inspection (e.g. Coolahan. & O'Donovan, 2009). This is partly because inspection can easily create a sense of confrontation. For instance, a study into the impact of school inspection on teaching and learning in Tanzania (Matete, 2021) concluded that the process created a feeling of fear for many teachers. There was a randomness inherent in the system too, with the inspectors giving advice even though they typically did not visit classrooms or undertake lesson observations, and instead focused on the documentation.

School inspection may create a local sense of structure, which constructs and mobilises particular conceptions of knowledge, judgement and expertise, but these change over time and between systems. In the context of the

English system, Baxter and Clarke (2014) suggested that changes were not part of a logical progression in search of school improvement but were more about retaining control of a system with widely varying models of governance. As a result of this, forms of knowledge which would have more credibility with the teaching profession were ignored, reducing the relevance of inspection to school practice. Similarly, in an examination of governance and school inspection in Scotland, England and Sweden (Lawn et al., 2014), each system demonstrated a different view of the school, its relations and purposes. However, in all three there was a tension between inspection and local control, reflecting a need to motivate and discipline, to be effective, efficient and trusting. The inspections were meant to create confidence and improvement, and as such they had to both change the school and leave it in place.

Uncertain evidence

In many ways, all that has come before will be seen by many seekers of certainty as the inevitable and acceptable consequence of a system which needs to organise and control large numbers of children and young people. It is an obvious outcome of historical and political machinations. People accept that we argue and battle about the issues raised; we will not all agree about the materiality of the emerging approaches and that across time our processes will shift frequently. The uncertainty can be ignored because we currently have ordained (agreed?) priorities and those are the things we need to focus upon.

The final topic of this section though, evidence-based practice, is seen by many people as much more than this, because it arises from scientific method – our benchmark for (getting close to) certainty. It is our means to provide a more permanent certitude. It would be simply absurd to suggest that evidence-based practice is not good practice.

The problem is that this too (evidence-based practice) is a mythical beast.

The first challenge is the difficulty in undertaking research deemed top quality by seekers of certainty. The resources and costs of implementing or researching evidence-based practices at scale are considerable (Horner, Sugai & Fixsen, 2017). Even for those who are well networked such an approach can prove hard to achieve. For example, in order to identify best practices in relation to the grouping of students, researchers from three UK universities were funded by the Education Endowment Foundation to undertake a randomised controlled trial, with sampling run by the National Foundation for Educational Research (Taylor et al., 2017). Despite the high standing of all these parties and the weight of research evidence in favour of mixed grouping, it proved impossible to recruit the required number of schools to the mixed attainment trials (even though the target for the 'setting' trial was 120 schools and for 'mixed attainment' was only 20 schools). To make things worse, once recruited, numbers dropped further. Various self-fulfilling, circular reasons for this shortfall emerged from the study, underlining the unreliability of human practice; but it also underlined the reality of undertaking research in complex social systems only a limited number of approaches can be tested in a manner which will be accepted as robust in the context of models of certainty.

A second challenge is the nature of studies which can produce a satisfactory evidence base. Putting to one side the fundamental contradiction in undertaking research involving categories that are contested and have been shown to be unreliably diagnosed, there is a bias towards certain research methods. For instance, in exploring the methodological challenges faced by autism educational research in impacting on practice, Guldberg (2017) notes the dominance of experimental research designs evaluating interventions. She suggests that there needs to be a more balanced range of methodologies if it is going to impact on the lives of individuals with autism, their families and the practitioners who work with them. This includes recognising that practitioner knowledge arising in the classroom has equivalent value to that of researchers. It should also involve participatory approaches situated in real-life contexts, taking into account everyday concerns and experiences. As further evidence of this lack of appliable evidence, Pellicano et al. (2014) identified that over a ten-year-period in the UK over half of funding into autism research went to studies focused on biology, brain and cognition, and just over 1% on societal issues and explorations of people's lived experience.

Thirdly, there is a problem with the research which is undertaken. In my last book, I cited a whole range of systematic reviews which demonstrated the poor quality of research across the field of special education. A similar observation has more recently been made by a leading figure in the field of children and adolescents' mental health, Leonard Bickmann (2020). Drawing on extensive systematic reviews he talks about:

- the poor quality of research.
- the overpromising of earlier studies.
- the lack of fidelity in process.
- the huge variation in results of interventions across populations.
- the contradictory evidence.
- the failure to improve outcomes over many decades.

He concludes that our psychotherapeutic responses fail because a 'plethora of other factors influence mental health'. An excellent example of the compromised research which underpins such failure comes in a paper exploring ideas of neuroscience for early years education. Vandenbroeck (2014) points to the high level of conflict of interest in many studies. They give an example of a parenting support programme called 'Triple P', where 32 out of 33 studies in a systematic review were authored by Triple P affiliated personnel and only two of them made note of their connection.

Fourthly, if you feel you can be certain about the overall quality of the research related to an issue, there is a challenge in identifying which evidence-based practices to apply. For example, a well-conducted study of school-based food and nutrition interventions identified four outcome measures that can enhance children's health: i) promoting knowledge about healthy eating and improving ii) dietary behaviour, iii) dietary attitude and iv) physicality (Chaudhary et al., 2020). However, in looking at the evidence, it is hard to know precisely what it is that will work. In coming to their conclusion, they ranked 43 studies against these four outcome measures. However, only one study had effect measures in all four, one of which was only partially effective. Of the 65 outcomes they recorded, 19 were seen as very effective (29%), 23 as effective (35%), 9 as partially effective (14%) and 14 were regarded as ineffective (21%). So how do you choose which one to use? Some interventions are effective for some outcomes and ineffective for others. And if you choose any one of these approaches, can you be certain it will work, even if it has been marked as 'very effective'? What does very effective mean? Is it 100% certain? (Obviously not).

Last but not least is the issue of applying the evidence base. As Bickmann concludes, services rarely deliver evidence-based practice and when they do it loses effectiveness. Here are some examples mostly from the United States, involving large-scale studies and doctoral studies in mainstream and special education settings undertaken in a range of school types with various student groupings. Studies looking at the implementation of evidence-based interventions, for instance, can show how the vast majority of practitioners and/or settings do not follow a recommended schedule, content and strategies (Ennett et al., 2011), or that anywhere from a sizeable minority to a sizeable majority of children do not reach reliable change criterion and might have achieved changes without the intervention (Lee, 2019). This lack of fidelity and consistency has also been observed in both school leadership and practitioners, leading to a suggestion that only interventions which require minimal support and training are not constrained by organisational issues (Melgarejo et al., 2020). Similarly, even if some schools report carrying on with an intervention beyond the initial study, they will not continue with all of them, particularly if they are complex (Pavez, 2017). It is also clear that school leaders may not recognise the impact of evidence-based programmes nor see them as being better than ones that are non-evidence-based (Hecht, 2016) and that practitioners can feel unprepared to assess skills and implement strategies in the way that the evidence-based intervention require (Mitchell, 2019). To cap this all off (and perhaps unsurprisingly), when a flexible (uncertain?) process is being evaluated using randomised controls, the inherent lack of fidelity presents a considerable challenge for the trial and can be used to explain inconsistent outcomes and any lack of gains (Carroll et al., 2020).

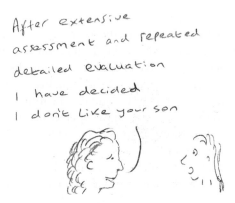

FIGURE 3.2   Just my luck?

Uncertain in theory

I would hope by this point in the book I have clearly outlined the ways in which people seek, expect and plan for certainty in education but experience and manage ongoing uncertainty. This fundamental contradiction between our idealised aspiration and everyday reality is echoed in the contradictions in our resulting policy and practice. It is consequently something which our school systems have to constantly deal with.

So let us turn to the ideas of inclusion. It has to be stated at the outset that the practices associated with much of the inclusion literature I am about to cite are very rarely evident on a large scale, and so would fail under any banner of evidence-based practice. It is also important to point out (as we will discuss in Chapter 4) that much which is done in the name of inclusion is exclusionary and bears many of the hallmarks of a quest for certitude. As Haussтätter (2014) notes, 'there is a force trying to make the unfinished finished, by transforming it from suggested to designed'.

Inclusion emerged in the 1980s and 1990s as resistance to the marginalisation of disabled people within the mainstream and special education 'continuum'. This is not to say that issues now associated with inclusion do not have a longer history. In the 19th and early 20 centuries, people were presenting evidence that generally children made better social and academic progress in ordinary classes (Cole, 1989); there were also active debates about types of education, risks to children and the desirability of segregation (Read & Walmsley, 2006), with school inspectors recognising that separation was not the solution and that 'slum clearance, good nutrition and school health services would be better cures' (Cole, 1989).

As policy documents around the globe began to pick up on the ideas and language of inclusion, it was possible to see these being appropriated and absorbed into the institutions they were trying to disrupt (Rix, 2011;

Slee, 2019). Consequently, in much school-related discourse and practice, 'inclusion' is shorthand for special education (or the equivalent national terms). At the same time, the idea behind inclusion has opened up so that now it is a term which goes far beyond education and disability. Allied with terms such as diversity, participation and equality, it is now frequently applied to all groupings that may be marginalised within education and social systems. It has become a go-to phrase for gender, ethnicity, race and sexuality and so forth. In universities, for example, it is widely used with this broader meaning even though very few people identified with special educational needs in school would ever be allowed into 'our' hallowed halls.

The ideas associated with inclusion within education are generally those which have arisen from practice (Florian, 2014), leaving a disconnect between everyday classrooms and theoretical understandings of inclusive provision (Finkelstein et al., 2021). Generally, the theory is focused upon people's understandings of inclusion and/or the rationale to include (Amor et al., 2019), with an absence of theory to inform the development of teaching practices (Forlin et al., 2013; Waitoller & Artiles, 2013). To the vast majority of academic authors, however, inclusive education reflects an ontological position which views practice as fundamentally uncertain and knowledge as emergent and situated (Rix, 2020). From this perspective, understanding is always incomplete, there is no single correct way to support the learning of any child, and our thinking and conclusions must be questioned (Hart, 1996).

Across a broad sweep of literature, inclusion can be seen as an 'assault on oppressive vestiges of the past as a way of contributing to alternative futures' (Slee & Allan, 2001) with 'change as an essential part of educational activities' (Dovigo, 2017). It involves a change in the 'behaviour' of adults (Ainscow & Sandill, 2010), a matter of 'solution finding' (Robinson, 2017), adopting a pedagogy that is underpinned by a principle of transformability (Hart, 2010). It is about drawing flexibly upon a class-community and co-operative learning structures (Naraian, 2011), not ignoring individual needs but addressing them 'within a larger framework of "we" as a class' (Bannink et al., 2020), with a curriculum based on values and rights (Booth, 2011). It has also been widely represented as an ongoing process (UNESCO IBE, 2008), active and without end (Flem & Keller, 2000), evolving and changing continually (Hausstätter, 2014). It is a commitment to eliminate barriers proactively, to respond flexibly and to create change in the policies, practices and cultures of 'regular' schools (CRPD, 2016). There is a strong message that people work towards reaching out to all learners, that they continually strive for this goal, even though they will not arrive (Ainscow, 2000). It can be seen as mixed with exclusion in 'a messy series of compromises, adjustments and individual preferences' (Corbett, 1997).

Some other sources of uncertainty

Inclusion can be seen as 'good education', interrupting the democratic order, with a beautiful risk at its heart (Biesta, 2010, 2013), but it is not the only approach to learning which draws upon notions of doubt. Dewey (1916), for instance, described the vagueness attending every situation and how thinking begins with uncertainty. There is plenty to disagree with Dewey about (Egan 2002), but in developing a pragmatic position, he described the need for teachers to be open minded, to recognise that the aims of education vary indefinitely, between people and as they move through life. He suggested that teachers need to support intellectual growth through the ongoing expansion of horizons with the reforming of purposes and responses.

A socio-cultural view of learning is rooted in an understanding that we live in continuously transforming social networks and relationships. These are the dynamic source of the fundamental uncertainties inherent in knowledge (Agrafiotis, 2002). This is why learning can be seen as a highly complex nego-tiation and creation of meaning within a wider community (Bruner, 1996). It means a community of learners within a classroom need to be engaged in a perpetual process of renewal and change as part of their own ongoing contin-uation (Rogoff et al., 1996). As a result, curricular content needs to undecided (Kirby & Webb 2021), with learning organised so that cracks are allowed to open up to create space for student agency (Dixon et al., 2018).

Drawing on similar socio-cultural roots, Moll (2005) talks about classrooms in which outcomes are an open question, processes are interactively constructed and come about through the quality of teachers' and students' work. The qual-ity of the space and the experience are also seen to play a central role in learn-er's development. This can be seen as taking place in zones of uncertainty, full of contradictions and unexpected interactions with cultural artefacts and practices – interactions that are not always beneficial to the individual or the setting (Engeström, 1996). It also requires a recognition of our interactions beyond the classroom, for example, Moll's notion of the funds of knowledge, and Biesta's (perhaps more philosophical than socio-cultural?) pedagogy of interruption (2010). Moll talks about the need to engage with the knowledge which emerges from people's life experiences, while Biesta calls for education to be open to a disruption of the everyday order, to a recognition that the uniqueness of learners is more than what happens within a singular space.

Beyond such socio-cultural advocates, there are also numerous calls that arise from critical pedagogy. This begins with a recognition that education must be 'the experience of a reality in the complexity of its constant "becom-ing"'. (Freire, 1970, p. 89) or requires 'shifting paradigms and talk about the discomfort it can cause' (hooks, 1994, p. 43). From this perspective, teaching in its current form has been described as impossible and to work with it requires us to accept 'the undecidability of pedagogy, and the indeterminacy of its address' (Ellsworth, 1997, p. 55). Dennis (2018), focusing upon decolonising the curriculum, includes in her ten defining approaches the need to reject a singular dominant voice or authoritative perspective. She suggests a need to be indeterminate, to accept conclusions as tentative and agreements as temporary (including her suggestion). Such a problematising approach also finds voice in indigenous insights. For example, a recognition that pedagogy is invariably troubled in ways we cannot predict, not only because of the ideas which underpin it but also because of its past, present and future (van Groll & Fraser, 2022). It calls for spaces to be opened for other ways of knowing, doing and being (Fellner, 2018), to ask difficult questions and to work with the diversity of students' different experiences and knowledge bases (Morcom & Freeman, 2018).

Recommendations to recognise the importance of uncertainty come from beyond these critical voices too. The demand for '21st-century skills', with its roots firmly embedded in corporate technology (Rix, 2010), is also rooted in a recognition that learners have to learn how to deal with and manage uncertainty. The OECD (2019), for instance, gives examples of immersive, transformative pedagogy in which students have agency and are encouraged to have an open mindset towards new ideas, perspectives and experiences. In contrast to the many of the voices above, however, it is typically claimed that 21st-century skills can be achieved by adapting the current processes and curricula. This seems to carry with it a similar inherent contradiction as special education's engagement with inclusion, but for now I will leave that concern with you.

Where uncertainty (maybe?) leads

So, let's now move on, to consider the process that is followed when people approach an issue from a position of uncertainty. In considering this process I have to offer a similar proviso as Dennis above about being tentative and temporary, since the model I propose is (probably) not true to itself. A model is an attempt to represent something. It is a framework (if you like). This means it is implying a certitude. It is clearly not possible to offer a certain model of uncertainty. However, I ask for some latitude (as I did with the model of certainty); this is intended to be a tool for reflection, a starting point for discussion. Reflecting on the nature of that tool itself might (perhaps as part of that discussion) go without saying.

A 'model of uncertainty' (see Figure 3.3)

We begin with uncertainty about the issue in question, while probably acknowledging our interdependent, relational life experiences and the complex nature of the context we are in (a).

We may simply accept or recognise that uncertainty or seek to use it as a means of confronting the issue or thinking about it (b).

We might, for example, adopt a critical approach, or seek to be pragmatic, developing hypothesis or exploring dilemmas, perhaps reflecting upon or reacting to the situation while accepting any outcome as doubtful (c).

In considering the situation, we will seek to consider possibilities arising from it (d).

To more fully appreciate those possibilities, we will ask questions about those involved in the situation and the processes at play (e).

This questioning will be informed by the uncertainty which underpins our approach and the emerging possibilities, leading us to momentary positions (f).

The momentary position will give us a point of focus, which itself can be open to further reflection and questioning (g).

In engaging with this point of focus, and accepting how it is likely to interact with other foci that are emerging, we will see a possibility emerge, an opportunity for action. This will open up boundaries and identities, presenting itself as a risk, with the potential for disruption. It will itself become a point of uncertainty (h).

The challenge for uncertainty

So how can approaches to education adopt a model of uncertainty when seeking certainty is dominant? I am not going to try and answer this question entirely in what remains of this chapter, partly because (you won't be surprised) I am uncertain I can but also because it is an issue I will return to. In particular, I intend to build upon this model in Chapters 5, 7 and 8, by considering who might be involved in these processes and how these processes might be structured/enabled/embraced. This will bring us back to the aim of this book to resolve the dichotomy between our embraces, confronting how our technologies of certainty struggle in the face of our individual and collective insecurities.

To help you situate the model, at this stage, I will provide some imagined examples of it operating in theory. Hopefully, this will help clarify my thinking and give a starting point for further discussion. It will soon become obvious that in trying to resolve the conundrum around an uncertain model of uncertainty, I have settled upon a standard format. I pose questions. I am not suggesting that these will be the only questions that could be asked; I see them as reasonable starting points. It is also worth noting that I have chosen to apply these questions to three issues that arose in the context of the model of certainty: school quality, areas of knowledge and evaluating additional support. I will return to this contradiction at the end of the chapter.

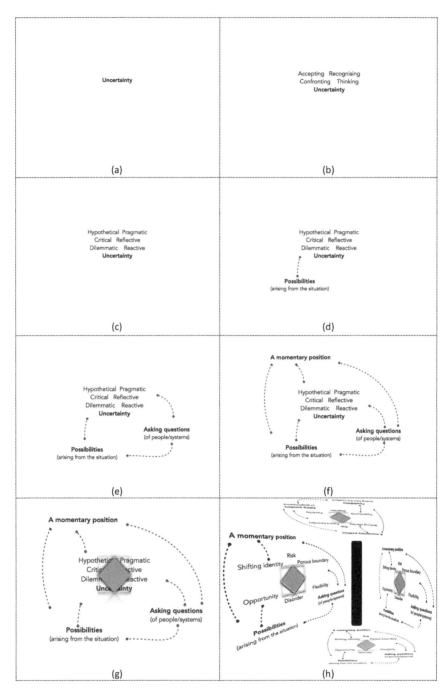

FIGURE 3.3 A 'model of uncertainty'.

FIGURE 3.4   A model of uncertainty – Applied to the notion of school quality.

Uncertain example 1 – School quality (see Figure 3.4)

We begin by opening up possibilities

For instance, what are the limits of this institution 'school'? Where are the spaces in which learning takes place? Who plays a role in these spaces?

We explore these possibilities through the understandings of those involved

What are the views of the people involved in these spaces? In what ways does the organisation influence and/or try to influence what goes on in those spaces? What do these people wish to attain from this space? In what ways are these views/goals in competition with or supportive of each other? Does this space have the resources it needs to achieve these goals? Does this space have the experiences necessary to achieve these goals? How do people assess whether these goals are being achieved? How can they best represent the strengths and weaknesses of the institution in reaching these goals?

In finding ways to answer each of these questions, we begin to open up new possibilities and potential points of agreement

For example, the first question may lead us to ask: Are we happy to begin with consideration of the school building, the outside environment, the homes, community and policy-making settings associated with the institution? If so, which should be our priority? Of course, in speaking to those involved in the setting priorities will (probably?) vary. This in itself may be a worthy point of future exploration. It highlights too a central challenge for those engaging through a model of uncertainty, the ongoing issue of balancing priorities and how this can be reasonably achieved.

Uncertain example 2 – Areas of knowledge (see Figure 3.5)

We begin by opening up possibilities

For instance, what is the knowledge content? Where is this knowledge valued? Who uses this knowledge? When does it have to be used?

We explore these possibilities through the understandings of those involved

Why do we frame this knowledge in this way? How else might we frame this knowledge? How might we apply this knowledge in different contexts? How might different people or systems apply this knowledge? Why might we focus upon one type of context for this knowledge? Why do we want to share such knowledge?

In finding ways to answer each of these questions, we begin to open up new possibilities and potential points of agreement

For example, we may consider the notion of erosion; we may associate it with geomorphology or engineering or biology or as an everyday experience with

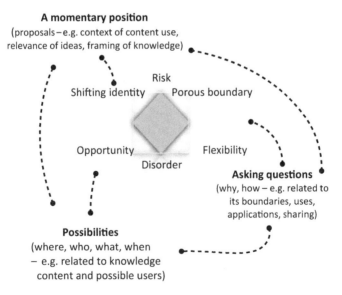

FIGURE 3.5 A model of uncertainty – Applied to the notion of areas of knowledge.

material forms or as a metaphor with applications across discourses – but at this moment, we may propose that our focus is upon its association with landscapes. This becomes the next starting point for our consideration of possibilities and what it is that we wish to achieve with this understanding.

Uncertain example 3 – Evaluating additional support (see Figure 3.6)

We begin by opening up possibilities

For instance, where is the practice that needs support situated? Who is affected by this issue? Who is involved in the support process? What are the practices that need support? When is this support required?

We explore these possibilities through the understandings of those involved

Why might this challenge have emerged? How might our collective and individual processes contribute to this issue? How might we provide support? Why is this support additional? How can our support benefit everyone involved? How can we understand the strengths and weaknesses of our support?

In finding ways to answer each of these questions, we begin to open up new possibilities and potential points of agreement

For example, we may agree that there are three young people in a class who have particular (and different?) challenges in communicating with their peers and so are struggling to make social relationships. We might recognise that

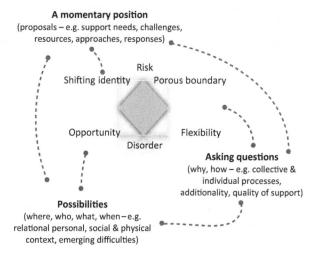

FIGURE 3.6   A model of uncertainty – Applied to the provision of additional support.

we need to create more collaborating opportunities which build upon their established skill sets. We might also wonder whether this could be achieved without the need for the activity to be additional to everyday practice. This brings us back round to an exploration of the collective possibilities and the need to explore the views of people concerned.

An uncertain solution

So why have I applied the three examples of the model of uncertainty to three issues identified in relation to the model of certainty? If I was a true believer, surely, I would understand that everything is relative, that an area of knowledge or quality of school or any form of support is only conceptually meaningful if we reify it. None of these things exist; they are all a matter of perspective; their being is in the moment and gone. Well, if you pushed me, that is probably what I do believe. In the next couple of chapters, for example, I will be exploring participation through an underpinning notion that only experiences in the actual now are really real.

BUT.

These words are written.

This book in some sense will be material.

And other people are more comfortable if they can plan and create structures. They do not want to see this as constant rebuilding but as tradition or culture or a reliable form of reality.

Given this yearning for certitude, it seems (dare I say it) pragmatic to start from the possibility that if we apply the model of uncertainty as outlined above, when we ask questions of people and systems, they will draw upon the certainty they feel they know. It therefore seems incredibly unlikely that we could see a complete transformation of the current system, so that approaches of uncertainty replace approaches seeking certainty. Can we really expect a shift in practice across all aspects of the system? People have tried such things before and, as discussed in the opening chapter, the existing system manages to (at the very least) cling on. This is the approach which is implied by much of the inclusion literature, of course – a system transformation. I would love to see this happen, but I am doubtful (is that a surprise?). It would speak to a timeless dream of humanity – a unanimity of approach. An ideal as unachievable as the goals and processes of certainty.

I will return to the challenge that this creates in Chapter 8. I think I have an answer ... or at least a good starting point for reflection.

But before we go there, let us consider a little more broadly and deeply our participation in learning and in our social systems. Let's explore how this can help us understand our experiences of certainty and uncertainty.

References

Agrafiotis, D. (2002). Knowledge and interdisciplinarity as socio-cultural uncertainties. *Ekistics*, 69(412/413/414), 10–18.

Ainscow, M. (2000). 'Profile'. In P. Clough & J. Corbett (Eds.), *Theories of inclusive education: A students' guide* (pp. 39–42). Paul Chapman.

Ainscow, M., & Sandill, A. (2010). Developing inclusive education systems: The role of organisational cultures and leadership. *International Journal of Inclusive Education*, 14(4), 401–416.

Allodi, M. (2017). A critical review of ideology, policy and circumstances in the Swedish context related to inclusive education organisational climate and students' wellbeing. In F. Dovigo (Ed.), *Special educational needs and inclusive practices: An international perspective*, Springer.

Amor, A., Hagiwara, M., Shogren, K., Thompson, J., Verdugo, M., Burke, K., & Aguayo, V. (2019). International perspectives and trends in research on inclusive education: A systematic review, *International Journal of Inclusive Education*, 23(12), 1277–1295.

Antoniou, F. (2021). Integration of Knowledge in textbooks: The case of five taught subjects in Greek junior high school. *Journal of Research in Humanities and Social Science*, 9(4), 41–51.

Bannink, F., Nalugya, R., & Van Hove, G., (2020). 'They Give Him a Chance'-parents' perspectives on disability and inclusive primary education in Uganda. *International Journal of Disability, Development and Education*, 67(4), 357–375.

Bate, E. (2020). Justifying music in the national curriculum: The habit concept and the question of social justice and academic rigour. *British Journal of Music Education*, 37(1), 3–15.

Baxter, J., & Clarke, J. (2014). knowledge, authority and judgement: The changing practices of school inspection in England. *Sisyphus: Journal of Education*, 2(1), 106–127.

Beach, D. (2017). Personalisation and the education commodity: A metaethnographic analysis. *Ethnography and Education*, 12(2), 148–164.

Behzad, A. (2013). Lesson planning in Afghan school: A quantitative study on the use of lesson plans in primary schools of Parwan, Afghanistan, Doctoral dissertation, Karlstads University.

Benevides, T., Barker, K., Lamb, M., Knight, D., Long, T., Bloder, M., Crews, T., & Su, S. (2022). Teachers and occupational therapists as interprofessional teammates: Implementation of an adapted social-emotional learning curriculum, *Journal of Interprofessional Education & Practice*, 29, 100573.

Bickman, L. (2020). Improving mental health services: A 50-year journey from randomized experiments to artificial intelligence and precision mental health. *Administration and Policy in Mental Health and Mental Health Services Research*, 47(5), 795–843.

Biesta, G. (2010). *Good education in an age of measurement: Ethics, politics, democracy*. Paradigm Publishers.

Biesta, G. (2013). *The beautiful risk of education*. Paradigm.

Boaler. (2008). *The elephant in the classroom: Helping children learn & love maths*. Souvenir Press.

Booth, T. (2011). 'The name of the rose: Inclusive values into action in teacher education' *Prospects*, 41(3), 303–318.

Bradbury, A., Braun, A., & Quick, L. (2021). Intervention culture, grouping and triage: High-stakes tests and practices of division in English primary schools. *British Journal of Sociology of Education*, 42(2), 147–163.

Bruner, J. (1996). *The culture of education*. Harvard University Press.

Capel, S., Bassett, S., Lawrence, J., Newton, A., & Zwozdiak-Myers, P. (2019). How trainee physical education teachers in England write, use and evaluate lesson plans. *European Physical Education Review*, 25(4), 964–982.

Carroll, C., Hurry, J., Grima, G., Hooper, A., Dunn, K., & Ahtaridou, E. (2020). Evaluation of Bug Club: A randomised control trial of a whole school primary aged reading programme. *The Curriculum Journal*, 31(4), 605–625.

Caslin, M. (2021). 'They have just given up on me'. How pupils labelled with social, emotional and behavioural difficulties (SEBD) experience the process of exclusion from school. *Support for Learning*, 36(1), 116–132.

Chaudhary, A., Sudzina, F., & Mikkelsen, B. E. (2020). Promoting healthy eating among young people—A review of the evidence of the impact of school-based interventions. *Nutrients*, 12(9), 2894.

Cinoglu, M. (2014). Evaluation of school uniform policy in Turkey: A case study. *International Journal of Progressive Education*, 10(3), 97–108.

Cole, T. (1989) *Apart or A Part?* Open University Press.

Committee on the Rights of Persons with Disabilities (CRPD). (2016).*Convention on the rights of persons with disabilities, general comment No. 4 (2016) Article 24: Right to inclusive education*, United Nations.

Coolahan, J. & O'Donovan, P. (2009). *A history of Ireland's school inspectorate, 1831–2008*. Four Courts Press.

Corbett, J. (1997). Include/exclude. *International Journal of Inclusive Education*, 1(1), 55–64.

Courcier, I. (2007). Teachers' perceptions of personalised learning, *Evaluation & Research in Education*, 20(2), 59–80.

Dennis, C. (2018). Decolonising education: A pedagogic intervention. In Gurminder K . Bhambra, Kerem Nişancioğlu, & Dalia Gebrial (Eds.), *Decolonising the university* (pp. 190–207). Pluto Press.

Dewey, J. (1916). Democracy and education. Retrieved from https://manybooks.net/

Dixon, C., Martin, L., & Betser, S. (2018). *Making uncertainty work: How youth manage uncertainty to shape learning trajectories in a school makerspace*. International Society of the Learning Sciences, Inc [ISLS].

Dovigo, F. (2017). Linking theory to practice in inclusive education. In F. Dovigo (Ed.), *Special educational needs and inclusive practices: An international perspective*, Springer.

Dulin, C. (2016). Impact of school uniforms on student discipline and the learning climate: A comparative case study of two middle schools with uniform dress codes and two middle schools without uniform dress codes, Doctoral dissertation, North Carolina State University.

Edwards, A. (2012). The role of common knowledge in achieving collaboration across practices. *Learning, Culture and Social Interaction*, 1(1), 22–32.

Egan, K. (2002). *Getting it wrong from the beginning: Our progressivist inheritance from Herbert Spencer, John Dewey, and Jean Piaget*. Yale University Press.

Ellsworth, E. (1997). *Teaching positions: Difference, pedagogy, and the power of address*. Teachers College Press.

Engeström, Y. (1996). Development as breaking away and opening up: A challenge to Vygotsky and Piaget. *Swiss Journal of Psychology*, 55, 126–132.

Ennett, S., Haws, S., Ringwalt, C., Vincus, A., Hanley, S., Bowling, J., & Rohrbach, L. (2011). Evidence-based practice in school substance use prevention: Fidelity of implementation under real-world conditions. *Health Education Research*, 26(2), 361–371.

Fellner, K. (2018). Embodying decoloniality: Indigenizing curriculum and pedagogy. *American Journal of Community Psychology*, 62(3–4), 283–293.

Finkelstein, S., Sharma, U., & Furlonger, B. (2021). The inclusive practices of classroom teachers: A scoping review and thematic analysis. *International Journal of Inclusive Education*, 25(6), 735–762.

Flem, A., & Keller, C. (2000). Inclusion in Norway. *European Journal of Special Needs Education*, 15(2), 188–205.

Florian, L. (2014). What counts as evidence of inclusive education? *European Journal of Special Needs Education*, 29(3), 286–294.

Forlin, C. I., Chambers, D. J., Loreman, T., Deppler, J., & Sharma, U. (2013). Inclusive education for students with disability: A review of the best evidence in relation to theory and practice. The Australian Research Alliance for Children and Youth.

Fowler, T. (2020). 2: What is a child?. In *Liberalism, childhood and justice*. Bristol University Press. Retrieved July 4, 2022, from https://bristoluniversitypressdigital.com/view/book/9781529

Freire, P. (1970). *Pedagogy of the oppressed*. Penguin.

Gaitas, S., & Martins, M. (2017). Teacher perceived difficulty in implementing differentiated instructional strategies in primary school. *International Journal of Inclusive Education*, 21(5), 544–556.

Gericke, N., Hudson, B., Olin-Scheller, C., & Stolare, M. (2018). Powerful knowledge, transformations and the need for empirical studies across school subjects. *London Review of Education*, 16(3), 428–444.

Guldberg, K. (2017). Evidence-based practice in autism educational research: Can we bridge the research and practice gap?. *Oxford Review of Education*, 43(2), 149–161.

Harlen, W., & Deakin Crick, R. (2002). A systematic review of the impact of summative assessment and tests on students' motivation for learning (EPPI-Centre Review, version 1.1*). In *Research evidence in education library* (Issue 1). EPPI-Centre, Social Science Research Unit, Institute of Education.

Hart, S. (1996).*Beyond special needs: Enhancing children's learning through innovative thinking*. Sage.

Hart, S. (2010). Learning without limits. In J. Rix, M. Nind, K. Sheehy K. Simmons, J. Parry, & K. Rajni (Eds.), *Equality, participation and inclusion 2: Diverse contexts*. Routledge.

Hausstätter, R. (2014). In support of unfinished inclusion. *Scandinavian Journal of Educational Research*, 58(4), 424–434.

Hecht, L. (2016). The impact of evidence-based bullying prevention programs on school climate and on bullying of students, including students with disabilities, Doctoral dissertation, Baker University.

Holt-White, E., Montacute, R., & Tibbs, L. (2022). *Paving the way: Careers guidance in secondary schools*. The Sutton Trust.

Hood, P., & Mitchell, H. (2017). Assessment and school readiness. British Educational Research Association Early Childhood Special Interest Group and TACTYC: Association for Professional Development in Early Years, 83.

hooks, b. (1994). *Teaching to transgress*. Routledge.

Horner, R., Sugai, G., & Fixsen, D. (2017). Implementing effective educational practices at scales of social importance. *Clinical Child and Family Psychology Review*, *20*(1), 25–35.

Hrstić, I., Marinović Golubić, M., Mestvirishvili, N., Sylla, C., Marmer, E., Seukwa, L. H., Chatterjee, C., Dyahadro, S., Romanovska, A., Deák, D., & Ferrer-Fons, M. (2019). National curriculum review reports.

Huang, Q. (2021). Exploring teacher roles in relation to classroom activities in an activity-dominated English class: The learners' perspectives. *European Journal of English Language Teaching*, *6*(6), 168–188.

Iskandar, D., & Lusiana, L. (2019). An analysis of teacher strategies on the eleventh grade students learning activities in EFL classroom at SMA Babus Salam Tangerang. *Jurnal Inovasi Pendidikan MH Thamrin*, *3*(1), 43–49.

Kennedy, S., & Stewart, H. (2011). Collaboration between occupational therapists and teachers: Definitions, implementation and efficacy. *Australian Occupational Therapy Journal*, *58*(3), 209–214.

Kidman, J., Abrams, E., & McRae, H. (2011). Imaginary subjects: School science, indigenous students, and knowledge–power relations. *British Journal of Sociology of Education*, *32*(2), 203–220.

Kippin, S., & Cairney, P. (2022). The COVID-19 exams fiasco across the UK: Four nations and two windows of opportunity. *British Politics*, *17*(1), 1–23.

Kirby, P., & Webb, R. (2021). Conceptualising uncertainty and the role of the teacher for a politics of climate change within and beyond the institution of the school. *Educational Review*, *75*(1), 134–152.

Korp, H., Sjöberg, L., & Thorsen, C. (2019). Individual development plans in the Swedish comprehensive school: Supporting high quality learning and equity, or rote learning and social reproduction? *Scandinavian Journal of Educational Research*, *63*(2), 229–244.

Lawn, M., Baxter, J., Grek, S., & Segerholm, C. (2014). The new local: System shifts and school inspection. In S. Grek & J. Lindgren (Eds.), *Governing by inspection* (pp. 96–115). Studies in European Education, 1. Routledge.

Leckie, G., & Goldstein, H. (2017). The evolution of school league tables in England 1992–2016: 'Contextual value-added', 'expected progress' and 'progress 8'. *British Educational Research Journal*, *43*(2), 193–212.

Lee, K. (2019). Translating evidence-based practice into an autism specific special school: Model, evaluation and outcomes, Doctoral dissertation, Bangor University.

Matete, R. E. (2021). Evidence based impact of school inspection on teaching and learning in primary school education in Tanzania. *Huria: Journal of the Open University of Tanzania*, *28*(1), 105–126.

McKeon, D. (2020). 'Soft barriers'–The impact of school ethos and culture on the inclusion of students with special educational needs in mainstream schools in Ireland. *Improving Schools*, *23*(2), 159–174.

Melgarejo, M., Lind, T., Stadnick, N., Helm, J., & Locke, J. (2020). Strengthening capacity for implementation of evidence-based practices for autism in schools: The roles of implementation climate, school leadership, and fidelity. *American Psychologist*, *75*(8), 1105.

Mitchell, S. P. (2019). Evaluation of evidence-based practice in a separate day school for students with emotional disabilities, Doctoral dissertation, The College of William and Mary.

Moll, L. (2005). Reflections and possibilities. In N. González, L. C. Moll, & C. Amanti (Eds.), *Funds of knowledge: Theorizing practices in households, communities, and classrooms*. Lawrence Erlbaum.

Monroe, F. (2009). The impact of uniform dress code on attendance, discipline, and academic achievement among students in a south Texas high school, Doctoral dissertation, Texas A&M University.

Morcom, L., & Freeman, K. (2018). Niinwi-Kiinwa-Kiinwi: Building non-Indigenous allies in education through Indigenous pedagogy. *Canadian Journal of Education/ Revue canadienne de l'éducation, 41*(3), 808–833.

Mulongo, G. (2017). Cross-national learning assessment: Relationship to educational policy, curriculum and capacity development in Kenya, Tanzania and South Africa, Doctoral dissertation, University of the Witwatersrand, Faculty of Humanities, School of Human and Community Development.

Nally, D., Moore, S. S., & Gowran, R. J. (2022). How governments manage personal assistance schemes in response to the United Nations convention on the rights of persons with disabilities: A scoping review. *Disability & Society, 37*(10), 1728–1751.

Naraian, S. (2011). Seeking transparency: The production of an inclusive classroom community. *International Journal of Inclusive Education, 15*(9), 955–973.

OECD. (2019). Future of education and skills 2030: OECD learning compass – Concept notes, organisation for economic and cultural development.

OFSTED. (2021). SEND: Old issues, new issues, next steps, Crown Copyright.

Patel, B. (2022). An investigation into the impact of government austerity measures on school-based approaches to adolescent neglect in England. *Children & Society, 36*(5), 821–839.

Pavez, B. (2017). An evaluation of the sustained use of evidence-based practices by high school personnel instructing students with autism spectrum disorder, Doctoral dissertation, Claremont Graduate University and San Diego State University.

Pellicano, E., Dinsmore, A., & Charman, T. (2014). What should autism research focus upon? Community views and priorities from the United Kingdom. *Autism, 18*(7), 756–770.

Puttick, S. (2015). Chief examiners as Prophet and Priest: Relations between examination boards and school subjects, and possible implications for knowledge. *The Curriculum Journal, 26*(3), 468–487.

Qamar, A. (2021). What is a child? Exploring conceptualization of Pakistani adolescents about children. *Journal of Childhood Studies, 46*(2), 34–50.

Read, J., & Walmsley, J. (2006). Historical perspectives on special education, 1890–1970. *Disability & Society, 21*(5), 455–469.

Rix, J. (2010). 21st century skills…All dressed up in the technology of the Knowledge Age in K. In R. Ferguson Sheehy & G. Clough (Eds.), *Controversies at the frontier of education (Education in a competitive and globalizing world)*. Nova Science.

Rix, J. (2011). Repositioning of special schools within a specialist, personalised educational marketplace. *International Journal of Inclusive Education, 15*(2), 263–279.

Rix, J. (2015). *Must inclusion be special? Rethinking educational support within a community of provision*. Routledge.

Rix, J. (2020). Our need for certainty in an uncertain world: The difference between special education and inclusion? *British Journal of Special Education, 47*(3), 283–307.

Rix, J. (2023). Re-examining special needs – What could be better? In R. J. Tierney, F. Rizvi, & K. Erkican (Eds.), *International encyclopedia of education* (Vol. 9). Elsevier.

Robinson, D. (2017). Effective inclusive teacher education for special educational needs and disabilities: Some more thoughts on the way forward. *Teaching and Teacher Education*, *61*, 164–178.

Rogoff, B., Matusov, E., & White, C. (1996). Models of teaching and learning: Participation in a community of learners. *The handbook of education and human development* (pp. 388–414). Wiley.

Sabic-El-Rayess, A., Mansur, N. N., Batkhuyag, B., & Otgonlkhagva, S. (2019). School uniform policy's adverse impact on equity and access to schooling. *Compare: A Journal of Comparative and International Education*, *50*(8), 1122–1139.

Sahlberg, P. (2010). Rethinking accountability in a knowledge society. *Journal of educational change*, *11*(1), 45–61.

Savage, J. (2021). The policy and practice of music education in England, 2010–2020. *British Educational Research Journal*, *47*(2), 469–483.

Sidik, E. (2020). The implementation of the national examination in Indonesian: Evaluating its usefulness and drawbacks. *Tamansiswa International Journal in Education and Science*, *1*(2), 25–33.

Slee, R. (2019). Belonging in an age of exclusion. *International Journal of Inclusive Education*, *23*(9), 909–922.

Slee, R., & Allan, J. (2001). Excluding the Included: A reconsideration of inclusive education. *International Studies in Sociology of Education*, *11*(2), 173–191.

Speizer, I. S., Mandal, M., Xiong, K., Makina, N., Hattori, A., & Durno, D. (2020). Impact evaluation of scripted lesson plans for HIV-related content in a life orientation curriculum: Results from two provinces in South Africa. *BMC Public Health*, *20*(1), 1–16.

Steinberg, C., & Waspe, T. (2016). The struggle for academic rigour in assessment education. *Perspectives in Education*, *34*(1), 53–67.

Taylor, B., Francis, B., Archer, L., Hodgen, J., Pepper, D., Tereshchenko, A., & Travers, M. (2017). Factors deterring schools from mixed attainment teaching practice. *Pedagogy, Culture & Society*, *25*(3), 327–345.

Tuckwell, K. (2017). *Death, dying and devolution*. Institute for Policy Research. Accessed February 2, 2018, from http://www.bath.ac.uk/publications/death-dying-and-devolution/

UNESCO IBE. 2008. *Inclusive education: The way of the future. Conclusions and recommendations of the 48th session for the International Conference on Education (ICE)*, Geneva, 25–28 November 2008.

van Groll, N., & Fraser, H. (2022). "Watch Out for Their Home!": Disrupting extractive forest pedagogies in early childhood education. *Journal of Childhood Studies*, *47*(3), 47–53.

Vandenbroeck, M. (2014). The brainification of early childhood education and other challenges to academic rigour. *European Early Childhood Education Research Journal*, *22*(1), 1–3.

Vanner, C. (2018). 'This is a competition': The relationship between examination pressure and gender violence in primary schools in Kenya. *International Journal of Educational Development*, *62*, 35–46.

Wagner, D., Lockheed, M., Mullis, I., Martin, M. O., Kanjee, A., Gove, A., & Dowd, A. J. (2012). The debate on learning assessments in developing countries. *Compare: A Journal of Comparative and International Education*, *42*(3), 509–545.

Waitoller, F., & Artiles, A. J. (2013). A decade of professional development research for inclusive education: A critical review and notes for a research program. *Review of Educational Research*, 83(3), 319–356.

Walker, K. (2021). Engaging with community: exploring the role of primary school governing boards in developing and implementing a 'Vision' for special educational needs, Doctoral dissertation, The Open University.

Waszczuka, M., Zimmerman, M., Ruggero, C., Li, K., MacNamara, A., Weinberg, A., Hajcak, G., Watson, D., & Kotov, R. (2017). What do clinicians treat: Diagnoses or symptoms? The incremental validity of a symptom-based, dimensional characterization of emotional disorders in predicting medication prescription pattern, *Comprehensive Psychiatry*, 79, 80–88.

Wiliam, D. (2010). Standardized testing and school accountability. *Educational Psychologist*, 45(2), 107–122.

Williams, J., & Wong, A. (2009). The efficacy of final examinations: A comparative study of closed-book, invigilated exams and open-book, open-web exams. *British Journal of Educational Technology*, 40(2), 227–236.

Wilshire, C., Ward, T., & Clack, S. (2021). Symptom descriptions in psychopathology: How well are they working for us?. *Clinical Psychological Science*, 9(3), 323–339.

Wuthrich, V., Jagiello, T., & Azzi, V. (2020). Academic stress in the final years of school: A systematic literature review. *Child Psychiatry & Human Development*, 51(6), 986–1015.

4

PARTICIPATING WITH INEQUALITY

(Would) I like to apologise (?)

I enter into this chapter in the full knowledge that I have played my part in the marginalisation of many people over the years. For example:

- one of my earliest memories is also my first knowing experience of shame, when I publicly humiliated a boy, Dennis, at school by destroying a birthday present he had given me, just so I could gain approval from my peers.
- one of my best mates at school for quite a few years, Mark, had a Malaysian heritage, and I used a typically 1970's racist epithet regularly in our conversations. When my mum heard me use the term, she was horrified, but I reassured her: 'Oh we all call him that. He doesn't mind'.
- as an adolescent in defending another boy, I mocked his tormentor by saying he had an even smaller penis than (purportedly) our sports teacher, and both he and the sports teacher (who had heard) were cowed into silence in a way that filled me with guilt but taught me a lot about power.
- as a trainee teacher in Coventry in 1981, I made a racist joke out of the word 'blackmail' when it was used by a young black boy in my class, and though I immediately knew I had done wrong I could never withdraw the doing.
- as a teacher in a training session, I used a throw-away trope about an Irish colleague going for a drink, which in exasperation she had to rebut in front of all our colleagues.
- I was part of a national system where recent immigrants were made to repeat courses year on year because they could not pass the English-based exam deemed essential to their entry-level vocational qualifications.

DOI: 10.4324/9781003281405-4

- I failed to get a class of white US students to hear a young man as he reflected at the end of the semester on his negative experience as the only African-American on their collective study abroad program.
- I disabled my son by not fighting harder to get everyone (including myself) to use key word signing with him.

These are all issues which have haunted me in their own way. I cannot ask for forgiveness. I cannot be sure what the actual impact was. But I know I was either directly or indirectly in the wrong. There are also plenty of others where I did things I thought were right, but I do not know if I made people feel excluded. For example:

- I explained to a particularly disengaged student that the economic and education systems were based on some people failing so others could succeed, and that by not working she was playing into the hands of the systems that made her so angry.
- I sat down with a lovely and lonely young person and (gently?) explained that part of the reason she lacked friends was to do with having body odour – this was someone who was basically a domestic servant for her aunt and did not finish the chores until midnight.
- I deeply upset a group of US students by asking them to recognise that negative stories about Israel in the UK media did not necessarily make UK media antisemitic.

There is also the underlying nature of my self. Something about which I can do nothing. I am (and always have been) male, white, upper-middle/middle class, not yet disabled (until recently), (mainly) heterosexual, economically stable and living in Europe and human. By the nature of my existence, I have benefited at the expense of others on the basis of my gender, ethnicity, class, well-being, sexuality, socio-economic condition, nationality and biology. I have recognised this advantage for nearly all my life, though my understanding of its ramifications and its true nature is still being (and will continue to be) revealed to me.

A real challenge that I (we all) face is how we can engage with the marginalisation that our being and our institutions' being create and perpetuate. The tales above are never simply about a single category of diversity or even an intersectional experience; they are always situated in a hugely complex interaction of possibilities; marginalisation is just one part of that interaction.

In this chapter, I will attempt to outline a useful model to help us explore this complexity. It is not an answer. But it is a way to reflect upon the uncertain. I will then use this model to explore some of this evidence about people's struggles within schools across the globe. I aim to demonstrate why/how the system they/we <u>will be/are/have been</u> participating in is so problematic ... and so begin to consider what we could do about it.

FIGURE 4.1 Independent thinking?

Is participation an education?

I was writing this chapter while there was a campaign going on to choose a new UK prime minister. One of the two remaining candidates said something which (I feel sure) most people would agree with. Rishi Sunak (he failed to become Prime Minister first time round but was appointed without opposition a few months later) said:

> A good education is the closest thing we have to a silver bullet when it comes to making people's lives better.
>
> *(PA Media, 2022)*

When I read this, I found myself asking something that I often ask. Why can people simply trot out such comments? Why is a claim about the universal value of education uncontentious?

[A simple answer is to conclude that this is just part of a wider discourse which dominates our times, a matter of economic correctness. He was using a style of talking about our system which unquestioningly accepts the current economic model of growth and each person's individual responsibility for their destiny within it. This way of seeing the world concludes that the best way to improve people's lives is for them to develop literacy, numeracy and so forth. I would like to suggest that providing better pay rates for jobs without such skills would be far closer to a silver bullet. However, while an economist can talk about education, an educationalist should not stray into economics; so, I shall leave my comment in a smaller font.]

I am always surprised that people do not see the fundamental contradiction in claiming our school system can provide the best answer to this (and many other) problem(s). In a world which cries out for us to follow the evidence, there seems plenty to show that school is not a very good answer at all.

It is tempting to reach for standard markers of difference to demonstrate that school is bad for a lot of us (therefore all of us?). For example, in 2016 in England, 39% of people taking national exams at 15/16 years of age had been identified with special educational needs at some point in their school career (Hutchinson, 2021), which is about the same number as failed to achieve a pass in five key subjects (33.1%). In addition, levels of exclusion are very high, so that over 7,000 pupils were permanently excluded from all types of state schools in England in 2017, with over 400,000 fixed-term exclusions issued (Selfe & Richmond, 2020). But since experiences of exclusion are part of a hugely complex interaction of possibilities, consider some of the additional issues at play in England. For example, factors that increase chances of exclusion include special educational needs; social, emotional and mental health needs; coming from some minority ethnic groups; being bullied; having poor relationships with teachers; life trauma; poverty and having a history of low attainment and challenges in home life (Graham et al., 2019). To give a further sense of scale: in 2021 over 20% of pupils were on free school meals, over 30% were from a minority ethnic background and over 19% had a language other than English as their first language (ONS, 2021).

Negative experiences may have many roots, but they are commonplace. For instance:

- in a survey of over 12,000 ten-year-olds from 15 countries (Gomez-Baya et al., 2022), more than 2,500 (20.8%) of them had suffered harassment and over 2200 (17.6%) of them had felt excluded twice or more in the last month.
- in a sample of over 5,500 adolescents in Brazil, over 1,500 students failed in their progression through school, with over 30% saying they felt unsafe and over 7% saying they were unhappy (Cunha et al., 2019).

For people who are struggling the issues can also be compounded, but others will be affected too. For example,

- in a survey of nearly 1,000 young women aged 13–20 in Sweden, 59% of pupils who had some kind of offending reported having had six or more problems in school, but so did 32% of the non-offending reference group (Azad & Hau, 2018).
- in a survey of over 1,600 secondary students in England, those who had been formally excluded were also far more like to have been bullied at school and reported that their school dealt with this badly. The study concluded that this is not an individual problem but a whole school issue (Fazel & Newby, 2021).

The negative experiences that result from everyday school practices are fundamentally embedded in the way that we do things. Consider the standard commitment to literacy. It is commonplace to read (ironically?) that literacy levels for children leaving primary school, internationally, remain a cause for concern (Carroll et al., 2020). If it is such a problem, why don't we stop using it as the main way of teaching and assessing learning? We know that this is not just a problem of younger children. In a study of 23 countries (mainly European with the United States and Japan), about 48% of people were operating at a functional literacy level of 2 or below (Desjardins et al., 2013), with only three nations below 40%. This means in every country nearly half of the population will struggle with:

- texts that are often dense or lengthy and include continuous, non-continuous, mixed, or multiple pages of text.
- text and rhetorical structures that are central to navigating texts and completing tasks.
- identifying, interpreting or evaluating one or more pieces of information, with varying levels of inference.
- constructing meaning across larger chunks of text or perform multi-step operations.
- disregarding irrelevant or inappropriate content.
- managing competing information which is not more prominent than the correct information.

These are the sorts of texts you might associate with contracts, workplace documentation and academic books. Perhaps more importantly this is what is required of young people in a classroom context, using school textbooks and having to sit written exams.

[It is interesting that I cannot find any more recent statistics on functional literacy. It would appear that this area of study had a brief moment in the sun. There are some concerns (inevitably) about the methods used, but I wonder if its certainty has not been embraced because it revealed an uncomfortable truth?]

As the examples above begin to demonstrate, even if our education systems may be good for some, for a great many others our school systems are not going to make their life better and could make it worse. To continue with Rishi Sunak's vampirical metaphor: school sucks the blood out of a lot of us. [Some might also suggest that it ensures the continued survival of those the same dread creatures of the night but that may be a matter of perspective].

The problem begins with a presumption that participation within a system is inherently (or predominantly) beneficial. From the earliest models of participation, however, it has been necessary to present different degrees of participation. For example, Arnstein intended her ladder of community participation (1969) to be provocative, with five of her eight rungs equating to non-participation or tokenism. This was because her primary concern was about where power lay (Thomas, 2007). Hart built on this idea with his influential Ladder of Participation (1992), but he pointed out that children do not always need to be on the upper rungs of the ladder. He suggested that different children might prefer different degrees of involvement at different times. Other models aimed to focus upon this positive engagement. Shier (2001) for example has five levels of participation ranging from 'Children are listened to' to 'Children share power and responsibility for decision-making'. He also recognises the necessary commitment of practitioners and the different stages of commitment they will show. There have also been attempts to represent participation as different levels of control and empowerment experienced by adults and young people (e.g. Wong et al., 2010), reaching a point of shared control. It is in later models that we start to see the fluid nature of participation represented, while acknowledging that not all participatory outcomes are positive (Cahill & Dadvand, 2018).

The emergence of these models echoes a tension which has also been evident in educational theory. Broadly speaking this is played out in two dominant pedagogic approaches; one is adult-centred and sees schools as the transfer of knowledge and the other is child-centred, with the children as active constructors of knowledge. Both of these models assume that learning primarily functions in one direction, with the control sitting with one party (Rogoff et al., 1998). There is a third model however, a participation-centred model. Arising for socio-cultural theorists, this is not a compromise between the other models but sees learning as a process involving the transformation of and through participation.

This approach recognises adults and children as together in the learning context; they are in a shared endeavour, contributing support and direction to each other. In contrast to the models of participation discussed above, these theories of participation do not see power as sitting with one group or other but as being within a relationship. This view of participation sees individuals and the cultural context as mutually constituting (Rogoff, 2003).

Participation from this perspective views events as not external to people. Our involvement is both a transformation of ourselves and that with which we are involved. It is a generational relationship, interacting with the current moment as well as the past and the future. This relationship will be influenced by all kinds of mundane things, from daily routines and habits to issues on a wider scale such as community values or institutional structures (Rogoff et al., 2018).

From this perspective, participation is not something you/we/they cannot be doing; by *being* you/we/they are *doing*. The issue is therefore about the nature of that experience of being.

So, this is where we go now. I am going to discuss a model of participation which emerged from participatory research and then give examples of how this model can help us to consider experiences of education. This model is called the *while* of participation.

The while *of participation (see Figure 4.2)*

Heidegger (1996) recognised that 'being' is defined by its historicity. Beings are 'always already together' (p. 99). Things show themselves by being within the world and by turning their attention to aspects of that world. This 'being-in' is not a quality which being sometimes has and sometimes does not have, nor is it a sum of momentary realities. Only experiences in the actual now are really real. Participation therefore happens in the moment, while you are doing something. It defines the person's experience of being within that moment; it is the experience that emerges from and contributes to the 'they' within which we all are; it is where we can discover our understandings of our separateness and of our boundaries. It is both a personal and physical experience, socially created from the collective resources, understandings and interactions. The *while* is the relational experience that occurs while the group and a participant are in the moment, and it defines their experience of being at that moment; it is the experience that emerges from and creates the boundaries in which people find themselves.

The understanding of the *while* did not emerge from a school-based project. It arose from a European Union-funded, access-to-heritage project called ARCHES, on which I was research lead. Between October 2016 to December 2019, four participatory 'exploration groups' were established in London, Madrid, Vienna and Oviedo. These groups involved over 200 disabled people, working alongside friends, family and other supporters including educators from six museums (some of whom would also identify as disabled). The groups also involved six partners developing a variety of technologies which aimed to enhance access to the space and learning within it. The access preferences and needs of these four groups were diverse, but we chose not to be defined by traditional impairment categories.

As part of this project, we undertook a review to learn from other participatory projects and inform the development of our practice. The review included 54 papers. This review confirmed what was evident in smaller, earlier studies; involvement in participatory projects is partial at best. For example, Stack and McDonald (2014) rated just over 28% of their studies to be high in participation, while across our study the overall figure was slightly lower (24%). The research area which excluded people most was data analysis, where only 35% of studies involved disabled people and nearly half of these just to check that they agreed with findings that the academics had come up with. In many ways what has been framed as participatory research could be better described as consultative (echoing the earlier models discussed above). However, as we went through these papers and explored the ideas and experiences contained within them, there emerged a picture of the nature of people's involvement, their participation.

FIGURE 4.2   The tensions, outcomes and component parts within the *while* of participation.

The tensions (that underpin moments of participation – see Figure 4.2)

The narrative emerging from these studies suggested that underpinning every moment in which people are participating are underpinning tensions around power, voice and support. Power was at the heart of much discussion in the papers, about practice and the capacity of participants to make individual and collective decisions about the structures, topics and outcomes of what was produced and how it was used. Many studies recognised that they were rarely led by participants. This was not just an issue about whether one can 'hand over' power but also about people having the inclination and capacity to use it. The use of power is something which can be/needs to be learned and facilitated. The negotiation of power and with power is never a singular point of action but is linked to ongoing questioning. It requires time to develop voice and relationships and the space for people to be honest about their experiences.

This focus upon voice was also linked to the need to listen. Talking together and spending time in people's company allows you to hear other perspectives. This enables you to see if participants feel represented, respected and have opportunities to participate, as well as hearing those who are saying 'no' to what is being done in their name. It is also, clearly, not without challenges.

For example, contradictory voices emerged in studies, as did communication differences that caused an impasse, frustration and fatigue. Papers also reported a need to continuously evaluate, recognising that those who speak more than listen will lack trust and rapport.

Supporting people to be heard was as important as supporting their understanding and physical access. Support came in many forms, but at its heart was collaboration and mutual support built around peers. Projects recognised they must not underestimate the support that individuals may require, as once underway it could be very challenging to get additional resources. The role of the supporters had to be clear to all. They were frequently interpreters, go-betweens or gatekeepers and so they had to want to be involved. However, groups needed to be aware that supporters' priorities could clash with participants', and it was not uncommon for them to have limited aspirations and ambitions on behalf of the group. Supporters needed to recognise that the process of learning is not one way and that it is important to have high expectations about what can/will be achieved.

These tensions around power, voice and support which arose in these studies were evidenced through the meaningful nature of outcomes within the *while*. So, let's turn to the outcomes which emerged from the 54 research papers.

The meaningful outcomes (that reveal the tensions around power, voice and support within the moments of participation – see Figure 4.2)

Across the studies the dominant outcomes appeared as:

- the value of the project to the participants themselves.
- the moments of learning which emerged.
- the capacity of projects to represent the lives of participants.

At the core of the literature was the participant's sense of involvement and enjoyment in projects. A small part of this was facilitated by payments or reimbursement for travel or with food (about 25% of projects), or the satisfaction that comes from developing new skills or having new life experiences. However, more typically, people talked about having fun, being part of a collaboration and not being defined by an impairment. For many, the process of being involved in the sharing of ideas was more important than the data which was generated.

The quality of participation was evident in the nature of the understanding which emerged, in moments of learning. This learning may impact upon supporters' or individuals' relationships within the group or beyond. It may be a realisation among the organisers about what was emerging, or it may be evident in people's agency, their developing skills and ideas, their actions or in the things they produced. People valued being able to articulate something in a new way and being part of an ongoing learning process. There was value too in seeing a process of planning and interacting coming to fruition and recognising how a contribution can 'add value'. This understanding could also relate to personal development and a deeper insight into oneself and/or how to do things.

These two outcomes were closely linked to a third, people's (and the project's) capacity to represent the lives of others and those involved within the research. It involved asking if perspectives:

- came from the participants themselves
- were moving beyond description.
- were avoiding using language and ideas that marginalised them.

It also involved reflection upon the approaches used to represent these ideas. There was a recognition that the process could get in the way of representing people's understandings.

Some claims were also quite general in nature and were more of a belief about the outcomes of their research rather than a conclusion based on evidence. Researchers often recognised such limitations in their work, particularly in relation to how 'participatory' it had been and whether it might impact on future research and practice. They often reflected upon the degree to which areas under discussion arose from the participants or from the priorities of others. This issue of power, voice and support was also reflected in the ease with which different participants were able to make their ideas known and the relevance of such ideas when mediated through others.

In looking across the papers, there were also a range of factors which researchers identified as a key means of achieving the outcomes of their research. We came to see these as the practical means by which participation was delivered. So, let's turn to these practicalities of the *while*.

The component parts (of participation – see Figure 4.2)

We recognised the practicalities of participation as the component parts of the *while*. These component parts in reality are fundamentally interactional, but for purposes of thematic analysis and reflection they were identified as *languages, roles, adaptation, enjoyment, relationships, time, listening, beliefs, flexibility and space.*

The sharing of ideas was a key element of participatory practice, with an emphasis upon the spoken word. This emphasis was challenged in many different ways by the language 'skills' of those involved and their capacity to deliver a complete, linear, 'reliable' narrative. Consequently, projects sought ways to get the information they needed using alternative means, but it was not clear whose priorities were being served in this process. Similarly, it was noted that the 'necessary' outputs of studies would exclude many of the people they purported to represent. There was often an acceptance that not everyone could engage with everything.

An alternative approach involved finding ways to share experiences in the moment, using personal responses, images and recordings to encapsulate feelings. This required adapting communications (visual, aural, emotional and sensory) to the moment, adopting different language forms to ensure ideas were shared and different voices were heard. This kind of flexibility was also seen as necessary to the different roles that people played across a project, often related to their shifting interests and desire to do particular things. This included people coming and going from groups and moving between insider and outsider positions. The identity which roles gave people was also recognised as important (or contested) in different projects, as were the responsibilities and possibilities which came with those roles.

In all projects, the attitudes of participants informed their involvement. The ways in which people were classified or not, for example, reflected and directed the manner in which they were responded to. Frequently, people adopted deficit thinking without being aware of it, but in other instances it was an important point of reference both during the project and in the write-up. These attitudes and beliefs were evident too in the barriers and opportunities people faced as participants.

The kinds of adaptations which emerged also reflected these attitudes. For example, some projects viewed it as necessary to adapt the individual through training, while others sought to adapt their method or the available roles to enable positive experiences of participation. Such adaptation was also associated with a frequent focus upon creativity and fun so that the individuals enjoyed themselves. Fun was seen as requiring planning and when it was present suggested that other components of the participatory process were in a positive place.

Planning was also evident in the ways in which groups built relationships. This included ensuring that there were organised social elements in projects, with opportunities to relax, while building up trust and rapport. The importance of demonstrating trust (for example, by being open to questions or sharing resources) was also widely recognised. Relationships were frequently discussed as being at the heart of projects and key to communications. Their complexity was also noted, as were their changing nature over time and their vulnerability to dynamic personal and group emotions.

The need for extended engagement over time was seen as key to being able to meaningfully enable all the other components of participation. This was not only a recognition of the evolving nature of groups but also the practical consequence of trying to work in ways that balanced power, support and voice. This balance between the underpinning tensions was widely associated with listening too. It helped participants:

- to engage with each other's perspectives.
- to find a balance across the dynamics of the groups and their various roles.
- to be responsive to negative and positive feelings.

The capacity to adapt, to act upon what is said, as well as to offer appropriate spaces and practices were also strongly linked to listening. This offer of appropriate spaces also required flexible management. This might be both in providing points of greater privacy or to facilitate coming together more widely. It could be both an issue of practical organisation (for example travel or room layout) and of cultural significance. It was through the space that all the other component parts of the *while* could be played out, but in turn the nature of that space was a result of the interaction of those parts.

While *in education?*

I hope that the description of the *while* has shown the interwoven nature of the tensions, outcomes and component parts out of which and through which the experience of participation emerges. When we consider any participatory activity, people and their activities are 'being' through/within/around them. These interactions form around each other; they are moments, but (to steal a famous metaphor) they are both a wave and a particle. Any experience of participation therefore emerges as a flow from many directions and is more than a sum of any preceding moments. This is why I feel that the *while*, even though it emerged from a study of participatory research projects, is just as relevant to an education context in which people of all characteristics are engaged.

So let us return to my earlier confusion about why people believe that school is the solution when it has the capacity to do so much damage. I am going to use the framework of the *while* to explore this conflicted (and frequently marginalised) experience of participation. This will I hope not only help examine the trouble with school, but it will also demonstrate the value of this model in seeking a better understanding of these troubles and how we may work towards overcoming them.

I have clustered this section using eight of the component parts of the *while* (I will return to the missing two component parts at the end):

- languages, listening and beliefs
- roles, relationships and enjoyment
- space and time

Given the interweaving nature of these parts, I could have brought these together in many different ways. This is just what felt right to me at the time of writing.

This exploration is framed around dozens of qualitative and quantitative research papers from all around the world. They include large-scale longitudinal studies, randomised control trials, surveys, interviews, observations, literature reviews and ethnographies. I hope that in using these technologies of certainty, I am once more underlining their value as tools for reflection, while at the same time reassuring readers that this is not just me spouting off.

Some thoughts about languages, listening and beliefs

I mentioned above that nearly one in five pupils in England had a language other than English as their first language in 2021. This is largely a result of immigration. In many countries, of course, having more than one language is part of the national identity. For example, there are more than 50 million speakers of Spanish in the United States, while in India there are more than 20 official languages. This does not stop school systems operating primarily with a single language though, with predictable outcomes. For instance, a small-scale random controlled trial in Zimbabwe showed that a monolingual primary class had statistically significantly worse academic outcomes to a class using a translanguaging approach (Charamba, 2022).

Such barriers are evident even when practitioners are aware of the problems too. For example, a South African study (Manga & Masuku, 2020) noted the educators' frustration at their lack of knowledge on deaf-blindness and approaches to effective communication. The young people in turn expressed their frustrations through challenging behaviours. The educators noted that these issues were exacerbated by the diversity of learners and educators, their backgrounds, cultures and languages. Other studies demonstrate the social nature of such barriers too; for instance, staff can be reluctant to use key word signing because they find it embarrassing or because they fear that it will be stigmatising (Rombouts et al., 2016).

The language of schools is more than just the means of teaching, of course. For instance, the introduction of criterion-referenced grading systems in Sweden (changing from language about low grades to fail grades) turned the weakest children into failures and did not improve results as anticipated (Arensmeier, 2022). While a small-scale study in one primary school in England showed how children (particularly of the same gender) cooperated and offered each other support when given the space to do so but did not cooperate when grouped in competitive structures or given individualised tasks (Ambreen & Conteh, 2021).

Edwards-Groves and Davidson (2020) note that we are co-participants in any communication. They suggest we need to recognise and respond to contextual challenges in the classroom and wider school context as well as how a contribution sits in the flow of the moment. This has many consequences. For example,

- teachers who demonstrate interest, understanding and respect by listening will have to deal with less discourteous and disruptive behaviour (Weger, 2018).

- ignoring requests for meetings and supports will compound the difficulties of teenage boys who had been excluded and 'misused' drugs (Martin-Denham, 2020).
- students who are deaf or hard of hearing will struggle because of unthinking behaviours (e.g. teachers walking and talking, writing while facing the board, general noise from beyond the class), but they will frequently do nothing about it (Nelson et al., 2020).

The capacity and desire to listen is often constrained in practice. For instance, primary teachers who know about the need to engage with the child's voice will still often ignore that voice because they believe that they know what is best for the children (Shaw, 2019). This adult control emerges in Norwegian kindergartens too. Here, there is a preference for harmonious and joyful interaction, while anger (particularly to an adult) is seen as an emotion to be eradicated. This emotion is not understood as a potentially legitimate response nor as a message to be interpreted but as a sign of an aggressive child (Grindheim, 2014).

The beliefs of teachers have a profound impact upon experiences of participation in many other ways. For example, their attitudes to the background of children and their families. Parents of early school leavers in Ireland have reported teachers' low expectations of their children and how they are left to their own devices (such as colouring at the back of the classroom). The parents felt there was a stigma associated with where they lived too and that their life experiences meant they could not always share the educators' priorities (Doyle & Keane, 2019). Similarly, case studies of adoptive families in Australia concluded that teachers had a lack of awareness, understanding and sensitivity about the potential impact of topics in the curriculum. On the surface, these topics seemed benign, but they actually brought up many challenges around memories and identity, challenges which might be problematic for other children too (such as family histories or personal biographies) (Sempowicz et al., 2018). The impact of background was also evident in interviews with 18 primary teachers in England about children who have experienced migration. It showed how some practitioners did not trust the children as decision-makers. These practitioners drew upon categorical perspectives while deciding for the children; in contrast, where the practitioners had a focus on personal relationships, all children were trusted to be agentive and capable of voicing their interests (Farini & Scollan, 2021).

This variability of belief within settings and between staff is evident in many research contexts (e.g. keyword signing – Sheehy & Duffy, 2009). A survey of over 1,200 teaching and support staff in Sweden, showed how nearly half:

- viewed a diagnosis as important for support.
- felt that 'special' groups were valuable.
- believed that special educators should lead on pedagogical content.

In contrast, the special educators downplayed this deficit view; they were more likely to identify school and teacher factors as problematic (Lindqvist et al., 2011). The special educators however would find themselves having to support children within the deficit framework and unable to make the kinds of changes they see as necessary. As part of an extended observational analysis of how teachers differentiate, Merl (2021) concluded: 'equal participation' cannot be achieved while ability norms 'are structurally inscribed into schools'. This perception of ability can be seen to affect the teacher's response to similar behaviours in different children and/or situations; it is also evident in the opportunities and resources which the children are offered.

Teachers enacted beliefs will invariably affect the nature of the classroom in which they and the students participate; however, these are often not the same as the beliefs they claim to have. So, for instance, traditional teacher-controlled practices dominated even when science teachers professed a constructivist philosophy (Mansour, 2013), and in multilingual contexts foreign language teachers resisted first language use but were happier with its use if that first language was shared (Gallagher, 2020). A key issue is that teachers are frequently not aware of such contradictions or the issues surrounding their practices. For example, a study involving over 1,000 Portuguese teachers showed that most teachers were not aware of gender differences in school failure and dropout and ascribed such failings to personal and family factors (Cavaco et al., 2021).

These kinds of attitudinal issues are not simply at play in teacher–student relationships. For instance, narratives of two student teachers with a visual impairment identified the challenges they faced. Colleagues' attitudes defined the kinds of support that were available to the two trainees; these then constrained them in terms of time and space (Parker & Draves, 2017). Student peer-interactions will be affected too. For instance, research with Arab and Jewish students suggests that even when groups are brought together and are willing to talk, minority opinions are silenced or blurred (Poyas, & Elkad-Lehman, 2022).

Clearly, there are a great many challenges associated with languages, listening and beliefs. My purpose, of course, is not to lay out all such challenges that exist in relation to these component parts of the *while* but to use these components to highlight the conflicting experiences of participation that arise as part of everyday schooling. So, let's broaden that exploration by looking at three more practical components.

Some thoughts about roles, relationships and enjoyment

Reflecting the fundamental uncertainty in schools are the shifting nature of people's roles, their sense of self and their relationships. Practitioners, for example, walk a fine line between controlling and providing self-direction for children and young people. In discussions with 40 US teenagers, students wanted teachers:

- to be experts in explaining things.
- to be caring and passionate about them learning.
- not to be constrained by the curriculum but see each group of children as different.
- to have an interest in students yet maintain a personal distance.

(De Bruyckere & Kirschner, 2016)

That is a tough balancing act.

Similarly, young people need to negotiate various roles across institutions, reflecting the different communities of which they are part. For instance, a narrative from a young black person shows her simultaneously negotiating race, class and gender constructions within a mathematics classroom (Gholson & Martin, 2019). She felt a need to perform toughness, coolness and confidence in and out of school, but it was punctured occasionally in vulnerable moments of learning and in seeking micro-confirmations from a supportive teacher. This kind of tension informs teachers' interpretation of students' capabilities, behaviours and attitudes.

The variable nature of the educational relationships is something to which the children and young people are attuned too. A Dutch study, for example, explored how secondary students valued close connections, low in conflict, but reported having difficult relationships in the subjects they didn't like (Roorda et al., 2019). While young people in Denmark, Norway and the UK recognised that relationships with peers and teachers linked to their sense of belonging, achievement and investment within a school (Stuart, 2020).

Such relationships are variously entwined with trust and respect too. For instance, a study of Aboriginal students suggested that building relationships included providing a meaningful role for other members of the children's community. This involved recognising their history with educational institutions and acknowledging different policy, family and school interpretations of issues and priorities (Lowe et al., 2019). Inversely, Welsh and Little (2018), drawing on wider literature, suggested that young people's relationships with school are damaged by punishing behaviour deemed inappropriate. They appear to lose days, lack supervision and support, disengage from education, experience stigma and struggle with reintegration.

Practitioners too find themselves in conflicted spaces as a result of their relationships and roles. Within the Italian system, for instance, even though support teachers have more training than classroom teachers, they have less social recognition and are seen as secondary roles (Ianes et al., 2020). Similarly, surveys and interviews with over 200 primary and support teachers in South Africa highlighted the lack of collaboration and how responsibility shifts to support staff for learners who experience barriers to learning, seeing them as the solution to their problems (Dreyer, 2014). Systemic responses are also evident in a life-history study of three black male educators. This study showed how they felt that other people (including students) did not give them the freedom to step away from the stereotypes to express their racial, gendered and sexual identities in diverse ways (Woodson & Pabon, 2016).

Such experiences of marginalisation as a result of participating in school systems is also evident for school leaders. A study of 36 women teachers in boys' secondary schools in Australia, for example, showed how they were stopped from rising up the management chain, only being allowed to find their niche in caring roles (Acquaro & Stokes, 2016). While interviews with 19 deputy principals in Israel highlighted their lack of social relationships with colleagues and the resulting sense of loneliness. They identified issues around an imbalance in commitment, expectations and responsibility at work, as well as distrusting school leadership and/or their lack of accountability (Dor-Haim, 2021).

The lack of consideration of social relationships within schools has also been shown to be at the heart of both causes and possible solutions to their students' disengagement (Wenham, 2019). This is not just an issue for people on the margins either. Following a review of literature, Valiente et al. (2020) concluded that a focus upon improving socialisation of everyone in the classroom can promote students' emotional and academic learning. An Austrian study highlighted how positive relationships with teachers and other students were interwoven with liking school and had an important role to play at moments of transition (Hagenauer et al., 2018), while a Greek study concluded that friendship quality had a significant effect on whether children liked school and did not feel lonely (Antonopoulou et al., 2019).

This issue of loneliness underlines the precariousness of relationships within schools. For example, studies of children and young people around the world have reported:

- 15.5% being lonely in Brazil (Antunes et al., 2022).
- over 60% experiencing occasional loneliness in Finland and 10% prolonged loneliness (Lyyra et al., 2018).
- 15.3% being lonely in four Caribbean countries and 19.8% being regularly lonely in Morocco (Pengpid & Peltzer, 2021, 2021b).

In all these large-scale studies, experiences of bullying and victimisation had a role to play, with mention often being made of school absences. A study in England also showed that loneliness is strongly connected to lower levels of social and emotional well-being (Palikara et al., 2021).

This complex interaction between well-being and relationships seems to be played out in United Nations estimates that around 20% of adolescents experience mental health difficulties. But its interconnection with learning is also suggested by some countries seeing enjoyment and happiness as an essential part of pedagogy (e.g. Budiyanto et al., 2017), as well as in data suggesting that children who enjoy reading are successful at school (e.g. Kucirkova et al., 2017). The double-edged nature of enjoyment and success is evident over the long term too. For instance, data from over 3,300 children in the UK showed that at age six girls were over two and half times more likely to report enjoying school than boys, and if they were enjoying school, they were 72% more likely to get high grades at age 16 (Morris et al., 2019). While another UK study showed the interaction between school enjoyment, connection to a school, depressive symptoms and academic outcomes (Cadman et al., 2021). Enjoying what goes on outside the school is also (not surprisingly) important. For example, a survey of nearly 700 adolescents in Korea showed experiential activities led to greater enjoyment of school and so too did more frequent family and group trips (Kang et al., 2019).

I feel I am dancing around between ideas here and that this makes it hard for the reader to follow. This is part of the challenge that we face though, in exploring issues of participation (and also inclusion?). Uncertainty is experienced against a shifting context. The perspectives we choose to engage with are momentary points of insight. What is a relationship? What is a role? What is enjoyment? Where are their boundaries? We can never fully answer these questions, we can only reflect on some answers (and seek more?).

So, let's move on...

Let's consider how the use of space and time might affect experiences of participation.

Some thoughts about space and time

A review into effective strategies for student engagement (Franklin & Harrington, 2019) highlighted the importance of different aspects of the learning space (e.g. crowding, group work, noise, organisation, visual complexity, traditional and multi-centric layout). For instance, poor, reverberating acoustics make it harder for everyone to follow what is said (Prodi & Visentin, 2022) so that even an audio-visual presentation will not enable people to follow easily (Nirme et al., 2019). The pupil's place in the room will also have an impact. A Czech study, for instance, showed teachers rarely made direct eye contact, gave some students up to 80 more single gazes in a lesson and tended to focus on the first and mid rows (Smidekova et al., 2020). While the pace of the space will also matter. For instance, being given time to think about a question before answering will benefit students but not if they are merely being asked to demonstrate knowledge (Alsaadi & Atar, 2019). The traditional practices of the space will also have an impact, such as boys getting more attention, while lower-achieving pupils receive less feedback and opportunities.

van Groll and Fraser (2022) talk about our need to reconsider our relationship with spaces, particularly if we recognise that pedagogy is a troubling of past, present and future, requiring the privileging of unknowing and uncertainty. They suggest we use them as a means to explore our imperfect relations with the environment and to understand them not as a resource but as a something which the children are in relationship with. A study of Polish high school graduates concluded that they had lacked an aesthetical and cultural education not only because of a lack of interest in their background, their experiences, knowledge and creativity but also because they studied in uninspiring surroundings (Krasoń, 2018). While in a South African study, teachers in rural schools were seen to be embedded ecologically through interlinked systems within the local and wider community as well as within the physical landscape. When schools had a teacher who was resident near the setting, they were able to benefit from such insider, community knowledge, but since the teachers frequently had to commute to work they often could not physically build relationships and make connections to available resources (Ebersöhn & Ferreira, 2012).

These complex relations are also evident in relation to dominant practices of a setting. For example, a narrative of a black male teacher's experience shows how he experienced isolation, marginalisation and suspicion within education spaces, both as a student and a practitioner. These spaces were/are framed by the dominant culture, with middle-class, white values evident in daily, mundane and iterative moments. These demonstrated ongoing, systemic othering, scrutiny and surveillance, frequently associated with negative stereotyping (Callender, 2020).

Not being within the dominant school space will also create a different participatory experience. The nature of the difference might seem quite small too. For instance, in a study in Flanders, 20% of pupils felt they were looked down upon because they were following a vocational, non-academic curriculum (Spruyt et al., 2015). But the nature of the difference can be far more extreme. For instance, official figures show that only 64.77% of pupils with a formal decision of special educational needs are in EU mainstream classes for more than 80% of the week (EASNIE, 2020). Inversely, 35% of them are in classes with their peers for less than 20% of the week. This is a result of the ongoing pre-eminence of the continuum model where children are slotted into provision regarded as appropriate (Lemons et al., 2018). This model is underpinned by deficit views of need, leading to increasingly individualised assessments, planning, funding and assistance. Additional support is frequently experienced as an alternative curriculum and segregated provision or additional time and additional space (Rix et al., 2013).

An observational study in Norway (Snipstad, 2020) explored the experiences of a young man labelled as intellectually disabled who spent most of his school time segregated from his peers. Not only does the young man construct a universe of imaginary companions, he is also aware that he is subject to different rules, with his actions being interpreted in a different light to others. While he recognised the injustice of much of this, his teacher maintains he is segregated for the benefit of the other children. Similarly, caregivers of autistic children excluded from schools in England reported their inadequate support (e.g. time-out breaks, a quiet space to go to, sensory support and a visual timetable) even if they had paperwork requiring it. This included one boy being held down by teachers as a regular school strategy (incorrectly claiming that it was a positive behaviour technique) and resulted in deeply upset children, some having suicidal thoughts (Martin-Denham, 2022).

The notion of the different time and space within the continuum is also evident in the widespread use of ability grouping (e.g. setting, streaming, tracking). Differentiation and use of group work can be seen to lower expectations and reduce opportunities for many students, while channelling them towards different possible futures. In a Swedish study, both students and teachers came to blame students for poor personal and school results (Gustafsson, 2018). While national data in England showed that pupils aged 7–11 were less likely to enjoy (or continue to enjoy) studying Mathematics and English (with less statistical certainty) when put into low-ability groups (Boliver & Capsada-Munsech, 2021).

It is clear that selection and separation on the basis of notions of intelligence:

- impacts on the lives, identities and relationships of individuals, families and communities across the lifespan and within and between generations.
- creates and perpetuates hierarchies and divisions according to ethnicity, social class, gender and disability.
- has a fundamental influence on individual and community educational experiences.

(Rix & Ingham, 2021)

Yet this practice continues across the world.

So, let's finish with an extreme example of how time and space are interwoven with marginalising participatory experiences. These are evident in UK schools but can also be found in other countries – isolation booths. In one survey, across a year over 220 students in 200 schools had spent a whole week in one of these booths. In some schools, these isolation areas were permanently staffed and pupils could not leave the area all day (Titheradge, 2018).

FIGURE 4.3 Perfect makes practice.

What's missing?

In the section above, I have not made any direct mention of two of the component parts, flexibility and adaptation (see Figure 4.2). This is partly because it is quite hard to find meaningful research looking into how they play out in schools, but it is also because they are inherently associated with all the examples above and the underpinning models of certainty and uncertainty. All the examples above demonstrate the coming together of uncertainty with the idealised certainty of our school systems and the people within them. In many ways the examples above are about the lack of flexibility and adaptation within the system. The people's experiences of participation outlined above are taking place in a constrained and constraining, risk-averse system. In the next chapter, we will return to these notions and how they play out if we are willing to open ourselves to greater uncertainty.

In the section above, I have also not made any direct mention of the underpinning tensions (power, voice and support) nor the meaningful outcomes (value to selves, moments of learning, representing lives). This is a pragmatic decision based on the length of the chapter and book. Unpacking such things is like opening up a fig. In opening, it is sliced apart and (probably) rolled back upon itself, destroying its structure to reveal its innards. Each step has taken us away from the wider nature of the fruit, such as its connection to the plant from which it came, the soil from which it grew and our relationship to it (Caroline, the photographer who took the cover photo, has loved figs since childhood but I avoid them because they spike my blood sugar levels and I am diabetic, etc). Looking into these issues is like looking into an Escher painting. This is why we attempted to create a three-dimensional image of the *while* (see Figure 4.2), leading both upward and downward, inward and outward, forward and backward, representing the positive, the negative and the in-between. If you want to think about these tensions and outcomes, they are there in all the examples; you just need to look.

Schools are fundamentally based around asymmetric power relations. For example, a study looking at five projects where children participated in designing technology noted that as well as schools being slow and inflexible partners, children lacked power in these educational settings. They were ostensibly 'forced' to do things. Consequently, they were not used to having to understand and explore why they were involved in something. Their learning goals were externally defined, while their opinions and insights about these were not wanted (Iivari & Kinnula, 2016). Similarly, a systematic review of student voice literature concluded that many initiatives begin with the notion of children as lacking competence in some way. Adult leaders retain power over the spaces to be heard. They exclude voices that they see as not acceptable, relevant or intelligible. The goals and structures of activities are also frequently framed by and for the institution. Consequently, they reinforce existing school power relations and maintain the marginalisation of those on the boundaries (Pearce & Wood, 2019).

This however does not mean that the participation is not going on.

Regardless of whether the settings adopt adult-centred or child-centred approaches, the component parts of participation are practically and inherently engaged. The problem is that the systems and people within them are not taking advantage of the possible opportunities participation brings.

I hope that in this chapter I have demonstrated the endless permutations surrounding people's participation in a marginalising educational experience. I hope I have shown how the *while* of participation can help us to focus our understanding of such challenges. In the next chapter, I will return to the research project out of which the concept of the *while* emerged. I will explore how this understanding of participation came about (and continues to come about) and then go on to the lessons I learned about participation and how to align people's experiences in practice.

References

Acquaro, D., & Stokes, H. (2016). Female teacher identities and leadership aspirations in neoliberal times. *International Studies in Educational Administration (Commonwealth Council for Educational Administration & Management (CCEAM))*, 44(1), 129–144.

Alsaadi, N., & Atar, C. (2019). Wait-time in material and classroom context modes. *International Journal of Contemporary Educational Research*, 6(1), 53–69.

Ambreen, S., & Conteh, J. (2021). Children's interactions in ability-based groups in a primary classroom. *European Educational Researcher*, 4(1), 85–107.

Antonopoulou, K., Chaidemenou, A., & Kouvava, S. (2019). Peer acceptance and friendships among primary school pupils: Associations with loneliness, self-esteem and school engagement. *Educational Psychology in Practice*, 35(3), 339–351.

Antunes, J., Machado, Í. & Malta, D. (2022). Loneliness and associated factors among Brazilian adolescents: Results of national adolescent school-based health survey 2015. *Jornal de Pediatria*, 98, 92–98.

Arensmeier, C. (2022). Institutionalizing school failure: From abandoning to reintroducing a failing grade—The rationales behind Swedish grading reforms. *Journal of Educational Change*, 23(2), 221–252.

Arnstein, S. (1969). A ladder of community participation. *American Institute of Planners Journal*, 35(4), 216–224.

Azad, A., & Hau, H. (2018). Adolescent females with limited delinquency – At risk of school failure. *Children and Youth Services Review*, 95, 384–396.

Boliver, V., & Capsada-Munsech, Q. (2021). Does ability grouping affect UK primary school pupils' enjoyment of Maths and English? *Research in Social Stratification and Mobility*, 76, 100629.

Budiyanto Sheehy, K., Kaye, H., & Rofiah, K (2017). Developing signalong Indonesia: Issues of happiness and pedagogy, training and stigmatisation. *International Journal of Inclusive Education*, 22(5), 543–559.

Cadman, T., Hughes, A., Wright, C., López-López, J., Morris, T., Rice, F., Smith, G., & Howe, L., (2021). The role of school enjoyment and connectedness in the association between depressive and externalising symptoms and academic attainment: Findings from a UK prospective cohort study. *Journal of Affective Disorders*, 295, 974–980.

Cahill, H., & Dadvand, B. (2018). Re-conceptualising youth participation: A framework to inform action. *Children and Youth Services Review*, 95, 243–553.

Callender, C. (2020). Black male teachers, white education spaces: Troubling school practices of othering and surveillance. *British Educational Research Journal*, 46(5), 1081–1098.

Carroll, C., Hurry, J., Grima, G., Hooper, A., Dunn, K., & Ahtaridou, E. (2020). Evaluation of bug club: A randomised control trial of a whole school primary aged reading programme. *The Curriculum Journal*, 31(4), 605–625.

Cavaco, C., Alves, N., Guimarães, P., Feliciano, P., & Paulos, C. (2021). Teachers' perceptions of school failure and dropout from a gender perspective: (Re)production of stereotypes in school. *Educational Research for Policy and Practice*, 20(1), 29–44.

Charamba, E. (2022). Pushing linguistic boundaries: Translanguaging in a bilingual science and technology classroom. *Journal of Multilingual and Multicultural Development*, 43(10), 951–965.

Cunha, I. P. D., Pereira, A. C., Meneghim, M. D. C., Frias, A. C., & Mialhe, F. L. (2019). Association between social conditions and oral health in school failure. *Revista de Saúde Pública*, 53, 1–15.

De Bruyckere, P., & Kirschner, P. (2016). Authentic teachers: Student criteria perceiving authenticity of teachers. *Cogent Education*, 3(1), 1247609.

Desjardins, R., Thorn, W., Schleicher, A., Quintini, G., Pellizzari, M., Kis, V., & Chung, J. E. (2013). OECD skills outlook 2013: First results from the survey of adult skills. *Journal of Applied Econometrics*, 30(7), 1144–1168.

Dor-Haim, P. (2021). Expressions of loneliness: Different perspectives of loneliness among school deputy principals. *Educational Management Administration & Leadership*, 1–19.

Doyle, G., & Keane, E. (2019). 'Education comes second to surviving': Parental perspectives on their child/ren's early school leaving in an area challenged by marginalisation. *Irish Educational Studies*, *38*(1), 71–88.

Dreyer, L. (2014). Exploring collaboration between mainstream and learning support teachers. *Education as Change*, *18*(1), 179–190.

Ebersöhn, L., & Ferreira, R. (2012). Rurality and resilience in education: Place-based partnerships and agency to moderate time and space constraints. *Perspectives in Education*, *30*(1), 30–42.

Edwards-Groves, C., & Davidson, C. (2020). Noticing the multidimensionality of active listening in a dialogic classroom. *The Australian Journal of Language and Literacy*, *43*(1), 83–94.

European Agency for Special Needs and Inclusive Education (EASNIE). (2020). In J. Ramberg, A. Lénárt, & A. Watkins (Eds.), *European agency statistics on inclusive education: 2018 dataset cross-country report*. European Agency.

Farini, F., & Scollan, A. (2021). Between marginalisation and agency. Primary school teachers' narratives in London and the position of children with migrant backgrounds. *Migration Studies Review of Polish Diaspora*, *182*(4), 79–96.

Fazel, M., & Newby, D. (2021). Mental well-being and school exclusion: Changing the discourse from vulnerability to acceptance. *Emotional and Behavioural Difficulties*, *26*(1), 78–86.

Franklin, H., & Harrington, I. (2019). A review into effective classroom management and strategies for student engagement: Teacher and student roles in today's classrooms. *Journal of Education and Training Studies*. *7*(12), 1–12.

Gallagher, F. (2020). Considered in context: EFL teachers' views on the classroom as a bilingual space and codeswitching in shared-L1 and in multilingual contexts. *System*, *91*, 102262.

Gholson, M., & Martin, D. (2019). Blackgirl face: Racialized and gendered performativity in mathematical contexts. *ZDM*, *51*(3), 391–404.

Gomez-Baya, D., Garcia-Moro, F. J., Nicoletti, J. A., & Lago-Urbano, R. (2022). A cross-national analysis of the effects by bullying and school exclusion on subjective happiness in 10-year-old children. *Children*, *9*(2), 287.

Graham, B., White, C., Edwards, A., Potter, S., & Street, C. (2019). School exclusion: A literature review on the continued disproportionate exclusion of certain. Retrieved August 15, 2022, from the Department for Education: https://assets. publishing.service.gov.uk/government/uploads/system/uploads/attachment_data/ file/800028/Timpson_review_of_school_exclusion_literature_review.pdf

Grindheim, L. (2014). 'I am not angry in the kindergarten!' Interruptive anger as democratic participation in Norwegian kindergartens. *Contemporary Issues in Early Childhood*, *15*(4), 308–318.

Gustafsson, J. (2018). Differentiation through individualisation – An ethnographic investigation of how one Swedish school creates inequality. *Ethnography and Education*, *13*(1), 52–68.

Hagenauer, G., Reitbauer, E., & Hascher, T. (2018). "It's cool but challenging" The relevance of basic need fulfillment for students' school enjoyment and emotional experiences at the transition from primary to secondary education. *Orbis Scholae*, *7*(2), 23–42.

Hart, R. (1992). *Children's participation: The theory and practice of involving young citizens in community development and environmental care.* UNICEF.

Heidegger, M. (1996). *Being and time: A translation of Sein und Zeit.* SUNY Press.

Hutchinson, J. (2021). How fairly and effectively special educational needs and disabilities (SEND) are identified? Trends in SEN identification: Contexts, causes and consequences, SEN Policy Research Forum. *Journal of Research in Special Educational Needs, 21*(1), 22–28.

Ianes, D., Demo, H., & Dell'Anna, S. (2020). Inclusive education in Italy: Historical steps, positive developments, and challenges. *Prospects, 49*(3), 249–263.

Iivari, N., & Kinnula, M. (2016, October). Inclusive or inflexible: A critical analysis of the school context in supporting children's genuine participation. In *Proceedings of the 9th Nordic Conference on Human-Computer Interaction* (pp. 1–10).

Kang, S., Lee, W., Moon, J., & Kim, W. (2019). The influence of leisure and travel experiences on the school enjoyment of adolescents: A panel analysis. *Leisure Studies, 38*(4), 548–557.

Krasoń, K. (2018). Marginalisation of culture and aesthetics in the Polish school seen through the eyes of its students. *The New Educational Review, 54*, 98–109.

Kucirkova, N., Littleton, K., & Cremin, T. (2017). Young children's reading for pleasure with digital books: Six key facets of engagement. *Cambridge Journal of Education, 47*(1), 67–84.

Lemons, C. J., Vaughn, S., Wexler, J., Kearns, D., & Sinclair, A. (2018). Envisioning an improved continuum of special education services for students with learning disabilities: Considering intervention intensity. *Learning Disabilities Research & Practice, 33*(3), 131–143.

Lindqvist, G., Nilholm, C., Almqvist, L., & Wetso, G. (2011). Different agendas? The views of different occupational groups on special needs education. *European Journal of Special Needs Education, 26*(2), 143–157.

Lowe, K., Harrison, N., Tennent, C., Guenther, J., Vass, G., & Moodie, N. (2019). Factors affecting the development of school and Indigenous community engagement: A systematic review. *The Australian Educational Researcher, 46*(2), 253–271.

Lyyra, N., Välimaa, R., & Tynjälä, J. (2018). Loneliness and subjective health complaints among school-aged children. *Scandinavian Journal of Public Health, 46*(20_ suppl), 87–93.

Manga, T., & Masuku, K. (2020). Challenges of teaching the deaf-blind learner in an education setting in Johannesburg: Experiences of educators and assistant educators. *South African Journal of Communication Disorders, 67*(1), 1–7.

Mansour, N. (2013). Consistencies and inconsistencies between science teachers' beliefs and practices. *International Journal of Science Education, 35*(7), 1230–1275.

Martin-Denham, S. (2020). Riding the rollercoaster of school exclusion coupled with drug misuse: The lived experience of caregivers. *Emotional and Behavioural Difficulties, 25*(3–4), 244–263.

Martin-Denham, S. (2022). Marginalisation, autism and school exclusion: Caregivers' perspectives. *Support for Learning, 37*(1), 108–143.

Merl, T. (2021). In/sufficiently able: How teachers differentiate between pupils in inclusive classrooms. *Ethnography and Education, 16*(2), 198–209.

Morris, T., Dorling, D. Davies, N., & Davey Smith, G. (2019). School enjoyment at age 6 predicts later educational achievement as strongly as socioeconomic background and gender. *SocArXivPaper*, August 10th. Retrieved from https://osf.io/preprints/socarxiv/e6c37/

Nelson, L. H., Anderson, K., Whicker, J., Barrett, T., Muñoz, K., & White, K. (2020). Classroom listening experiences of students who are deaf or hard of hearing using listening inventory for education – Revised. *Language, Speech, and Hearing Services in Schools*, 51(3), 720–733.

Nirme, J., Haake, M., Lyberg Åhlander, V., Brännström, J., & Sahlén, B. (2019). A virtual speaker in noisy classroom conditions: Supporting or disrupting children's listening comprehension? *Logopedics Phoniatrics Vocology*, 44(2), 79–86.

Office of National Statistics (ONS). (2021). Schools, pupils and their characteristics. Retrieved from https://www.iicsa.org.uk/key-documents/27114/view/INQ006503.pdf

PA Media. (2022). Rishi Sunak vows to end low-earning degrees in post-16 education shake-up. *The Guardian*, 7th August. Retrieved August 8, 2022, from https://www.theguardian.com/politics/2022/aug/07/rishi-sunak-vows-to-end-low-earning-degrees-in-post-16-education-shake-up?CMP=Share_AndroidApp_Other

Palikara, O., Castro-Kemp, S., Gaona, C., & Eirinaki, V. (2021). The mediating role of school belonging in the relationship between socioemotional well-being and loneliness in primary school age children. *Australian Journal of Psychology*, 73(1), 24–34.

Parker, E., & Draves, T. (2017). A narrative of two preservice music teachers with visual impairment. *Journal of Research in Music Education*, 64(4), 385–404.

Pearce, T., & Wood, B. (2019). Education for transformation: An evaluative framework to guide student voice work in schools. *Critical Studies in Education*, 60(1), 113–130.

Pengpid, S., & Peltzer, K. (2021). Prevalence and associated factors of loneliness among national samples of in-school adolescents in four Caribbean countries. *Psychological Reports*, 124(6), 2669–2683.

Pengpid, S., & Peltzer, K. (2021b). Prevalence and associated factors of loneliness among a national sample of in-school adolescents in Morocco. *Journal of Psychology in Africa*, 31(3), 303–309.

Poyas, Y., & Elkad-Lehman, I. (2022). Facing the other: Language and identity in multicultural literature reading groups. *Journal of Language, Identity & Education*, 21(1), 15–29.

Prodi, N., & Visentin, C. (2022). A slight increase in reverberation Time in the classroom affects performance and behavioral listening effort. *Ear and Hearing*, 43(2), 460–476.

Rix, J., & Ingham, N. (2021). The impact of education selection according to notions of intelligence: A systematic literature review. *International Journal of Educational Research Open*, 2, 100037.

Rix, J., Sheehy, K., Fletcher-Campbell, F., Crisp, M., & Harper, A. (2013). Exploring provision for children identified with special educational needs: An international review of policy and practice. *European Journal of Special Needs Education*, 28(4), 375–391.

Rogoff, B. (2003). *The cultural nature of human development*. Oxford university press.

Rogoff, B., Dahl, A., & Callanan, M. (2018). The importance of understanding children's lived experience. *Developmental Review*, 50, 5–15.

Rogoff, B., Matusov, E., & White, C. (1998). Models of teaching and learning: Participation in a community of learners. In D. Olson & N. Torrance (Eds.), *The handbook of education and human development: New models of learning, teaching and schooling* (pp. 373–398).

Rombouts, E., Maes, B., & Zink, I. (2016). Attitude and key word signing usage in support staff. *Research in Developmental Disabilities*, 55, 77–87.

Roorda, D., Jorgensen, T., & Koomen, H. (2019). Different teachers, different relationships? Student-teacher relationships and engagement in secondary education. *Learning and Individual Differences*, *75*, 101761.

Selfe, L., & Richmond, R. (2020). *A review of policy in the field of special needs and inclusive education since the 1990s*. SEN Policy Forum, Department for Education.

Sempowicz, T., Howard, J., Tambyah, M., & Carrington, S. (2018). Identifying obstacles and opportunities for inclusion in the school curriculum for children adopted from overseas: Developmental and social constructionist perspectives. *International Journal of Inclusive Education*, *22*(6), 606–621.

Shaw, P. (2019). Engaging with young children's voices: Implications for practitioners' pedagogical practice. *Education 3–13*, *47*(7), 806–818.

Sheehy, K., & Duffy, H. (2009). Attitudes to Makaton in the ages on integration and inclusion. *International Journal of Special Education*, *24*(2), 91–102.

Shier, H. (2001). Pathways to participation: Openings, opportunities and obligations, *Childhood*, *15* (2), 107–117.

Smidekova, Z., Janik, M., Minarikova, E., & Holmqvist, K. (2020). Teachers' gaze over space and time in a real-world classroom. *Journal of Eye Movement Research*, *13*(4), 1–20.

Snipstad, Ø. (2020). Framing inclusion: Intellectual disability, interactive kinds and imaginary companions. *International Journal of Inclusive Education*, *24*(10), 1050–1063.

Spruyt, B., Van Droogenbroeck, F., & Kavadias, D. (2015). Educational tracking and sense of futility: A matter of stigma consciousness?. *Oxford Review of Education*, *41*(6), 747–765.

Stack, E., & K. McDonald. (2014). Nothing about us without us: Does action research in developmental disabilities research measure up? *Journal of Policy and Practice in Intellectual Disabilities*, *11*(2), 83–91.

Stuart, K. (2020). A critique of 'Early School Leaving', 'Drop Out' and 'NEET' from the UK, Denmark and Norway: Marginalisation and co-created education research project. *Journal of Higher Education Theory and Practice*, *20*(7), 55–70.

Thomas, N. (2007). Towards a theory of children's participation, *International Journal of Children's Rights*, *15*(2), 199–218.

Titheradge, N (2018). Hundreds of pupils spend week in school isolation booths. *BBC News*. Retrieved August 8, 2022, from https://www.bbc.com/news/education-46044394

Valiente, C., Swanson, J., DeLay, D., Fraser, A., & Parker, J. (2020). Emotion-related socialization in the classroom: Considering the roles of teachers, peers, and the classroom context. *Developmental Psychology*, *56*(3), 578.

van Groll, N., & Fraser, H. (2022). "Watch Out for Their Home!": Disrupting extractive forest pedagogies in early childhood education. *Journal of Childhood Studies*, *47*(3), 47–53.

Weger, H. (2018). Instructor active empathic listening and classroom incivility. *International Journal of Listening*, *32*(1), 49–64.

Welsh, R., & Little, S. (2018). Caste and control in schools: A systematic review of the pathways, rates and correlates of exclusion due to school discipline. *Children and Youth Services Review*, *94*, 315–339.

Wenham, L. J. (2019). Misunderstood, misinterpreted and mismanaged: Voices of students marginalised in a secondary school, Doctoral dissertation, UCL (University College London).

Wong, N., Zimmerman, M., & Parker, E. (2010). A typology of youth participation and empowerment for child and adolescent health promotion. *American Journal of Community Psychology, 46*(1), 100–114.

Woodson, A., & Pabon, A. (2016). "I'm none of the above": Exploring themes of heteropatriarchy in the life histories of Black male educators. *Equity & Excellence in Education, 49*(1), 57–71.

5

SEEKING FAIRER PARTICIPATION

Is this me speaking?

I was born to famous parents. My sister lived in a long-stay institution established by the namer of Down syndrome. I grew up with incredible privilege, while being a witness to profound unfairness.

I was never successful at school. But I went to a place that got people through exams, so even though I failed many, I scraped by in enough to be allowed qualified entry to adulthood. And I was lucky in other ways. From a very young age, I knew I loved teaching and I loved writing. My other passions faded but not these.

In my twenties, my famous, campaigning father began working for greater museum access for mentally handicapped people (on the cusp of becoming people with learning disabilities – in the UK). I was writing for a theatre in Education company at the time. My dad asked me to write a pilot script for an audio tour guide of the Overlord Museum, and so I undertook some trials with users. As a consequence of this nepotism (let's not argue the toss), I ended up writing over 50 basic language audio tour guides all around the UK. This was not the sort of nepotism which brought with it large amounts of money, but it was really interesting. Perhaps unsurprisingly, a fascination with access to heritage burgeoned.

I never knew if the work based on those initial trials was delivering what I intended though, and I always wanted to explore this further. In my forties, I wrote a research application to develop a team of community assessors at Portsmouth Historic Dockyards. The aim was to explore issues of access. The application was not successful, but at the suggestion of my father, I got in touch with a charity (MENCAP) in Liverpool. Another funding application

DOI: 10.4324/9781003281405-5

was submitted (related to Merseyside) and was once more refused. A series of meetings followed with the local community, and during these the museums involved made it clear that they did not really want an access audit project but would rather have an arts project, with an exhibition at the end. This siloed workstream would not challenge the status quo, of course, and it was not something I wanted to be part of. After many months of working on a different idea entirely, I decided to withdraw. As I left that last meeting, I asked (or strongly suggested) that any final decision should be based upon the views of the people with learning difficulties (a term being recommended at the time). I asked them to listen to those at the meeting and those who had been involved in the project so far. A while later (to my delight), when the people with learning difficulties finally got to vote, they made it clear they wanted to stick with the audit plan.

In 2005, the Access to Heritage project was set up, with funding from a wide variety of local and national sources. Participants undertook audits of numerous settings. Their work went on to be showcased in practitioner journals, as well as national and international press; they won many awards and then undertook a range of Sensory Arts projects. At the time of writing, many of the participants are still actively involved in the field. I was a regular visitor to the project, supporting the co-ordinator in small ways. I am delighted to say that what was achieved was little to do with me and much more to do with the involvement of hundreds of other lives, spaces and places.

In the chapter that follows, I will talk in detail about the European Union-funded project that emerged as part of my experiences with this Merseyside-based project. But before I get there, I want to ask you some questions.

So here are some simple ones. Would this have all happened if:

- my father was not famous?
- my sister had had a fairer life?
- I had been a success at school?
- I had been at a school not focused on exams?
- I had not loved writing and teaching?
- my father had not believed in nepotism?
- we had been successful in either of our funding applications?
- others did not agree with my reasons for resigning?

And here are some (possibly?) less simple ones. Would this have all happened if:

- I was not white, middle-class, English-speaking, male, not-yet-disabled, etc?
- the social model of disability had not been developed?
- many long-stay institutions had not been shut down (in the UK)?
- the sensory arts movement did not exist?
- technology had not enabled recorded audio tours?

Or more obscurely. Would all of this have happened if:

- tarmac had not been invented?
- The East India Company had not been set up?
- sheep had not been introduced to (what we now call) Europe?
- how did these pasts affect the futures that were now?

Participating in more-than-me

Of course, all of these questions are unanswerable in a categorical way. But they do speak to the diverse and competing nature of the historicity at play, when we stop to reflect upon something that has caught our attention (whatever that may be). The reality of any moment is a point of experience. At any such point are endless possibilities. Unless one believes that we are participating in a preordained narrative or are under direction from a higher force (which I do not), then any moment is fundamentally random. Every aspect of that moment is random. Any explanation in retrospect is partial. That aspect may reflect a mathematical likelihood, but any deduced causality will never be singular or absolute; it will always rest in a moment of doubt.

The *me* in a moment of participation therefore is much more-than-me. Being more-than-me though is not just about understanding us as individuals drawing on our collective knowledge, with connection to ancestors and standing on the shoulders of previous generations of scholars (Blalock, 2015). The more-than-me participating in any moment is an inter/intra/into-weaving, a multiplicity of random moments of personal being in that space. It/we/they is in an in/tangible relationship with that space and all that is being within it. This is why any moment of being is never part of a linear pathway. Neither is it a multitude of pathways (akin to a river basin), with many sources leading to one point of flow. The more-than-me (the more-than-us) is the random coming together of all those random moments at this random point of experience.

In a room of 20 people, we may 'feel' we are 20 'me's, but it is not as simple as 20 lives lived, brought together in 20 singular identities or even 20 individual clusters of multiple identities. There is one existing life in that moment. This one-life involves every aspect of that space and our relationship to/with/through it. Yet, we perceive/understand/explain our existence as fundamentally material and social. We respond to/emerge from the space/relationship we are in, the space/relationships around us and the space/relationship between this all. This response/emergence is informed by such things as tradition and rules and memories. Such things are never absolute or complete of course. They are always emerging. They are purely a perspective. They can 'feel' real. They can 'feel' agreed. They can 'feel' like a truth. They can feel like our best ethical/mathematical/cultural way forward. But they will always be partial. They will always be leaching back into random

FIGURE 5.1 Our story.

possibility. They can 'feel' solid, but they are always in the process of changing. The past, the present and the future therefore are metaphors for the confusion of now. This is where 'we' are.

Of course, it may also feel as if none of this is particularly helpful if 'we' want to get things done. But perhaps it is helpful in reflecting upon the everyday practical problems 'we' face.

[By the by, before we go on to think about participating in theory, I would like to offer you a detour. This may a useful reflection on the notion of more-than-me, which in turn may be a useful way to think about any learning moment. Is it up to you whether you take it?]

Every part of the tale *I* have told above is more-than-me. (The *I* that is writing this is more-than-me). Each moment is a moment of randomness to which I have applied a retrospective meaning; a meaning based upon the more-than-me as I (think about) (replay the) present in the past. I find it particularly interesting to think about how more-than-me participation influenced so much that the embodied me was not there for. I was there/I was not there. Thus, our absence/presence/influence is a way to describe endless number of 'being's who are both more-than-me and more-than-us (but to themselves are *me* and to ourselves are *us*).

Participating in theory

Before we go together to visit ideas related to participation within a European Union-funded project, *I* want to provide some theoretical points of reference. *I* want to offer some background to the nature of those reference points, how they emerged and the reasons why (*I* feel?) they might be relevant.

In the last chapter, *I* introduced the *while* of participation, having spoken about socio-cultural understandings of participation and then making links to Heidegger's (1996) notions of being. The idea and these connections did not arise fully formed of course. Their emergence was iterative (and populated by randomness?).

The *while* of participation began with:

- a commitment to our understanding of the contested areas of emancipatory and participatory research.
- an understanding of systematic reviewing.
- a request from participants to explore other research which had been called participatory.

We chose search terms, search engines and inclusion/exclusion criteria; then we read abstracts and papers, identifying meanings which spoke to us as readers. Next, extracts of texts were identified, coded, categorised and thematically grouped and analysed. At each point, it was possible for something else to have arisen. Our process sought to operate systematic parameters, but it was fundamentally a relational experience. It involved beings as technologies, texts and researchers. It required us to constantly question whether we should be doing it otherwise. Maybe we should. We certainly kept having to go back and forth, filling gaps that suddenly appeared where no gap had seemed to be before.

It was only after the first (very long and dry) report of the study was submitted to colleagues on the project that the socio-cultural framing arose. The more-than-me had for many years been thinking about the socio-cultural notions of learning and participation. Perhaps, these voices were talking to me/us throughout, but it was only after the themes emerged that more-than-me began to discuss the *while* with others and that the connections began to be made. At around this time too, another colleague made it clear that they did not like the term the *while*; they felt the *moment* of participation would be better. The issue was contested until we presented the review to one of the participatory groups. When asked, one member of the group (labelled as having learning disabilities) piped up her approval: 'It's simple. Participation happens while you are doing things'. On another day (with a different support worker?), she would not have been there (together in that space). But she was, and the term was adopted.

It was at about this point too that a colleague suggested revisiting Heidegger. As with all thinkers, there are critiques of their arguments and views, but in the case of Heidegger this includes questions about his involvement with National Socialism during the time of Hitler. *I* am a voyeur on this issue, knowing not enough to come to judgement, but *I* have another unease based upon a far less in-depth reading than many of his critics. As *I* read

Being and time, I was excited by how his thoughts related to the core idea of being within the *while*, but *I* was also disturbed by how other ideas of his could justify the removal of those that Kristeva (1982) termed the abject. Heidegger concluded that being with one another creates averageness, squashes down on what is allowed, what is proper, what is success, what can be ventured and what has been gained. He sees this as 'levelling down of all possibilities' (Heidegger, 1996 translation, p. 119). *I* profoundly disagree with such a notion, not only because it feeds into arguments commonly associated with advocates of eugenics. I also disagree because my life experience has taught me that being with another only creates averageness or reduces opportunities if we are closed to possibilities and have a limited view of:

- people's abilities/knowledges/experiences.
- what the normal or average is.

This book is premised on the opposite view that when we are open to possibilities then it creates far more than we can imagine or predict, taking us in new and unexpected ways that can benefit a great many.

Given the problematic aspects of Heidegger's work, it was tempting to step away from his other ideas, but there seemed a fundamental contradiction here. Participation is not just a cuddly experience. Participation is about involvement in where we are. And where we are is always full of ethical challenges. Engaging with Heidegger exemplifies the tensions inherent in being more-than-me within the wider them. It also aligns with the views of knowledge that more-than-me held as part of the ARCHES research project. We talked about the multiple views and understandings of participants situated across numerous shifting boundaries. It was recognised that these ideas spread through the group like a ripple and outwards beyond the project. It was also recognised that these ripples were constrained by our relationship with gatekeepers, institutionalised cultures and individualised/collective priorities. Ideas were therefore understood to be things which permeated, shifting as they moved through us. Engaging with Heidegger's notion of being within the *while* is perhaps such a ripple, one which emerged from more-than-me and informed our interactions?

The emergent process was/is ongoing too. Over the next year or so, other people read about the *while*. More-than-me began to recognise ideas in our discussions of 'being' that spoke to other theoretical notions, including some which spoke to our fundamental entanglement with ethical challenges. So let us turn to these now, broadly defined under three headings:

- post
- cross
- trans

Post

In discussions with a research student, Petra Vackova, and other members of the Open University post-humanist collective, strong connections with ideas associated with post/humanism/materialism/structuralism/etc emerged. Post-humanism draws on poststructuralist, socio-cultural and other traditions, and so notions such as assemblage (a becoming that brings elements together) are applied to posthuman descriptions of encounters among humans, materials and learning. The emerging pedagogy builds on learners' interests and questions; with learning activities directed by problems that emerge. In this context, practitioners explore how to arrange all elements of the assemblage to enable this process (Toohey & Smythe, 2022).

Posthuman understandings also challenge dualist traditions (e g mind–body), in that all matter has vibrant thing-power and exists in an entangled state. This means that disability (and other identities) can be understood as ongoing entanglements (Jones, 2019) with the possibility of 'rupture' ever present. This allows practitioners to re-understand and rework these entanglements. Such entanglements involve no fixed division between self/other, past/present/future, cause/effect. Within them, space and time are not predeterminate givens (as we once thought?).

Such thinking undermines any notion we might have of individual bounded and propertied objects as actors operating in a linear narrative, since we are entangled with all aspects of the planet we are becoming with (Barad, 2010). From this perspective, all things within our entangling are seen as possessing agency, which itself is something emergent, as an effect in relation to context (Nelson et al., 2021). The capacity to have an effect in relation to the context is never a radical separation, however, but about making connections and new commitment. This also brings a focus onto the ethical nature of our being and a shift from old planes of thought to new planes. It challenges us to consider what 'new' is; to question our most-taken-for-granted beliefs; to acknowledge newness and belief as being emergent, without a linear beginning and end, but constantly undergoing creation (St. Pierre et al., 2016).

Another relevant poststructuralist concept is Kristeva's notion of the abject, mentioned above. Participation within schooling can be seen as a paradox involving double gestures that abject and exclude while claiming to include. Consider, for example, seeking the literate child in opposition to seeking the child a literacy focus leaves behind (Popkewitz, & Huang, 2021). This understanding of participation sees those on the periphery of society as being expelled, or as useless or repulsive to social hegemonic forces. 'These people' do not participate in the ways society values. By marginalising 'these people' from accepted participatory arenas, it is anticipated that they will seek to achieve acceptance. However, these individuals do not respond in this way. They are still participating; it is just that they do so by creating their own contrary understandings and counter-practices; creating norms, rights and responsibilities with their abject peers. Their experiences of abjection create an identity for their own in-group that in turn excludes others (Sharkey & Shields, 2008). These others include those who oversee the social structures in which 'these people' are participating.

Another range of ideas that have emerged as relevant to the *while* are those associated with cross-disciplinary and cross-theoretical understandings. So, let us turn to those next.

Cross

Under the broad banner of almost any academic field there will be important, nuanced differences, which create strong divergences. (For example, Hein (2016) focuses upon Deleuze's emphasis upon the inherent instability of structures and the need to open them up to new conceptualisations and forms, contrasting this with Barad's emphasis on indeterminacy and intra-activity, where matter is not a thing but a doing.) However, new/post/materialism/humanism/structuralism is open to cross-disciplinary engagement. Its priority is developing new orientations towards material and ever-emergent, entangled embodiments.

The lack of certainty about these issues and our need to treat them as emerging ideas (asking us to interact with them?) is just as it should be. It reminds me of Latour's (2004) use of Heidegger's notion of the 'thingness of the thing'. He sees the thing as a gathering, an issue, which has humans and non-humans as ingredients. He asks us to offer arenas in which to gather, which construct us as something other with care and caution and which generate more in the process.

Latour's notion of ethical worlds which attend to 'the common good', was also picked up by Taylor and Giugni (2012). They see/saw how the posthuman (more-than-human) understanding echoes the indigenous relational understanding of being, where people are inextricably connected with the land, the living entity of which they are. From this position, inclusion is dynamic and generative, involving an active process of assembling commonalities. The focus should be relational, not upon communications between already formed subjects but as mutually generative encounters with others (human and non-human). And it should be grounded in an engagement with actual places, not as theory but as practice engaged in ethical and political challenges. Participating in this context involves questioning relationships. This includes learning how to be responsible for and negotiate around common interests.

Participation is also central to indigenous understandings of teaching/learning and the many versions of the apprenticeship system across cultures. These emphasise participation in activity, often hands-on, often allied to the telling of stories and often involving the observation of experienced practitioners at work (Golafshani, 2023). Indigenous models see the learner participating in a reciprocal relationship too:

- with their ancestors and generations to come,
- with their place and the creator,
- with their traditional knowledge and the knowledge they are engaged with as learners.

(Lindbolm & Jannok Nutti, 2022)

There is a clear overlap in the application of such ideas and socio-cultural concepts in pedagogical terms, so for example:

- the use of mapping is central to the Mosaic approach developed by Clark and Moss (2001) and is also proposed as a new materialist approach to inquiring into children and youth's active engagement and movements across the educational terrain (Reddington & Price, 2018).
- the new materialist focus upon space and place, and personal relationship to objects can also be seen as central to established approaches such as Photovoice (Wang & Burris, 1994) and In-the-Picture (Paige-Smith & Rix, 2011).
- The invitation to rework conventional approaches to issues such as development and special education are already essential ideas in the inclusion literature and other approaches which begin with uncertainty and critical engagement.

(see Chapter 4)

The disruption of mind/body dualism is also a characteristic of many critical and radical pedagogies which argue for moving away from such divisions, to open ourselves, moving against and beyond boundaries, to allow emotions and feelings to work in concert with the rational. Unlike new materialism, however, such approaches focus upon the human within these relationships. For example, as with the notion of the *while*, they recognise the role of excitement, fun and laughter within learning situations. They accept that irreverence and frivolity are valuable ways to engage with (serious?) issues (Chalklin & Mulvey, 2016).

A third strand of relevant thinking emerged from a range of sources across the last couple of years. This arose from general reading or hearing people talking at meetings or seminars about educational and social matters. Part of this focus emerged because of a political interest in the concept too, and this turned me towards a range of studies. So, let's cross over to ideas associated with trans and their possible relevance to the underlying tensions, outcomes and component parts of the *while*.

Trans

In much the same way that post- and cross- are often associated with other concepts, there is a complex range of usage of Trans(-) (prefix/whole word). Chalklin and Mulvey (2016) use the prefix trans in trans-pedagogy to encapsulate the focus of critical pedagogy upon transgressing and transcending established assumptions and power structures. (Like ARCHES they are working in informal museum education contexts too and apply this model to capture insights and experiences related to teaching and learning in an art museum). But they also recognise the wider use of trans- in disrupting binaries and challenging dominant assumptions: For instance:

- transdisciplinarity
- transcultural
- trans-species
- trans-racial
- transgender

They see trans- as being both a verb and a noun, suggesting a broad movement across boundaries, and use it to reflect the situatedness of knowledge and the need to be in a constant state of crossing to challenge established power structures.

The issues of disability which informed the development of the *while* speak to the notion of trans. For example, the ethical concerns of trans*historicity help us understand the violence inflicted on minds and bodies by normativity (Long in Bychowski et al., 2018). The dynamic intermeshing of embodied beings within the material world, which transforms/is transformed by them is also at the heart of trans-corporeality. This view sees dissolved relations and interchanges across all matter, engaging in the ethics and politics of entangled biological, technological, economic, social, political and other systemic processes and events. These operate at vastly different scales in an ever-emergent world and can help us explore ongoing, material, intra-actions which we may not value as human. These might not only be in wider environmental terms but also in relation to issues such as impairment and sexuality (Alaimo, 2008, 2018). For instance, a study exploring students' responses to gender-inclusive toilets demonstrated how a critical trans/disability lens can raise questions around non-normative embodiment, which in turn raises fundamental questions of educational in/exclusions and patterns of institutionalised hierarchies (Adair, 2015).

The issues of listening and language which are component parts of the *while* are also well served by notions associated with trans. Translanguaging views language as fluid and dynamic, dependent on the speakers who are making meaning and constructing discursive practices, while trans-semiotising sees language as entangled with other meaning-making processes (e.g. visuals,

gestures and body movement). Lin (2019), drawing upon socio-cultural pedagogies, highlights the importance of acknowledging the spontaneity of these
processes and the challenge of translating these into the language of academic
genres. She notes the continuous, expanding nature of learning and the value
of considering these issues from new materialist perspectives. This notion of
emergence is also evident in educational practice related to bilingual learners.
Translanguage approaches in this context see the importance of drawing
upon the learners' language repertoires to expand their participation in learning opportunities. Adopting this in pedagogy and assessment means speakers
can choose their linguistic resources depending on context (Fine & Furtak,
2020). This means communications do not have to follow the dominant language forms; it supports sense-making through diverse linguistic resources.

PAUSE

TAKE A MOMENT

Ready?

Move

On...

A part of participation

I have been trying to demonstrate how aspects of the *while* can be understood through a variety of theoretical lenses which can be associated with
uncertainty. In the next part of this chapter, *I* want to explore the emergent,
situated and complex nature of the participatory experience by discussing
aspects of the European funded, access to heritage project, ARCHES. *I* will
firstly present three examples of the interplay within the *while* and then
explore how our approach was entwined with risk.

Some readers may feel that an understanding situated in a non-school context is not applicable to school-based situations, but *I* believe it is for (at
least) two reasons:

- Firstly, as Booth (1999) suggests, the value of comparative study is to
  make 'the strange familiar and the familiar strange'. Any educational
  case study *I* offer up will be limited by the differing cultural contexts in
  which it is situated and the parochial nature of many of the concepts in
  use. This does not stop them from offering a valuable point of reference
  and reflection.
- Secondly, *I* have fulfilled the role of teacher and learner in many spaces.
  The insights that emerged from more-than-me's engagement with ARCHES
  convinced me it serves as an excellent exemplar for/across formal/informal
  learning contexts.

So let's go back to the topic of toilets.

Material relations

Humanity has a complex relationship with toilets. They are inherently associated with our comfort and well-being, while reflecting considerable cultural variation in their design, availability and use. They are also (perhaps surprisingly?) closely allied with the tensions of power, support and voice which underlie participation. Let me begin, therefore, by underlining their social justice credentials and relevance beyond ARCHES:

- At the time of writing, over ¼ million people in the UK cannot use traditional UK toilets. As a result of lived experiences such as these, Loretto Lambe from PAMIS in Scotland had to begin The Changing Places Toilets campaign in 2003. This resulted in the development of facilities that can be used by people with profound and multiple disabilities. Of course, this does not just affect them, but all those other people associated with their lives.
- Different countries have very different responses to the gendered nature of toilets. So while the UK government in 2022 still had a single-sex policy for public buildings in Scandinavia it was a widely accepted practice to have gender-neutral toilets. Meanwhile, an Australian study looking at the development of gender-neutral spaces in schools demonstrated the complexity and potential negative consequences of applying a toilet policy which aimed to reduce marginalisation (Francis et al., 2022).
- School toilets are commonly a site for bullying. A South African study identified them as a space for violence and illegal activity. They noted that they were often positioned away from the centre of school activity, and avoided by teachers (Ngidi & Moletsane, 2018).

Within ARCHES, toilets cropped up a lot. The availability of toilets, associated signage and people's experiences of them were all seen as essential items in the surveys developed by groups across the three nations. The organisation of breaks, routines for accompanying people and their adjacency were all relevant to the running of sessions. Within the London group, we had a participant who was a wheelchair user and wished to explore the accessibility of the toilets in various museums we visited. *I* spent many a happy hour going around museums taking photos of her trying (and often failing) to get her wheelchair in and around the confines of supposedly accessible spaces. We also had a participant who was stuck in a toilet for over 15 minutes because he could not turn on the water to wash his hands. There was no way for a person with a visual impairment to know that the tap had a movement sensor.

The last two stories (hopefully) clearly speak to the underlying tensions of power, support and voice, which were in play during our visits. But the outcomes of our interactions with toilets were not just related to museum access.

They also revealed a great deal about our methods of collecting data, how we could represent our findings and how we could get our points across to the management of the museums. We found out, for example, while recording visits to the 'accessible' toilets that:

- our photographs were not stored on the app we were developing.
- museum management did not want to listen to the issues raised, particularly if we used our preferred method (videos of the problem) rather than theirs (written reports).

We also found ourselves interacting across and through all the component parts of the process. We needed to be flexible, shift roles, take our time, listen to each other, seek our different ways to communicate about issues and so forth. Through our interactions with toilets, we challenged our beliefs about access, museums and research processes, as well as largely enjoying ourselves as we revealed injustices. The toilets acted upon us. Our relationship with them profoundly affected our relationships to the institutions in which we met and the relationships within the groups.

FIGURE 5.2 Whose boundary is it anyway?

Getting it wrong

The tensions, outcomes and component parts of the *while* were all ever-present concerns as we tried to organise the sharing of ideas across the project's 169 sessions. Membership and numbers attending the four groups varied, with between 15 and 25 people regularly in attendance in each group. These groups met weekly or bi-weekly, undertaking activities of their own design or in response to requests from various participant partners. As part of these, a wide range of in-museum activities emerged, including access audits, relationship-building exercises, explorations of access preferences, the creation of access proposals, trials of ideas, advice on provision, the testing of software, providing feedback on products and developing tours and multisensory resources (see Garcia Carrizosa et al., 2019).

At the heart of these sessions was the need to communicate/develop our thinking and share our experiences. This need was informed by the diverse access preferences of the groups (e.g. audio description, signing, subtitles, easy-read, sensory objects and language). Many of these preferences might be associated with the labels of sensory impairments and intellectual impairments; however, we recognised that different communication approaches generally influenced the whole of the community to some degree, a community that drew on a huge array of cultural, economic, social and linguistic understandings.

From the outset, we organised our communications with multiple access supports, but we still got a lot wrong. The issues, solutions and ramifications kept emerging through our dynamic entangled interactions with more-than-us. For example, in setting up the group we had not arranged to have a note-taker to provide a real-time text record. As a result, it soon became clear that we were excluding a couple of regular attendees. Our first response emerged from the technological focus of the project. With the support of the people we had excluded, we explored the use of apps that offered real-time text, but none of them worked. We next identified touch-typers in the group (including me) to undertake the note-taking role, but this too failed to provide the required support. The participants were very patient, but it became clear that our failure to identify the necessary resource at the outset was part of difficulty in resolving the problem. It was still sending a message that some access preferences were more important than others, and thus that some people were more/less important too.

The solution required us to create a new permanent role within the project for a note-taker; to find the funds and demonstrate a commitment to the principles of the project. Yet, this happened a few weeks into the project. The underlying tension between support, power and voice was clear to see. It had been evident in how we were representing and valuing the participants and the ways in which the understanding of the issue had emerged.

It was also clear how this all played out through the component parts. This was an issue about language and the practicalities of listening and being listened to; it represented beliefs in action, informing our relationships and the capacity of participants to enjoy the experience; we had let time pass; our attempts to be flexible and adapt what we were doing had been cumbersome. This was not a positive or productive participatory experience.

Understanding each other

As well as the 200 disabled participants, their friends, family and other supporters, ARCHES also involved participants (some of whom would also identify as disabled) from six museums, five technology companies, two universities and one cultural education company. In a paper written by members of one of the technology partners (Travnicek et al., 2022), they describe how they intended to produce a tactile-relief and gesture-based system for people with a visual impairment, but ended up projecting a colour image onto the tactile relief, creating a full graphical user interface and offering multiple levels of text in diverse formats. They talk about the tensions they faced in being funded to deliver specific outcomes while having to be true to the underlying participatory principles of the project. They were not used to designing their work with the potential needs of all participants in mind nor with engaging with the participant's voice in all aspects of the project. They were caught between the emergent approach adopted by the project and their more traditional quantitative approach which positioned participants as subjects of research.

The technology partners arrived with a confident self-image of themselves as researchers and in their understandings of the research process; they were not prepared for the challenges of working in a project where multiple voices were given equal weight. They struggled to understand the ways of working where roles were disrupted and status was negotiated. They found it challenging to look beyond the typical boundaries associated with disability categories, professional expertise and research processes and to do so in a diverse mix of institutional, national and community cultures. At times it felt as if our focus upon universal opportunities was like trying to contain the infinite.

The technology partners not only had to change their ways of working and their understandings of participation. The project also confronted their own sense of self, both professionally and personally. They were faced with the different perceptions that people brought to the project about expertise and where power lay, and also about the nature of impairment and disability and how these should be supported and responded to. In achieving this, it also generated unanticipated costs and created challenges in delivering expected outcomes, meeting with resistance from other participants who could/would not move their boundaries of the possible.

These partners found the notion that everyone was a participant (not because they were a disabled person but because they were attending and engaging with the exploration groups) to be both disruptive and enabling. It required ongoing responsive dialogue, which called for shifts across cultures and contexts. They had to tussle with the realisation/internalisation that building a project around the uncertainty of participation was not simply about removing barriers but also threw up myriad (new?) ways to marginalise and disable any (or all) participants. They had to accept that what works in one moment may not work in the next. They had to accept the risks, the positives, the negatives and the in-betweens; they had to try not to see them as anomalies or something that could be planned away.

The focus of their paper is more positive than negative though. They describe how this disruptive experience was also productive. New relationships and conceptualisations emerged, as did new ways of understanding technologies and their audience. They also recognised that they could not have predicted at the outset how the project changed them. It had to be experienced and engaged with, in order to be appreciated. They needed to be part of the *while*.

Entwining

The ideas for the activities, out of which ARCHES emerged, were initiated by, and followed up by, regular attenders and the less regular. Participation was context dependent. The nature of it depended upon the experience of being involved in a session, but it moved across other spaces too. People came and went, often returning, sometimes not; leaving ideas behind them which continued to spread and have an influence. We relied upon participants' diverse skills and experiences to lead us in different directions; we recognised that we all had resources and motivations of which others were unaware, and which were only revealed within the evolving context of the groups and their activities.

Within the sessions, we established a routine. People would have an experience (for instance., trialling a piece of technology, visiting a gallery, exploring an access preference), they would then reflect upon the experience, share understandings and insights from that experience, summarise those experiences, record them and share them with other participants for clarification and verification. In nearly all these projects and activities, there were competing priorities, funnelling our ways of working and what could be achieved with the output.

In addition to a suite of apps, games and training materials, we also created local change that responded to needs identified by participants.

This included introducing new materials, approaches to access, enhancing communications and initiating new ways of working, through such things as:

- a tactile map with a supporting audio description to enable navigation around our base museum in Vienna.
- the introduction of Wi-Fi in our base museum in Oviedo, the inclusion of cameras and screens in their lifts and an agreement to announce the closure of the museum at the end of the day both verbally and by raising and lowering the lights.
- a sample QR code resource in a base museum in London, which showcased how to create a book in each room for different access preferences, with links to accessible, updatable information.
- a video in the base Madrid Museum to introduce the different resources available at the museum and enable potential visitors to prepare how to navigate around the museum space and find basic amenities.

In undertaking these activities, we were involved in an emergent process that brought together and shared multiple views and boundaries. All of these processes were underpinned by risk, which related to the tensions, outcomes and component parts of the *While*. We challenged ourselves in how we supported each other, enabled our voices and questioned the shifting of power within our relationships. These challenges were evident in the value that people put on what we were doing within and beyond the project, within the moments of learning that emerged and the ways in which we represented our lives and ideas. We took risks with the roles we asked each other to fulfil, by challenging attitudes, and proactively seeking to bring together people from diverse cultures and with a wide variety of access preferences. We had to be open to the complexities of multiple languages, willing to adapt practices and spaces to enable relationships, to be flexible and take the time for people to enjoy themselves.

As the stories above demonstrate, things could/would go wrong at any point. The space worked for some people but not others; the use of language was only good for some in the room; the speed of activities was not suitable for everyone. As a result, people felt marginalised or fell out with each other; often activities did not achieve what some of us had hoped and rarely did outcomes materialise in the way we might have anticipated. Yet, by taking such risks we developed a communal sense of ourselves. We were enabled to take ownership of the project, to go in unexpected directions and to experience unexpected relationships with people, places and the spaces we were part of. This is why (perhaps?) people talked about the empathetic power of the project, seeing this (perhaps?) as more significant than the new ways of working and unanticipated results that arose.

In taking these risks, we talked about how our ways of working, of being within the *while*, risked the overall quality of what we could achieve. We saw that this might influence how people viewed the overall project and all of us involved, effecting their trust in the processes and outcomes and how this was both a process internal to the project and externally, informing the ways in which people felt and behaved towards each other and interacted with their space and place. Since we were a research project, we were aware that this meant we were in some way taking a risk with the quality of research. The majority of people believe in the value of research because of researchers seeking to ensure the quality of the process, its legitimacy and rigour. However, in an emergent and participatory frame, it is particularly difficult to assure people that these are being delivered as part of the research processes.

The relational and uncertain nature of participation means the process is inherently chaotic. It is not what one might consider consistent, predictable, replicable and measurable. If it is situated in meaningful participation, therefore, it is premised upon participants' momentary positions (is this subjective/is this objective?). Many people (internal and external to a project) struggled to value the approach in comparison to neatly definable methods. So, while some partners opened themselves to seeing their own products, attitudes or ways of working in new ways, other partners in the project faced similar challenges but were not able to change their established focus. For them, the risk was too great. They held, for example, onto a view of a particular 'type' of user/visitor/human and a right way to do things. Consequently, they felt a need to adopt their previous approaches so as to deliver the product/experience that they had envisaged and/or sought before.

There is little doubt that by seeking to support an open, emergent approach, we lost something in traditional research terms, but (most of us felt) we enhanced the overall quality of our experience and what we produced, how we were seen by ourselves and others and by the nature our relations.

Reputations and relations

Participatory spaces are public. They involve revealing yourself in new contexts and in ways which you often have little prior experience of. In the context of ARCHES, we were in spaces with people who had a great deal of experience of marginalisation and of struggles with well-being, but we were also with: people using different spoken and signed national languages; people who preferred simplified language and text-supported communication; people who gained access through audio description, braille and through engaging with multisensory objects. This created a whole range of novel situations for participants, such as a person signing in one language being translated into another spoken language, which was being signed too, alongside an expectation that language would be kept simple and offer audio description and text output. In such situations, it is all too easy to get things wrong and to be judged accordingly.

There were also clear risks in representing the group beyond our own boundaries, in more-public situations. In presenting the group and its ideas, the participants invariably risked presenting the underpinning tensions around power, support and voice that underlay the group. Particularly, given the political nature of many issues associated with disability and impairment. For example, it might seem appropriate to use the 'best' communicators as presenters in such situations. But what does this mean? We wanted to confront such notions and encourage our audience to understand the possible. As a consequence, people who were 'difficult to understand' were supported to lead museum visits; signing was undertaken on videos by a range of people including untrained signers; presentations to the press involved participants who might focus in great detail on a very specific issue or talk a great deal or be very perfunctory and quiet. This openness was a huge step into the unknown for many of the participants. They had to be courageous, willing to represent others and accept they might be a target for disagreement. Even though these public sharings were generally successful, we had to argue about them, to plan but always be open to change. We could not sit in judgement when (at any point in the process) what we were doing had to change.

Such emergent experiences open us up to powerful emotions, understandings and beliefs. It is possible that we can experience a communal togetherness in such moments but are also likely to experience competing views that are not easy to conflate or compromise over. There is always the likelihood that someone is being disappointed. A focus upon enhancing people's participatory experiences underlines this disappointment too. It can provide a platform for emergent frustrations to come to the fore. For example, during one evaluation session one participant, who was used to being marginalised through dominant forms of communication, used an artwork to tell us how there was favouritism in the group and that she was not listened to. We could not deny this experience of course. We reflected (we felt) on whether we had:

- (unintentionally?) given too much weight to some people's views (perhaps out of concern for their well-being?);
  or
- not supported people enough to share their ideas;
  or
- needed to be much better at confronting our deeper social biases?

But we also recognised that we were in a messy space (Seale et al., 2015). Adopting democratic processes (where compromise is necessary for decisions to be made) means people can get used to seeing themselves as part of the majority or minority. Such democratic compromise can easily silence people's voices (or create a sense that they are being silenced) and over-project other voices.

But that does not mean there is no coming back from a situation. This particular person did return to the group, and it only reaffirmed to her that things had not changed; however, for others there was a way back. For example, one week an entire group of D/deaf participants simply stopped attending. Clearly, something had gone wrong. Perhaps the risk they had taken in participating was not seen to be paying off. However, after a few months, they did return. Partly this was because institutional changes were emerging, alongside an opportunity to design and deliver training to staff. But such coming back requires a recognition that we are not coming back to the same space. It had not only involved other members of the group maintaining an ongoing respectful dialogue but also an openness from those who had left that things might be moving on, informed by their own ideas.

There are numerous tales *I* could tell about this project and all of them are rooted in the relational nature of participation. They are about our interactions within a space with the material, the human, the conceptual, the intangible, the past, present and future. Participation is visceral, but it is also a deeply conscious experience. It is very hard (if not impossible) to practice participation. We have to get on and do it, because we are doing it anyway. However, if we wish to be part of a more rewarding participatory experience (and support each other to be part of a more rewarding participatory experience), we have to be willing to risk failure, ambivalence and 'no thanks'.

PARTICIPATION is just a bunch of letters on a page, or sounded out in passing, but when *I* hear this word *I* frequently find myself remembering rejection. Just as exclusion is a fundamental part of inclusion, so too is rejection a fundamental part of participation. We are in this together, but it is so easy to feel like we are in this alone. One large scale, research project cannot solve such challenges, but (*I* hope) telling stories from within the *while* might provide us with a starting point to ask questions about the underlying tensions and experience of outcomes within learning situations. *I* hope it can help us consider the broader possibilities that exist through a recognition of the ongoing and continuous practicalities of our participation in that space.

When does a chapter end?

In more-than-me's last book (Rix, 2015), *I* explored how an increased emphasis upon 'Us' might be a better starting point for developing our school practices. As part of this *I* suggested how notions of self (I and us) arise from our deeper notion of being a meaningless part of 'Them'. *I* pondered how the self only exists because our sense of separation evokes comparison which is (often?) channelled through the dominant cultural narratives in which we are participants. Our perceptions of any moment are socialised and biologised as part of our historicity; through them our moments are boundaried. We have moments of realisation of being, which take/are taking on the substance of our position.

However, as humans our point of focus within the relational is ourselves – it takes an act of imagination and definition in order for us to understand the other beyond a general presumption about who and what they are or to ascribe a general universalising aspect to 'us all'. This is why *I* return to the socio-cultural to understand how we can engage with our experiences in contexts intended to be educational. The broad range of theoretical positions that are situated in uncertainty offer powerful tools for describing our emergent situations; however, within a teaching/learning situation it is the socio-cultural context we interact through and through which 'others' act upon 'us'. The ubiquity and uncertainty of participation and learning seem to be captured by socio-culturalists who challenge assumptions about dominant models of learning and knowledge that see it as acquired, rather than situated in cultural practices. As Engeström (2001) notes, within institutions and our personal lives we are learning things that are not stable, not understood ahead of time, involving new forms of activity that are not yet there. In the everyday, what is being learned is being created in that moment. We are participating *while* we are being.

I hope that in this chapter, *I* have managed to help you reflect on the nature of participation. In the next chapter, *I* will use the community of provision model to explore how we can understand the context in which participation is situated, in ways that acknowledge the tensions between certainty and uncertainty. We will consider how certainty and/or presumptions of certainty exacerbate the tensions, inhibit the outcomes and constrain the component parts of participation. We will also begin to explore whether (the thingness of) things might be organised somewhat better.

We might even consider whether being 'organised somewhat better' is a yearning for certainty or simply a way of looking.

But that is up to you. We are participating in this together, after all.

References

Adair, C. (2015). Bathrooms and beyond: Expanding a pedagogy of access in trans/disability studies. *Transgender Studies Quarterly*, 2(3), 464–468.

Alaimo, S. (2008). Trans-corporeal feminisms and the ethical space of nature. *Material Feminisms*, 25(2), 237–264.

Alaimo, S. (2018). Trans-corporeality. In R. Braidotti & M. Hlavajova (Eds,), *The posthuman glossary* (pp. 435–438), Bloomsbury Publishing.

Barad, K. (2010). Quantum entanglements and hauntological relations of inheritance: Dis/continuities, spacetime enfoldings, and justice-to-come. *Derrida Today*, 3(2), 240–268.

Blalock, N. (2015). More than me. In A. Jolivétte (Ed.), *Research justice: Methodologies for social change* (pp. 57–62). Policy Press.

Booth, T. (1999). Viewing inclusion from a distance: Gaining perspective from comparative study, *Support for Learning*, *14*(4), 164–168.

Bychowski, M., Chiang, H., Halberstam, J., Lau, J., Long, K., Ochoa, M., Snorton, C., DeVun, L., & Tortorici, Z. (2018). "Trans* historicities" A roundtable discussion. *Transgender Studies Quarterly*, *5*(4), 658–685.

Chalklin, V., & Mulvey, M. (2016). Towards a performative trans-pedagogy: Critical approaches for learning and teaching in art and performance. *Performance Matters*, *2*(1), 62–77.

Clark, A., & Moss, P. (2001). *Listening to young children: The Mosaic approach.* Joseph Rowntree Foundation.

Engeström, Y. (2001). Expansive learning at work: Toward an activity theoretical reconceptualization. *Journal of Education and Work*, *14*(1), 133–156.

Fine, C., & Furtak, E. (2020). A framework for science classroom assessment task design for emergent bilingual learners. *Science Education*, *104*(3), 393–420.

Francis, J., Sachan, P., Waters, Z., Trapp, G., Pearce, N., Burns, S., Lin, A., & Cross, D. (2022). Gender-neutral toilets: A qualitative exploration of inclusive school environments for sexuality and gender diverse youth in Western Australia. *International Journal of Environmental Research and Public Health*, *19*(16), 10089.

Garcia Carrizosa, H., Diaz, J., & Sisinni, F. (2019). Towards a participatory museum. Retrieved from https://www.arches-project.eu/wp-content/uploads/2019/07/English Guide_Hyperlinks_mid.pdf

Golafshani, N. (2023). Teaching mathematics to all learners by tapping into indigenous legends: A pathway towards inclusive education. *Journal of Global Education and Research*, *7*(2), 99–115.

Heidegger, M. (1996). *Being and time: A translation of Sein und Zeit.* SUNY press.

Hein, S. (2016). The new materialism in qualitative inquiry: How compatible are the philosophies of Barad and Deleuze? *Cultural Studies? Critical Methodologies*, *16*(2), 132–140.

Jones, I. (2019). *Disability as an entanglement: A new materialist reimagination of disability*, Doctoral dissertation, The University of Waikato.

Kristeva, J. (1982). *Powers of horror.* Columbia University Press.

Latour, B. (2004). Why has critique run out of steam? From matters of fact to matters of concern. *Critical Inquiry*, *30*(2), 225–248.

Lin, A. (2019). Theories of trans/languaging and trans-semiotizing: Implications for content-based education classrooms. *International Journal of Bilingual Education and Bilingualism*, *22*(1), 5–16.

Lindbolm, A., & Jannok Nutti, Y. (2022). Conceptualising global indigenous and indigenist models of inclusive and equitable education. *World Studies in Education*, *23*(1), 135–154.

Nelson, P., Segall, A., & Durham, B. (2021). Between aspiration and reality: New materialism and social studies education. *Theory & Research in Social Education*, *49*(3), 449–476.

Ngidi, N., & Moletsane, R. (2018). Bullying in school toilets: Experiences of secondary school learners in a South African township. *South African Journal of Education*, *38*(Supplement 1), s1–s8.

Paige-Smith, A., & Rix, J. (2011). Researching early intervention and young children's perspectives – Developing and using a 'listening to children approach'. *British Journal of Special Education*, *38*(1), 28–36.

Popkewitz, T., & Huang, J. (2021). Rethinking critical theory and the study of education: Contributions of the 'Posts/New Materialism'. In R. Tierney, F. Rizvi, K. Ercikan, & G. Smith (Eds.), *Elsevier international encyclopedia of education fourth volume*. Elsevier.

Reddington, S., & Price, D. (2018). Pedagogy of new materialism: Advancing the educational inclusion agenda for children and youth with disabilities. *International Journal of Special Education*, 33(2), 465–481.

Rix, J. (2015). *Must inclusion be special?: Rethinking educational support within a community of provision*. Routledge.

Seale, J., Nind, M., Tilley, L., & Chapman, R. (2015). Negotiating a third space for participatory research with people with learning disabilities: An examination of boundaries and spatial practices. *Innovation: The European Journal of Social Science Research*, 28(4), 483–497.

Sharkey, A., & Shields, R. (2008). Abject citizenship – Rethinking exclusion and inclusion: participation, criminality and community at a small town youth centre. *Children's Geographies*, 6(3), 239–256.

St. Pierre, E., Jackson, A., & Mazzei, L. (2016). New empiricisms and new materialisms: Conditions for new inquiry. *Cultural Studies? Critical Methodologies*, 16(2), 99–110.

Taylor, A., & Giugni, M. (2012). Common worlds: Reconceptualising inclusion in early childhood communities. *Contemporary Issues in Early Childhood*, 13(2), 108–119.

Toohey, K., & Smythe, S. (2022). A different difference in teacher education: posthuman and decolonizing perspectives. *Language and Education*, 36(2), 122–136,

Travnicek, C., Stoll, D., Reichinger, A., & Rix, J. (2022). "It soon became clear" – Insights into technology and participation. *Qualitative Research Journal*, 22(2), 129–142.

Wang, C., & Burris, M. (1994). Empowerment through photo novella: Portraits of participation. *Health Education Quarterly*, 21(2), 171–186.

6
BUILDING EXCLUSIONARY COMMUNITIES

Is this belonging?

As a parent of a child receiving additional support, you engage with a school in ways that you do not if your child is functioning as the standard model. In preparing to write about this, I went back through some of the correspondence I/we have had with schools over the years, looking for a representative story about parental participation. I wanted to present an example of how our participatory experiences are (socially-environmentally) contextually situated and imbued with the tensions between certainty and uncertainty.

I had dozens to choose from. I had examples of things that had been shared between us and: head teachers, special education coordinators, class teachers, teaching assistants, heads of year, support staff, governing bodies, local authority administrators, as well as various therapists and medical folk. These took a wide variety of forms too, including letters, reports, bullet lists, research summaries, updates, plans, materials, observations, records, notes and a myriad of films and photos of things we and our son had done.

And that is when I realised that this huge wad of communication was the story itself.

Generally speaking, my/our communications with the systems were a discussion with silence or polite disinterest. I have often wondered why.

As a (fairly) senior academic, I am used to going into educational settings and to having my questions answered in open and (surprisingly) frank ways and/or my comments received with interest. But as a parent, I have rarely experienced this. There have been quite a few people who seemed to be interested or appeared to answer my/our questions but left me/us wondering about their sincerity, since very few of them then acted on that interest or demonstrated much commitment to the answer(s) they had given.

DOI: 10.4324/9781003281405-6

I have often concluded that this is something to do with the insider/outsider conundrum.

> As an insider, you can be relied upon. You are one of us. You understand the constraints under which we function. You come with some certainty.
> As an outsider, you cannot be relied upon. You are one of them. You do not understand the constraints under which we function. You come with quite a lot of uncertainty.

As a parent, I/we do have my/our official points of access. So, I have been asked to fill out forms, to write submissions for meetings, to come along as one more timetabled visitor on a busy day. Through the formal processes of parental choice and voice, I have been allowed entry, but my suggestions and offers of practical support have been (at best) tolerated (with some amusement) even though (ironically) they are based upon insider knowledge.

This negative participatory experience has been evident across the system, in the myriad of places where I have engaged. From policy and administrative fora to the domains of management and of governance; across many formal and informal school spaces as well as those places associated with support, involving all kinds of people, supporters, learners, staff and those on the margins.

The ubiquity of the experience suggests to me that should anyone want to resolve this sense of parental marginalisation (I am not the first; I am not the last), they will need more than innovative teacher training or an updated policy; it will require confronting a whole range of issues that are fundamentally integrated within the whole.

It is this then to which we now turn. We will reflect upon the context of our educational relationships through the lens of the community of provision, considering how tensions between certainty and uncertainty across our systems effect experiences of participation, not just for parents.

FIGURE 6.1 Are we trying?

Provision is/as a community

A much-quoted saying is that it takes a village to raise a child. This metaphor (I presume) is intended to help readers/listeners think about ways of working and being, to recognise how our lives are interwoven and dependent upon the support we give each other. However, plenty of these metaphorical villages are not (necessarily) doing the children any great few favours. They are likely to have a tendency towards insularity with a capacity to marginalise just as much as welcome people from inside and outside their boundaries. The ideal notion of the village may provide a sense of certainty, but communities are based upon uncertain, tenuous relationships. They are defined by the inter-weaving characteristics, resources, groupings and priorities of their members. Their shape is context dependent, with internal and external borders that may be restrictive but will also be porous. We come, we go. The village (if there is such a thing) is ever changing.

Accepting the complexity of our situation and the social mirage of our boundaries creates a problem. We need concepts to think with. This was a challenge that a group of 'us' were set by the National Council for Special Education in Ireland when examining special education globally (Rix et al., 2013). They wanted us to reconceptualise the continuum, that linear model of thinking which from the 1970s onwards has been widely associated with special education and social sciences more broadly (Rix et al., 2015). In Irish legislation, much was made of two continua, the continuum of support (see Figure 6.2) and the continuum of special educational needs (see Figure 6.3). The basic premise was that you can match a child with a particular type of need with a particular type of support. However, undertaking an extensive systematic review of the literature associated with the concept made it very clear that there are many limitations to describing provision in this way.

Overall, we noted more than two dozen continua models associated with special educational needs and numerous associated concepts. But we became increasingly aware of the gaps that emerged in the range of conceptualis-ations of the continuum, each one encouraging a simplified view of the issues that existed within the continuum being described.

We began to wonder about such things as:

- Could we exclude some continua and include others when considering provision?
- Could we ignore the oversimplification and the negative associations that arise from a linear focus upon a predetermined aspect of a far wider whole?
- Could we weave together multiple continua? If so, how?
- If we regard provision as a series of individual threads, do we not increase the chance that our focus opens up gaps between the continua, through which people will fall (or fear to fall)?

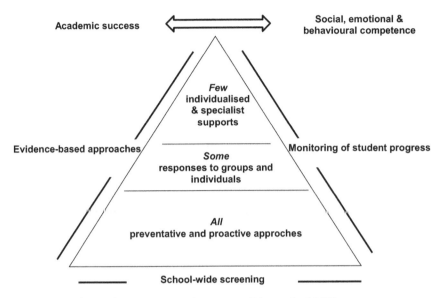

FIGURE 6.2 The Irish continuum of support. (Rix et al., 2013).

FIGURE 6.3 The Irish continuum of special educational needs. (Rix et al., 2013).

It was also noticeable across the review that the continuum encouraged a focus on the individual, yet aspired to provide services that worked in a collective manner. The continua were frequently framed as encapsulating provision for all at one end and provision for a select few at the other. They were developed too, to enable and represent shifts in thinking. They were usually meant to describe complex systems, capturing their multi-layered, interconnected nature. Their operation (increasingly) involved engaging with multiple perspectives; they were seen as a platform for multidimensional responses and (ironically) nonlinear, flexible thinking.

To encapsulate the diversity of provision and the complex interweave of relationships within which education and schools are situated, we chose to recommend a shift away from the continuum metaphor and a move to the community metaphor. We introduced the notion of a community of provision. Our broad definition was:

A community of provision is made from the settings and services which work together to provide learning and support for all children and young people within their locality.

By their nature, communities of provision (like villages?) are full of contradictions and challenges, opportunities and aspirations. They are not inhabited by people who agree with each other. Some of us will hold different theoretical positions, some of us will never think about theory at all and a great many of us will be unsure about what we think (or think we should think). The community is likely to involve excellent and less than excellent practice; it will involve people who like being there and people who do not, and the nature and experience of excellence and pleasure will likely be shifting across spaces. The community will also include all kinds of schools and support services, funding mechanisms and exam systems, sometimes (feeling) in competition with each other. Their seeming reality will vary from country to country, region to region, school to school, class to class, from child to child, despite there being apparent similarities at numerous levels of these systems.

We used our systematic review of the literature (associated with the continuum as applied to special education) to create a frame for considering the complex reality of provision. From 65 studies, we identified 194 concepts and 29 different types of continua, providing us with an empirical base for six perspectives associated with a community of provision:

- **Community systems**: concerned with issues of governance
- **Community strategies**: concerned with the quality of support
- **Community support**: concerned with the quantity and type of support
- **Community staffing**: concerned with who is providing the support
- **Community space**: concerned with where support takes place
- **Community of students**: concerned with who is being supported

In order to resolve the inherent limitations of the continua from which these clusters emerged, we recognised that each of these six perspectives have to be seen in relation to each other (see Figure 6.4 on page 131). Any educational issue involves the interplay of these perspectives. They are the means by which provision is described, but they are also the means by which it is delivered. They do not apply solely to a singular grouping or separate contained aspect of provision; the entirety needs to be understood through them.

Can we continua with this?

So, let's go back to my earlier parental participation story. As I was looking through the paperwork, it was clear to me that I/we had experienced issues: with where our support took place; with those who provided our support; with the quantity, quality and type of support we received; and with how the whole process was designed and organised. This was why there was no simple solution to our negative experiences.

Let me give you an example: Every year we had an annual review of our son's 'needs' and how those 'needs' could be supported. This followed a nationally legislated code of practice, involving legislated documentation, locally imagined, which had to be filled out in such a way that it outlined the 'needs' he had. The ultimate goal was for his support to be signed off by the funding agency (the local authority). When it was not done in the right way (including setting up the initial provision), it became a battle of legalities.

Prior to and during these meetings, we had to identify things which were seen as socially valued, demonstrating how our son was struggling/ inadequate/defective in this/these arenas. If we could attach a label to this/ these, all the better. This focus on the negative was despite people (and the paperwork) always saying they were interested in what he could do and wanted to 'celebrate' his accomplishments. The irrelevance of his 'strengths' was obvious because they had no bearing on either the support he got or the provision which the authorities would fund. And of course, the individualised focus of the meeting meant my son's (all our) needs were considered in isolation from the collective learning context of a classroom. He was always an individual (with individualised problems, outcomes, funding, developmental history, means of support, etc.), and the classroom was (at best) something in the background. The socio-cultural was not part of the official conversation.

Each year this meeting served as a point of transition. It was (meant to be) populated with reports from all kinds of services, funded locally or nationally, and always had the potential to bring us into conflict with authorities and governance structures. The paperwork was circulated before the meeting began. Each one spoke to the priority of the authors. So for instance, the teachers' reports talked about his behaviour in class, what he was learning/ failing to learn, and how he was measuring up to the curriculum targets; the therapists focused upon the tests they had done and how different parts of our son worked in relation to pre-established norms; the medical reports described his development against developmental and biological tests and checklists; while our report tried to sound knowledgeable, loving but bleak (to ensure we got the funding).

We would arrive in the official room (trying not to feel intimidated). Generally, there would be tables, with chairs, like in a job interview. Generally, there was us (or one of us) and somewhere between four and seven 'professionals', from the school, support services and the local authority. Generally, they all knew each other, some as collaborators in practice, others from attending other meetings like this one. Invariably, we would be invited to go first. The thrust of the meeting was always that this was a chance for us to be heard. People listened. Sometimes they agreed. Then they would offer a view in relation to what had been decided the previous year. The outcome (a pile of paper) was <u>always</u> a list of valued goals identified by the school/legislation/ curriculum, with targets they had predetermined. Then we went home.

Over the years the process did change slightly. A new law was introduced; the process had to follow a new code of practice and use new paperwork, with the notion of 'needs' reframed as 'outcomes'. There was even an increased focus upon hearing from the young person. But it was the same process and the same experience. It was mostly an unspoken confrontation (sometimes highly emotive and combative) that left us feeling sucked dry.

The other aspect of the experience that did not change was that the people in the meeting were (mostly) lovely, hard-working, committed and eager to do the right thing. [If we had had dinner together, we probably would have had a lovely time.] Yet it seemed (to me) that year on year each role came with a particular set of priorities:

- the special education coordinator wanted to ensure the funding was in place, the meeting was conducted as required and the paperwork was completed in a timely fashion.
- the teacher and other staff wanted to feel that what they were doing was appreciated and that they could carry on doing what they were doing pretty much unchanged.
- the local authority wanted to see if there was anything untoward happening, if they could reduce funding, while following procedures and appearing useful.
- the therapists were trying to get their voice heard about a particular way of working or resource they would love the school to use.
- the parents wanted to sound appreciative but were fighting for support that (virtually) never materialised as suggested.
- the young person was there (briefly) on display and could be used as a pawn in any negotiations, by representing/talking about their wishes.

Perhaps the only unified, point of focus was that everyone wanted to get the meeting out of the way, since we all knew this was what the system required of us and that it was about treading water.

Back in the community?

In writing this, I am struck by how the process I am describing reflects the criticisms we had (as researchers) of the continuum metaphor. The processes sound linear; they are about focusing upon the individual and fitting them into a predetermined space and the available provision. This is why we always felt like we were falling between the different services, their priorities and ways of working.

If we focus upon how we can overcome the experience of marginalisation in the narrative above, it also seems tempting to focus upon it as a collection of (individualised?) component parts. For instance:

- the nature of the paperwork and predetermined timetable.
- the character of the meeting room.
- the structure of the meeting.

- the (personal/role-specific) priorities of the professionals there.
- the formal(ised?) understanding of needs/outcomes.
- the availability of resources.
- people's understandings of what was possible and/or confidence in their own abilities.
- the relationships between all these mediating artefacts and between the people involved.

However, trying to resolve this by focusing upon the parts in separation from each other is futile. That is why the new legislation (introduced with hopes of transforming practice) was never going to work. It did not matter how good they made it; they were simply changing one part and leaving the rest as they found it.

However, viewing each issue through the six perspectives of the community of provision (see Figure 6.4) helps clarify the discordance we experienced in this process and encourages us to look beyond the strands and focus on the whole. For example, 'the character of the meeting room' cannot just be viewed as exemplifying the community space perspective. It is an educational issue which needs to be viewed through the six perspectives.

≅ There is the space itself, its layout, condition and position within the overall school building, but there is also the function that space plays in the organisation, the resources available in it, the funding, management and maintenance of the space and resources within it, and participant's experiences of using that space and therefore their relationship to it and finally (perhaps) there are our understandings of the space relative to other spaces that could have been used within the school or elsewhere in the local authority.

Not all of these will have a significant bearing on the nature of the meeting to discuss the paperwork, but I can recall instances across the years when all of these at some point had some sort of bearing.

Considering the interplay of these perspectives provides a relatively simple way to understand why/how the community of provision (as we experienced it in those moments) was looking in many different directions, despite official claims about a unified focus upon the needs and supporting the needs of a child. It also, hopefully, underlines the fundamentally interwoven nature of the process and its 'outcomes'. The meeting did/do not fail because of a single aspect but because of everything that goes into it.

As we begin to explore such issues, we invariably come face to face with the impossibility of being certain about any of it. The 'best' we can hope for is to recognise that we are facing uncertainty and that by asking questions it can lead us to:

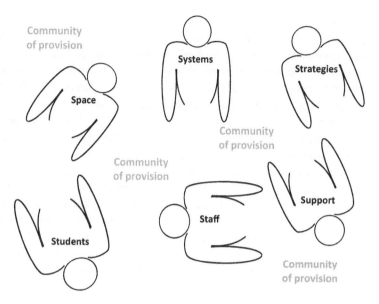

FIGURE 6.4 A discordant community of provision.

- possible answers.
- things to try that may be of benefit.

This does not rule out a role for wisdom, experience, innovation and tentative assertions about evidence; in many ways, it makes them even more important, but it does require that our structures/processes/roles are focused upon the uncertain rather than the certain.

And elsewhere, *while* in a community near you?

A similar interwoven story emerges from a report that was published by the Office for National Statistics (2022) the day after I started writing the section above; it looks at the experiences of young people who had either received special educational needs support or had an education, health and care plan in the English system. It was based upon 62 interviews with 11–16-years-olds and 64 parents and carers, as well as focus groups with 23 members of staff across England (with the support of the National Association for Special Educational Needs). Significantly, the focus was upon people's lived experiences of education, as well as their preferences, expressed needs and suggestions for improvement, and it was guided by a Youth Expert Panel alongside an advisory team of academics and non-governmental organisations.

This report talks about the everyday strategies which the young people use to manage their learning and emotional well-being, some of which are dependent upon what is made available within the space and some which emerges from their relationship with that space (e.g., wearing headphones or sunglasses, fidgeting, doodling and accessing sensory areas). They highlight how the lack of (or ineffective) support and feeling unsupported can generate feelings of anger and frustration. They recognise how this affects not just them but others around them, leading to being identified as troublesome and experiencing further isolation and exclusion.

The young people talked about their own preferences and how they felt the need to be supported in ways that did not identify them as different but which appropriately accommodated their needs (e.g., through curriculum and assessment that was more flexible, or by offering them their preferred modality such as hands-on activities or visual resources). They also talked about their use of spaces in the setting where they felt safe and the value of choice about such things as where and what they studied and issues such as uniform. The young people also focused upon their relationships with staff, who they wanted to feel comfortable with. They wanted them to be empathetic, respectful and caring and able to adapt things in ways that helped them. They also discussed the importance of social opportunities, through school activities and peer-to-peer support, which recognised what people achieved besides the academic, that helped them to enjoy themselves and create understanding between each other.

It seems to me that these issues raised by the young people speak to the six perspectives of the community of provision. They are talking about policies, processes, places, practices, personnel and peers, but they are doing so in ways which are rooted in uncertainty. They are discussing things in ways that are relational and are situated in the collective school context. This is in contrast to the staff and parents within the report. They raise issues more clearly associated with certainty. It was the staff who discussed the role of the inspectorate as well as the need for training about needs and how to meet them, and they and parents talked about the importance of plans and ensuring they were relevant, up to date and followed. It was parents who complained about navigating systems that were inconsistent, stressful, lengthy, complex and lacked accountability.

This (perhaps) unintentional divide between the certain and uncertain within the report, also reflects (perhaps) the underlying tensions in people's participation. The young people are asking for greater power, support and voice in relation to:

- shifting roles and attitudes.
- a capacity to adapt practices and spaces that emerge from and enable relationships.
- a recognition of the need for being flexible, taking time and for people to enjoy themselves and be understood.

While the adults are far less focused upon the practicalities of participation. They are not seeking greater flexibility or ways to better engage with the voice of the young person. They are looking for greater control over their roles and ways of working, clearer understanding of exactly how to adapt practices and spaces, greater consistency in the organisation and management of the outcomes.

I am not suggesting that the young people don't yearn for a bit of certainty and the adults would not like a bit more flexibility, but I am suggesting that when we consider their experiences of the *while* within school (just as within the community of provision), they/we are looking in different directions.

Participating in a discordant community

So, let's return to that discordant community and explore how our services work to produce negative participatory experiences. Any such analysis is going to be partial, of course. The perspectives we adopt and how we apply them will limit our capacity to explore experiences and practices; they will only ever partially reveal their interweaving, porous nature. In using the six perspectives of the community of provision to frame a discussion of our experiences in schools, I am seeking to provide a tighter focus for readers, but to be effective it needs to encourage you to go for a personal meander in your (own?) thoughts.

Starting from here...   1/6?

Interweaving with systems

Our education systems are (of course) inherently interwoven with our other social structures (e.g., serving as the means of entry into employment), but the ways in which we enable this to happen are not predetermined. They represent our collective beliefs about what participation is and how it should function. How we frame authority within the system, our approaches to accountability, how we control its outcomes and benefits is something which we create and recreate in both the design and the doing. Our top-down processes of governance can create marginalising pressures, which work against inclusive practices and the enabling of participation. For instance, educational policies in England and Wales seek to reduce inequality; yet, they do not seem to reduce the educational disadvantage gap (in relation to exam grades at 16). There is almost no closing of this gap over time while across the nations a clear ongoing post-code lottery is in evidence. Consequently, academics conclude that this educational issue requires a wider focus on child poverty not just across all parts of our education systems but across policy areas and public services (Cardim-Dias & Sibieta, 2022).

Education systems (the people, spaces, resources, values, rules and processes) also interact with the wider whole in creating, adopting and reinforcing social categories; this in turn drives the tension between power, support and voice for people within those education systems. Domina et al. (2017), for example, explore the ways in which schools give meaning to categories (such as dropout, A-student, gifted and talented, special needs) by creating boundaries and mediating resource distribution. They underline how schools give status to such categories (as well as to categories from beyond the school such as citizen, scientist, employable), while at the same time reinforcing even wider conceptualisations (such as class, race, gender, ability, sexuality, age). They explore the notion of schools as institutions seeking to be egalitarian but reproducing social inequalities. Even as our schools seek to compensate for racial, ethnic, gender or class inequalities, they are marginalising people by deciding who to enrol and sorting them into age, grades, ability groups, streams, tracks, sets, subjects and other formal and informal groups.

Decisions made at a systemic level will have consequences for how people value themselves and the nature of their learning experiences across roles and spaces in a school. For instance, in Sweden, where school grades determine admission to upper secondary school, policy makers introduced a criterion-referenced system with a sharp pass/fail distinction, presuming it would drive up results; however, a large proportion of students failed to pass, and the percentage of failures remained strikingly constant in subsequent years. As a result, some children are doomed to fail compulsory school. Their time is frittered away, because no matter how much pedagogical support they receive and how hard they work, they will not learn and develop as the system would like them to. The results are not just damaging for the children involved either but also for the schools and teachers who are identified as inadequate (Arensmeier, 2022).

Across the border in Oslo, similar damaging effects can be seen to operate at large scale and through a variety of mechanisms. Policy makers introduced school choice, per capita funding, school self-governance, standardised testing, evaluation, school comparison and incentives for school leaders. However, the result has been increased segregation, where the less-popular schools are dealing with increased violence and criminality. Interviews with teachers in these schools suggest that these governance mechanisms affect how people are represented in the system. They result in the 'best' students being selected, with increasing segregation at the class level and in local communities. The teachers' comments suggest that this process is classed, raced and gendered, with a different weight attached to the voices/views of parent and students who are marginalised or privileged (Haugen, 2020). Similarly, primary headteachers in England talk about how they respond to standardised assessment (even though it creates staffing difficulties): through the use of ability grouping, by prioritising of children on the cusp of grade boundaries (often through out-of-school sessions) and by withdrawing children for 'interventions' to fill 'gaps' in learning (Bradbury et al., 2021).

The use of time and space also reflects education's wider sorting function and the policy makers' beliefs that underpin it. Consider, for example, the ways in which school leaders undertake what is called exclusion in England, 'off-rolling' in Scotland and 'suspension/expulsion' in Northern Ireland. Many countries will follow the staged intervention model for school exclusion as in Scotland and Wales. This formally designed and managed structure often resembles the traditional continuum, with a narrowing and targeting of support from whole school to segregated, requiring the child to be fitted into the right slot or stage in the available interventions (McCluskey et al., 2019). This has a profound impact on a great many young people though. When I was preparing for my inaugural lecture in 2017, I looked at official and unofficial figures at the time. In England on average, the Department for Education reported over 35 children being expelled every school day. Victoria, whilst in Australia – across 2015 – 2.35% were suspended in Victoria and in New South Wales 3.8% had short suspensions and 1.6% had long suspensions.

Headteachers in England have reported that formal and informal exclusionary practices are both a necessity and helpful because they are constrained by the lack of support services and individual assessments (Martin-Denham, 2021). The same sense of being trapped by wider circumstances is clear in the response of school leaders in Ghana. They feel a need to be seen as firm leaders and to deliver other policies associated with social norms (such as using exclusion in response to student pregnancy). But a consequence of this approach is that it encourages teachers to focus more upon disciplinary measures in their classes, further lowering self-esteem among students and further deteriorating their relationships with the school (Gunu, 2018).

The effect of leaders' top-down governance on the relationships between students and teachers is also demonstrated in a study looking at teachers working in six high-poverty, urban schools in the United States. They concluded that three of the schools were predominantly closed systems and three predominantly open. Teachers in the more open system were working in a school that was an interdependent organisation, which tried to coordinate instruction, discipline and targeted support across the school. In contrast, the closed systems operated as a collection of semiautonomous classrooms, treating students as all similarly prepared, expecting them to respond positively to standardised predictable expectations. In the former, teachers felt they had increased opportunities to manage their students' uncertain lives, while in the latter they felt constrained in dealing with the uncertainty (Kraft et al., 2015).

Interweaving with strategies

So, let's consider how the quality of strategies for support can perpetuate and construct the problems they seek to resolve. In a previous book (Rix, 2015), I discussed a range of well-established and well-accepted everyday teaching practices that can exclude a variety of pupils (e.g., our use of subjects, the focus on the written word, approaches to mathematical problems). I also gave examples of strategies which are meant to enable access but frequently constrain participation (e.g., differentiation, the use of images or the simplification of language). Our use of such strategies and to whom we apply them speak to issues of support, power and voice. They are about how we define people, how we let them come to understand and represent themselves.

We continue to use such strategies even though we often have strong evidence to doubt their quality. Consider, for example, our embrace with special labels which I touched upon briefly in Chapter 1. Even though there is an overwhelming lack of certainty related to their design and application, we continue to use them with increasing intensity. For many people, the need to sort, label and categorise (and to do this better) are essential tasks. Many would claim that if we do not use labels within our systems, then disabled people are likely to be ignored (e.g., Kauffman & Hornby, 2020). These people are absolutely right of course, since the application of labels is a key component of the dominant support strategies; particularly those associated with continua of support, matching identified need to identified resources – strategies that can be seen to be creating counterproductive experiences of participation.

However, the application of most labels in educational contexts is of very limited value to practitioners in the classroom. This is because (to use the words of Timimi (2021), they are 'thin descriptions'. They leave out so many of the things that are important to teachers to understand in relation to somebody's life (friends, family, social life, social background and so forth) as well as their skills, capacities and interests. These issues of power, voice and support seem to pivot around our use of labelling as a strategy, and the way in which the associated language and beliefs create practical barriers in how people understand/enact/experience their roles as teachers, learners, administrators, etc. This focus upon assessment and categories reinforces social inequalities, undermines collective learning opportunities and encourages people to feel that they lack expertise.

It seems commonplace for our dominant strategies to undermine their own goals because they are recommending things which do not (seem to) happen in practice or (perhaps) help.

Two beliefs which fascinate me in this regard are:

1. planning and practice should be evidence based.
2. teacher/practitioner education/training is the best route to delivering (any number of) educational goals.

Consider a set of 'high-leverage practices for special education teachers', approved by the US Council for Exceptional Children (CEC), based upon syntheses of the research evidence (see Table 6.1).

TABLE 6.1 High-leverage practices for special education teachers, based upon syntheses of the research evidence

Collaboration
  1. Collaborate with professionals to increase student success.
  2. Organise and facilitate effective meetings with professionals and families.
  3. Collaborate with families to support student learning and secure needed services.

Assessment
  4. Use multiple sources of information to develop a comprehensive understanding of a student's strengths and needs.
  5. Interpret and communicate assessment information with stakeholders to collaboratively design and implement educational programs.
  6. Use student assessment data, analyse instructional practices and make necessary adjustments that improve student outcomes.

Social/Emotional/Behavioural Practices
  7. Establish a consistent, organised and respectful learning environment.
  8. Provide positive and constructive feedback to guide students' learning and behaviour.
  9. Teach social behaviours.
  10. Conduct functional behavioural assessments to develop individual student behaviour support plans.

Instruction
  11. Identify and prioritise long- and short-term learning goals.
  12. Systematically design instruction towards a specific learning goal.
  13. Adapt curriculum tasks and materials for a specific learning goal.
  14. Teach cognitive and metacognitive strategies to support learning and independence.
  15. Provide scaffolded supports.
  16. Use explicit instruction.
  17. Use flexible grouping.
  18. Use strategies to promote active student engagement.
  19. Use assistive and instructional technologies.
  20. Provide intensive instruction.
  21. Teach students to maintain and generalise new learning across time and settings.
  22. Provide positive and constructive feedback to guide students' learning and behaviour.

(adapted from McLeskey et al., 2017).

In the final report, each of the high-leverage practices was supported by a lengthy explanation of the background data. The final list therefore seems perfectly reasonable, backed by robust evidence. Its air of certainty permeates the text. It is filled with numerous statement that read as absolutes, full of 'must', 'will' and 'need to'. This includes conclusive statements about what a knowledgeable teacher is, what an effective special education teacher will be well-versed in and how these practitioners will apply standards using evidence-based practice and so forth, across tiers of instructional intensity, with fidelity. There is very little acknowledgement made (if at all) that:

- the strategies come from a wide variety of theoretical backgrounds (so that behaviourism sits alongside constructivism and socio-culturalism) without a recognition that each will create/require a very different teaching and learning environment;
- some of the strategies are still very much contested and have been shown to work (at best) with some but not all (e.g., functional behavioural assessments, providing intensive instruction and teaching social behaviours);
- much of what they are calling for has been recommended for a very long time, (e.g., collaboration, effective home/school relations, flexible grouping, developing a comprehensive understanding of strengths and needs), but it doesn't appear that people do it/them very well;
- in an earlier study creating similar recommendations around effective intensive practices (McLeskey and Waldron, 2011), the same lead author concluded that the recommended approaches were used rarely (if at all) in either separate provision or the mainstream.

FIGURE 6.5 Doubtless…

Interweaving with support

In discussing how the quality of strategies can perpetuate and construct the problems they seek to resolve, I touched upon many issues that concern the nature of support too. Consider the nature of continua as experienced in a South African context. Since the introduction of Inclusive Education goals in South Africa, various systemic changes have been introduced with the aim of providing quality education, including a continuum of support model. The support experienced by people identified with learning disabilities underlines how the perspectives of systems, strategies and support are inherently interwoven. Three levels of intellectual disability are now identified, requiring support at three intensity levels in either mainstream or special settings. The support comes through four programs (specialist services, curriculum differentiation, specialised support materials and technologies; training and mentoring of staff). This policy is increasingly being delivered through three curricula, allocated through screening (McKenzie, 2020). Setting aside the inherent unreliability of such screening processes, there are not enough special schools for this to operate as designed and many learners are being accommodated and marginalised in mainstream classes. Perhaps, unsurprisingly, the dominant view is that the teachers have inadequate training and support and that unrealistic expectations are made of them (Dreyer, 2017).

Another South African example relates to the use of a single language as a dominant support mechanism. This results in rural children (among others?) not having access to resources, being limited in how they can apply their knowledge and therefore being denied the opportunity to excel in their studies (Omidire, 2020). It also equates to three personal experiences over the years:

- the marginalisation experienced by participants in ARCHES due to our failure to include note-taking support (as discussed in Chapter 5).
- working with older teenagers who had recently arrived in the UK but who were kept trapped in a cycle of failure because they could not engage in the academic English (deemed) necessary to pass multiple choice tests – even though they could demonstrate considerable knowledge by practically applying it.
- the support offered to my son, which consistently held him back because it was constantly framed around the written and spoken, even though it was clear to all of us that words were a barrier to his involvement. As a consequence, practitioners were seeking to support him via his (profound and obvious) weaknesses rather than his strengths and interests.

Linguistic barriers permeate support across roles within the community of provision too. For instance, policy documents which aim to support the rights and practices of people within the system can be seen to frequently marginalise them. The discourse of these policy documents can easily exclude people who have to understand the content if they are to use it to navigate the systems. This can result in the absences of their voices from documents which are intended to be their platform, such as individual education plans (Heiskanen et al., 2021). Similar silencing has been identified within early intervention support, an approach very much at the forefront of early years policy and practice in many countries. In home visits, practitioners have been shown to dominate, initiate and control discussion topics, so that the parents they are supporting take up passive roles; there to provide information and follow advice (Hancock & Cheatham, 2021).

The nature of our support traditions clearly limits the possibilities for practitioners too. Much of this can be seen to be associated with our collective desire for consistency (not flexibility) in how we deliver and assess. Consider scientific practices, which in the wider world are largely concerned with managing and exploring uncertainty, not only in how they explain phenomena but in their ways of working. Within school learning environments, however, our classroom support focuses upon certainty and so does not encourage scientific practices associated with investigation, explanation and argument. Manz and Suárez (2018) give the example of a study topic exploring the needs of plants. Rather than engaging with uncertainty, typically students would count, measure and compare parts of the plant in two specified conditions, under the direction of teachers and the curriculum. Variability and surprise are not on the agenda, neither is critique nor the opportunity to participate in the construction and testing of knowledge. Such an approach also requires students to have the skills necessary for the activity as designed for them or (put my son in the room) they can do something else. [The irony is that this creation of something else is frequently held up as an example of adaptation or flexibility. It is labelled (perhaps) as personalisation or differentiation. Yet it fails to deal with the greatest barrier in the room, the absence of openness and flexibility in the original activity.]

(Unsurprisingly?) the nature of our support interacts with the learner's sense of self. It can work in a virtuous cycle so that if a student is enjoying an area of learning and is not bored by it, then the student is more likely to achieve well at formal assessment points, which in turn will lead to enjoyment and less boredom (Putwain, Becker, Symes, & Pekrun, 2018). But it can also trap the young person in negative ways. So being in a group identified as low ability means they will more frequently compare themselves to others, take the comparison more seriously than those in high-ability groups and are more likely to be affected by it in relation to their self-esteem (Webb-Williams, 2021).

As discussed in Chapter 4, different emotions are valued in different ways so that emotions which are seen as interruptive and disruptive identify an individual as problematic (Grindheim, 2014). This is particularly salient when we consider the young people's comments from the Office for National Statistics (2022) mentioned earlier, where they talk about frustration with support as a catalyst for such displays of emotion. The nature of emotions also effects the ways in which people engage with that support. For instance:

- feelings of enjoyment and boredom have been seen to have an effect upon people's reading (Wingard et al., 2020).
- enjoyment has a positive effect across subject areas, but each student's enjoyment varies across subjects (Goetz, Frenzel, Hall, & Pekrun, 2008).
- conflicts and problems with children's behaviour in Early Years settings are reduced when teaching seeks to provide emotional support (Khalfaoui et al, 2021).

From another perspective...   4/6?

Interweaving with staffing

Hopefully, it is clear by now that the six community perspectives are designed to be understood as a facet of each other, a prioritised way of focusing upon the whole. From the discussion above, it is evident that the approaches emerging from systems, strategies and support are related to a staffing perspective (e.g., people's roles in supporting learning, class and curriculum organisation, attitudes, dominance of particular voices and established routines). Let's now return to one of these discussions, the strategic role given to evidence-based practice and training and its unintended impact upon the practitioners it is meant to support.

Standards, such as those in Table 6.1, serve to undermine the power of the teachers and diminish their voice. Ironically, given that these standards make mention of collaboration and flexibility, they constrain the role of the practitioners. This begins with a false dichotomy because the standards are about where we want teachers to be rather than where they are. As a result, teachers recognise:

- if there are standards, you have to meet them.
- you have to effectively transfer the knowledge about the standards into your understanding and practice.
- you need initial training, you need more training, you need ongoing training.

- you are not good enough yet (others are better).
- if you are trying to meet standards and the students are not succeeding (or you are failing to deliver other forms of proof), then you are the one who is at fault.
- since other people know more than you, the easiest thing to do is rely on other people.

This reflects insights from interviews with UK teachers and school leaders who struggle with the challenges that emerge from such standards and their associated notions of accountability. It impacts upon how they understand themselves and undermines their sense of their own expertise and how it is valued (Skinner et al., 2021).

The staffing perspective also draws attention to the negative participatory experiences of additional adults working in classrooms across countries and systems, regardless of their title and level of training (e.g., Devecchi et al., 2012). Globally, it is commonplace to see an additional adult working in the class (e.g., special educator, support staff, Teaching Assistant, Learning Support Assistant, Inclusion support, Resource Teacher, Care Supporter, Vernepleier, social pedagogue). An English study that echoes research from around the world describes how these additional adults work 'under the radar' of teachers and schools, acting as 'go-betweens', for teachers, pupils and spaces (mainstream class and special education base) (Lehane, 2016).

As well as being witness to practice that is not inclusive and experiencing limited differentiation, these practitioners report not having advance information about lessons and having little or no contact with the teachers. They are gap filling, trying to keep 'their' pupils up to speed with the class, responding in ways they think are appropriate to the learner's perceived needs. Those students who cannot keep up are socially isolated too, in class and outside. The school spaces further reify this, with the special education base being more accepting and peaceful, while acting as a means for the staff to manage such pupils.

The literature describes how these additional adults have to fulfil unclear roles, while experiencing limited communication with other staff and limited time for collaboration; all this undermines their capacity to offer effective social and pedagogical support even though they are being relied upon by the lead teacher (Sharma & Salend, 2016). What is particularly dispiriting about this (above and beyond it being a really bad participatory experience for the people involved) is that the literature is also clear that students view staff, their beliefs and their relationships with them as the key factors (along with accessibility of appropriate resources and environments) that support inclusive education (e.g., Subban et al., 2022).

From another perspective...   5/6?

Interweaving with space

I mentioned above the tensions experienced by teaching assistants moving between the main class and special unit. This reflects my experiences as a teacher, researcher and parent. The special/inclusion space is frequently in the attic or cellar or implicitly separated from the main body of the building. I recall, for instance, a former teacher in Norway describing to me a hut that had been built as a classroom for a child with Down syndrome, which she felt had been well positioned, because the child could look out and see the other children playing. This is not some hangover from the early days of the continuum either. As part of a study in two schools a decade apart (Parry et al., 2013), we observed what happened when the special/inclusion space was moved. One school had seemingly sought to be more inclusive by relocating an annexe to a position in the main building, but this was described by staff as a school within a school. They said they now had little or no inclusion in the main school and limited easy access to ground-level communal areas. Similarly, the additional support staff in the other rebuilt school felt there had been no real benefits for them. Previously, they had been spread around the school but were now out of sight and out of mind, stuck away in smaller rooms, in the basement.

This ability of space to demonstrate the (lesser) value of some students (and the support and staff identified with them) is also evident globally in creations such as autism cages, isolation booths, consequence rooms and inclusion units. In England, one child was kept for 35 days in an isolation unit, only being allowed three breaks a day, for five minutes to go to the toilet (Perraudin, 2018). In such places, children are frequently expected to sit in silence all day, with no teaching. In 2017–2018, in one English academy chain, in just 14 of their 31 schools, students were sent to these rooms 31,000 times (Staufenberg, 2018). Such spaces can be seen as being on the extremes of the continuum (if you want to adopt that metaphor), as well as a continuation of the exclusion policies discussed above. It is not unusual to hear of school leaders, such as those in Wales (Power & Taylor, 2020), talking about the different types and lengths of exclusion they use, even hiring buildings to send those who are misbehaving (but need to be kept on the register), so they can experience therapeutic and alternative approaches.

The exclusionary space is not just physical. It is a social and relational dynamic underpinned by our experiences of power, support and voice. In spaces where these things are lacking, we feel marginalised. Gray et al. (2016) describe one teacher's experience as ontological exclusion. They apply this notion to a female LGBTQ teacher's experience of being a substitute teacher, teaching metalwork to a class full of boys who were writing mocking terms on the board. The teachers in this study did not feel imprisoned by such spaces of exclusion, however. They were able to deliberately confront the mechanisms at play, particularly the dominant understandings of gender and sexuality, in the knowledge that state-level policy was on their side.

This capacity to do something about it (perhaps) contrasts with the experiences of the children in the isolation booths and those who are unhappy in lower sets or tracks. A German study (Raufelder & Kulakow, 2022), looking at the responses of over 1,000 young people, concluded that being in the lower track engenders a feeling of powerlessness in many students, so they experience a sense of exclusion and disengage from schooling. Similarly, experiencing segregated schooling among black and white students in the United States shows how unconscious bias increases in individuals who have limited experience within diverse communities (McCardle & Bliss, 2019).

The nature of the space and our understandings of that space will inevitably have an impact on embodied experiences in that space. The material organisation of that space and the interactions within it will have an impact on people for a great many reasons (e.g., sound, heat, noise, smell, clutter, colours, light, crowdedness), but its nature will also be defined by (and arise from) the traditions of that space. In Chapter 1, for example, I talked about the inability of schools to use social media and mobile technologies with my son in ways that would have included him. This resistance to allow the use of such technologies ignores the role they play for disabled people as a means to contest discrimination, facilitate access and enable participation in exclusionary and inaccessible spaces (Saltes, 2018). Such social conventions will serve to marginalise people, in terms of expectations and what is allowed to happen in that space just as much as the conventions around behaviours, appearances and other cultural understandings.

The boundaries of schools are generally understood as the walls of the building, containing the people who study there and those who work there. As I explored in my discussion about responses to me as a parent at the start of this chapter, this notion of the institution creates a divide with the outside. But of course, schools are not just boundaried in this way. They are places within a wider community, a site to motivate actions and interactions. The being of them effects our identities within our collective historicities, so that if we have a role to play through any of the six perspectives, then we are participants within this space – open to the vagaries of the *while*.

From another perspective...   6/6?

Interweaving with students

In considering the previous perspectives, I have mentioned various groups, including students, parents, teachers, other classroom practitioners and school leaders. I could also have made mention of various governance or administrative roles too or the wide range of therapists or volunteers who are engaged in the community. As we turn to this final perspective, the community of students, I feel a need to raise an issue about where these other roles are situated in the whole and the nature of those roles.

As with all models, the terms and their boundaries are there for convenience. They are partial. They are inherently fallible. For instance, the community of staffing is defined as being *concerned with who is providing support* and the community of students is *concerned with who is being supported*. BUT as part of the community of staffing, we discussed training – surely this is a form of being supported. And students most definitely provide support to a great many people in the community; they are not simply recipients of support.

In a subsequent project which used the community of provision model as a framework for a collaborative professional development process, we dealt with this issue by recognising that the focus of support may be anyone within the community, and subsequently reframed this perspective as the community of service users (Twining et al., 2016). I was conflicted about whether to use this term in this book too. ... but in the end, I decided not to get hung up on the label, since obviously, other options are available. Instead, I leave it with you, dear reader. Where do any of the six perspectives start? Where do any of them stop?

The focus upon students in the original model was because this is what had emerged from the continua as the focus of support (associated with ratios, types and severity of need). It is of course perfectly reasonable to assume that those who are providing support can/need-to be the focus of support as well. The importance of this wider notion of support would also be particularly relevant in exploring strategies framed around such things as family-centred practice or if the nature of the support is understood within a socio-cultural, participation-centred model. But to keep things relatively simple, let's consider a couple of examples in relation to children and young people's representation and experiences in the system.

How we represent the lives of children is fundamentally tied up with access to schooling and our beliefs about difference. This is evident, for instance, in the over-representation and under-representation within different student groups across services in every country in the world. Across European and English-speaking nations, there is an over-representation of ethnic minority, immigrant and indigenous populations in relation to special educational provision, with social inequalities and cultural barriers as the mechanisms for the disproportionality (Cooc & Kiru, 2018). This is likely to lead to some form of 'ability' grouping either within schools or between schools, with a consequent impact upon expectations, pedagogy, curriculum, assessment, perceptions and identities (Francis et al., 2017).

There is a similar imbalance in relation to many other school processes; for example, black Caribbean young people in England are more likely to face formal exclusion. The consequence is not just an experience of being outside school for a time but will have a direct effect on in-class practices. Much like students in different sets/tracks/streams/ability groups, teachers respond differently according to who is placed where. These young people talk about being overlooked to answer questions. They experience teacher verbal aggression, harsher reprimands than other ethnic groups, stereotyping, as well as poor professional understanding of race and diversity issues (Demie, 2021).

Children and young people recognise that adults act as gatekeepers for them. They recognise their participation is based upon adults' views of their competence. They are used to having decisions largely imposed on them, being at best consulted, with their opinions only sought on peripheral matters. They know they have very limited influence over day-to-day activities and rules, and their experiences of teaching and learning (Horgan et al., 2017). Even when there are system-wide curriculum documents calling for children's joint responsibility, the restrictions are evident. For instance, in the early years, in Finland, where choice is called for in policy, it is largely limited to free-play activities. Children are not seen by practitioners as active meaning makers. They do not value the children's perspectives about their own learning and their membership of society (Kangas, 2016).

This issue of representation is also one evident across curricula, where particular cultural values, histories and social identities dominate the focus of study and the resources used to support that study. The consequence of such an absence is multifaceted. For example, the Australian curriculum attempts to ensure the relevance and connection with the Aboriginal people, **but** it does not effectively represent and create space for that community's aspirations for their children and young people (Parkinson & Jones, 2019).

All of which brings us to...

One last look (almost a footnote)

While developing my plans for this book, I came across a practitioner-focused article involving Participation Plans (Kurth et al., 2020). I became excited. I thought this was going to be a very teacher–learner friendly approach, open to socio-cultural understandings of participation. Its headline characteristics included accommodations and modifications to support access to the curriculum, embedding instruction into activities and observations of classroom routines over several days/sessions to explore their needs in context. But it did not take long to recognise the thinking about who the learner was at the heart of the process. It was an individual child who would benefit from 'standards-based' instruction with the focus on prioritised skills identified within an individual education plan.

The focus of the support was not the collective learning space. It was not about building on strengths. It was not about an openness to opportunity.

Once again, all six perspectives were looking in the wrong direction ... or that's how it felt to me.

In a certain while?

My aim in this chapter has been to explore the interaction of certainty and inequitable participation through the different perspectives associated with school communities. My sense is that a commitment to certainty:

- creates tensions between power, support and voice that play out in an imbalance of power, a limited notion of support and less opportunity to be heard.
- inhibits the possible outcomes, restricting the capacity of the participatory experience to represent people and find a personal sense of meaning, while constraining the nature of learning and what is valued about that learning.
- restricts the component parts (*time, enjoyment, roles, flexibility, beliefs, adaptation, space, languages, listening, relationships*) so that they perpetuate and construct negative participatory experiences, narrowing our capacity to respond to the range of need and opportunities.

This chapter has in many ways been quite challenging to write. I have been attempting to clarify how we limit people's participation and let them down through failures of support. I have attempted to illustrate this through a multitude of tales, none of which are particularly controversial. But in pulling these examples apart and reflecting upon them through the perspectives of the community of provision, I have been bathing in mundanity. The stories are not shocking. They are just everyday.

But I also believe our way of creating more inclusive experiences of participation is out there within the everyday.

So, that is where we will go next, asking if there are unextraordinary moments which we can hold up to the light, to see better possibilities.

References

Arensmeier, C. (2022). Three decades of school failure in Swedish compulsory school. *Scandinavian Journal of Educational Research*, 66(1), 14–27.

Boliver, V., & Capsada-Munsech, Q. (2021). Does ability grouping affect UK primary school pupils' enjoyment of Maths and English? *Research in Social Stratification and Mobility*, 76, 100629.

Bradbury, A., Braun, A., & Quick, L. (2021). Intervention culture, grouping and triage: High-stakes tests and practices of division in English primary schools. *British Journal of Sociology of Education*, 42(2), 147–163.

Cardim-Dias, J., & Sibieta, L. (2022). *Inequalities in GCSE results across England and Wales*. Education Policy Institute.

Cooc, N., & Kiru, E. (2018). Disproportionality in special education: A synthesis of international research and trends. *The Journal of Special Education, 52*(3), 163–173.

Demie, F. (2021). The experience of Black Caribbean pupils in school exclusion in England. *Educational Review, 73*(1), 55–70.

Devecchi, C., Dettori, F., Doveston, M., Sedgwick, P., & Jament, J. (2012). Inclusive classrooms in Italy and England. *European Journal of Special Needs Education, 27*(2), 37–41.

Domina, T., Penner, A., & Penner, E. (2017). Categorical inequality: Schools as sorting machines. *Annual Review of Sociology, 43*, 311.

Dreyer, L. (2017). Constraints to quality education and support for all: A Western Cape case. *South African Journal of Education, 37*(1), 1–11.

Francis, B., Archer, L., Hodgen, J., Pepper, D., Taylor, B., & Travers, M. (2017). Exploring the relative lack of impact of research on 'ability grouping' in England. *Cambridge Journal of Education, 47*(1), 1–17.

Goetz, T., Frenzel, A., Hall, N., & Pekrun, R. (2008). Antecedents of academic emotions: Testing the internal/external frame of reference model for academic enjoyment. *Contemporary Educational Psychology, 33*(1), 9–33.

Gray, E., Harris, A., & Jones, T. (2016). Australian LGBTQ teachers, exclusionary spaces and points of interruption. *Sexualities, 19*(3), 286–303.

Grindheim, L. (2014). 'I am not angry in the kindergarten!' Interruptive anger as democratic participation in Norwegian kindergartens. *Contemporary Issues in Early Childhood, 15*(4), 308–318.

Gunu, I. (2018). Alternatives to school exclusion in Ghana: Changing the rhythm of dealing with truancy in Ghanaian high schools. *Sage Open, 8*(4), 1–9.

Hancock, C., & Cheatham, G. (2021). Decision-making during early intervention home visits: From minimal to meaningful parent participation. *Journal of Research in Childhood Education, 35*(1), 68–90.

Haugen, C. R. (2020). Teachers experiences of school choice from marginalised and privileged public schools in Oslo. *Journal of Education Policy, 35*(1), 68–94.

Heiskanen, N., Alasuutari, M., & Vehkakoski, T. (2021). Intertextual voices of children, parents, and specialists in individual education plans. *Scandinavian Journal of Educational Research, 65*(1), 36–53,

Horgan, D., Forde, C., Martin, S., & Parkes, A. (2017). Children's participation: Moving from the performative to the social. *Children's Geographies, 15*(3), 274–288.

Kangas, J. (2016). Enhancing children's participation in early childhood education through participatory pedagogy, Doctoral Dissertation, University of Helsinki.

Kauffman, J., & Hornby, G. (2020). Inclusive vision versus special education reality. *Education Sciences, 10*(9), 258.

Khalfaoui, A., García-Carrión, R., & Villardón-Gallego, L. (2021). A systematic review of the literature on aspects affecting positive classroom climate in multicultural early childhood education. *Early Childhood Education Journal, 49*(1), 71–81.

Kraft, M., Papay, J., Johnson, S., Charner-Laird, M., Ng, M., & Reinhorn, S. (2015). Educating amid uncertainty: The organizational supports teachers need to serve students in high-poverty, urban schools. *Educational Administration Quarterly, 51*(5), 753–790.

Kurth, J., Miller, A., & Toews, S. (2020). Preparing for and implementing effective inclusive education with participation plans. *Teaching Exceptional Children*, *53*(2), 140–149.

Lehane, T. (2016). "Cooling the mark out": Experienced teaching assistants' perceptions of their work in the inclusion of pupils with special educational needs in mainstream secondary schools. *Educational Review*, *68*(1), 4–23.

Manz, E., & Suárez, E. (2018). Supporting teachers to negotiate uncertainty for science, students, and teaching. *Science Education*, *102*(4), 771–795.

Martin-Denham, S. (2021). Alternatives to school exclusion: interviews with headteachers in England. *Emotional and Behavioural Difficulties*, *26*(4), 375–393.

McCardle, M., & Bliss, S. (2019). Digging deeper: The relationship between school segregation and unconscious racism. *Smith College Studies in Social Work*, *89*(2), 114–131.

McCluskey, G., Cole, T., Daniels, H., Thompson, I., & Tawell, A. (2019). Exclusion from school in Scotland and across the UK: Contrasts and questions. *British Educational Research Journal*, *45*(6), 1140–1159.

McKenzie, J. (2020). Intellectual disability in inclusive education in South Africa: Curriculum challenges. *Journal of Policy and Practice in Intellectual Disabilities*. doi: 10.1111/jppi.12337

McLeskey, J., & Council for Exceptional Children, & Collaboration for Effective Educator Development, Accountability and Reform. (2017). *High-leverage practices in special education*. Council for Exceptional Children.

McLeskey, J., & Waldron, N. L. (2011). Educational programs for elementary students with learning disabilities: Can they be both effective and inclusive? *Learning Disabilities Research & Practice*, *26*(1), 48–57.

Office for National Statistics. (2022). released 7 November 2022, ONS website, statistical bulletin, Educational experiences of young people with special educational needs and disabilities in England: February to May 2022.

Omidire, M. (2020). Experiencing language challenges in a rural school: Implications for learners' life aspirations. *Early Child Development and Care*, *190*(10), 1619–1637.

Parkinson, C., & Jones, T. (2019). Aboriginal people's aspirations and the Australian Curriculum: A critical analysis. *Educational Research for Policy and Practice*, *18*(1), 75–97.

Parry, J., Rix, J., Sheehy, K., & Simmons, K. (2013). The journey travelled: A view of two settings a decade apart. *British Journal of Educational Studies*, *61*(4), 385–399.

Perraudin, F. (2018). Pupil brings legal action against school's isolation policy. *The Guardian*, December Tue 11, 2018. Retrieved November 25, 2022, from https://www.theguardian.com/education/2018/dec/11/pupil-brings-legal-action-against-schools-isolation-booths-outwood-grange-academies-trust

Power, S., & Taylor, C. (2020). Not in the classroom, but still on the register: Hidden forms of school exclusion. *International Journal of Inclusive Education*, *24*(8), 867–881.

Putwain, D. W., Becker, S., Symes, W., & Pekrun, R. (2018). Reciprocal relations between students' academic enjoyment, boredom, and achievement over time. *Learning and Instruction*, *54*, 73–81.

Raufelder, D., & Kulakow, S. (2022). The role of social belonging and exclusion at school and the teacher–student relationship for the development of learned helplessness in adolescents. *British Journal of Educational Psychology, 92*(1), 59–81.

Rix, J. (2015). *Must inclusion be special? Rethinking educational support within a community of provision.* Routledge.

Rix, J., Sheehy, K., Fletcher-Campbell, F., Crisp, M., & Harper, A. (2013). Exploring provision for children identified with special educational needs: An international review of policy and practice. *European Journal of Special Needs Education, 28*(4), 375–391.

Rix, J., Sheehy, K., Fletcher-Campbell, F., Crisp, M., & Harper, A. (2015). Moving from a continuum to a community – Reconceptualising the provision of support. *Review of Educational Research, 85*(3), 319–352.

Saltes, N. (2018). Navigating disabling spaces: Challenging ontological norms and the spatialization of difference through 'Embodied Practices of Mobility'. *Mobilities, 13*(1), 81–95.

Sharma, U., & Salend, S. (2016). Teaching assistants in inclusive classrooms: A systematic analysis of the international research. *Australian Journal of Teacher Education (Online), 41*(8), 118–134.

Skinner, B., Leavey, G., & Rothi, D. (2021). Managerialism and teacher professional identity: Impact on well-being among teachers in the UK. *Educational Review, 73*(1), 1–16.

Staufenberg, J. (2018). Isolation rooms: How swathes of schools are removing pupils from their classrooms. *Schools Week,* October Fri 19th, 2018, 5.00. Retrieved May 13, 2019, from https://schoolsweek.co.uk/isolation-rooms-how-schools-are-removing-pupils-from-classrooms/

Subban, P., Woodcock, S., Sharma, U., & May, F. (2022). Student experiences of inclusive education in secondary schools: A systematic review of the literature. *Teaching and Teacher Education, 119,* 103853.

Timimi, S. (2021). The social cultural construction of autism: Trends in SEN identification: Contexts, causes and consequences, SEN policy research forum. *Journal of Research in Special Educational Needs, 21*(1), 28–32.

Twining, P, Rix, J., & Sheehy (2016). *Developing point of learning: An innovative approach to enhancing professional learning.* Imagine Education.

Webb-Williams, J. (2021). Teachers' use of within-class ability groups in the primary classroom: A mixed methods study of social comparison. *Frontiers in Psychology, 12,* 1–16.

Wingard, A., Hermawan, H., & Dewi, V. (2020). The effects of students' perception of the school environment and students' enjoyment in reading towards reading achievement of 4th grades students in Hong Kong. *Indonesian Journal on Learning and Advanced Education (IJOLAE), 2*(2), 68–74.

7

INCLUDING OURSELVES

Somewhere between?

As a teacher, I have never been good enough. Same goes for being a parent, a cartoonist, a researcher, a friend, an expert on this and that ... and so on. ...

There have been days when I have done a good job, but even on the best, there was always the possibility to have done better, the likelihood that what I sought to be/do I was/did not quite as well as someone else might have (or maybe I would have done in another space/in another moment).

I live in a to and fro, always and never, being and not-being assured. I know I am (being) endlessly (being) situated. I have but one certainty – that is, my uncertainty.

This is perhaps why I feel so comfy in the confusion between inclusion and special. This is why I nod when (my friend) Rune wonders if inclusion has re-legitimised special education, and I think of the special teachers who tell me nothing has changed in their practice over the last 30 years. This is why I am so honest to friends who tell me about how a diagnosis of this (or that) has been so beneficial to them. This is why I acknowledge its power for them but can't help pointing out that the diagnosis is purely a place to hang their hat (someone built the wall upon which the hanger is hung ... no, no, not real). This is why I am endlessly disappointed by the everyday practice I witness in the name of either inclusion or special, and yet I always feel I understand why it is (probably) so.

I find myself in a similar space in writing this chapter too. This is not a binary argument that I can win even with myself, because in the end, I don't care what the label is (inclusion/special) as long as people are having a positive participatory experience.

DOI: 10.4324/9781003281405-7

FIGURE 7.1 Here I am?

Let me recap the point I made earlier: my fundamental theoretical position is socio-cultural. This is the position which all my experiences of teaching and research tell me best explains what has gone/is going on in the learning context. Even when I am placed in a space that is fundamentally traditional or people are delivering a behaviourist-based intervention or I am witness to a constructivist or progressive curriculum, what I see going on makes sense through this socio-cultural lens. (What is fidelity, after all? What is an assessment, after all? What is normal, after all? What is any institutionalised process, after all?) It could be that the approach is producing something positive, but I understand it as a relational entity. This too is why I do not see the need to understand the classroom through post- and trans- positions, as much as they interest me, and motivate my thinking. These approaches (all of them) can help me/us ask questions, but they do not focus upon the means through which the teaching/learning emerges. The behaviour, the construction, the material within any educational space will always be socio-culturally situated.

My starting point therefore is how can we best enable the socio-cultural way of working?

The classic model

Not all socio-cultural models are relevant to the classroom. For example, the *community of practice* model is something which Lave and Wenger (1991) say should not be applied to the classroom. They noted that school knowledge is fundamentally derived externally from the community of students. The valued knowledge within this community arises primarily from the values, behaviours, expectations and ways of thinking associated with communities of practice from beyond the school. In contrast, the *community of learners* model emerged as a school-based practice. It builds upon experiential learning, with a high adult–child ratio involving people from the local community as well as qualified teachers; it draws upon the expertise of families, focusing upon the child's own interests and (non-norms-based) progress. It recognises dynamic, complementary group relations, seeking for everyone to take responsibility for their learning and the functioning of the group. There is not a single expert providing instruction but a community working together as a resource for each other, with shifting roles as appropriate. It is about conversations, building upon each other's ideas, with a teacher leading and guiding (Rogoff et al., 1998). This is the model which represents my best understanding of a classroom operating with a socio-cultural approach to learning. It is a useful starting point.

The power of this model has been more widely recognised too. For example, by 2017 Finland had reformed their national core curricula so that at its heart the school was seen as a learning community. This community is supposed to develop through dialogue, to encourage learning together and from each other, as well as exploration and experimentation. It aims to develop democratic action, social participation, through both subject lessons and multidisciplinary learning modules, with students involved in planning and with teachers supporting their realistic and practical expectations (Halinen, 2018).

It is tempting to take this as the marker in the sand, to which all other systems can aim. However, I will resist this temptation because:

- firstly, many countries do not share Finland's social values, highly supportive welfare system and commitment to equity and cooperation. They do not have teachers who are very highly qualified (for free), socially respected and trusted to undertake innovative teaching strategies, while experiencing few external accountability practices (Morgan, 2014);
- secondly, Finland can offer us quite a few lessons in how not to do it;
- thirdly, there are plenty of other practices around the world which present us with an opportunity for reflection on the barriers and opportunities for positive participatory experiences.

So, let's explore some of the issues and ideas related to uncertainty and equitable participation as discussed in earlier chapters; and let's do this in light of opportunities and challenges that are spread around everyday practice from many countries. Once again, I will frame this discussion using the six perspectives of the community of provision. This will reflect the multi-layered nature of interactions that are evident in school research (e.g., Defever et al., 2021). It will also highlight how structures and strategies will have unanticipated outcomes, and how interactions with wider community networks can open up new resources for the school and learners, as well as creating unexpected learning possibilities.

As I said in Chapter 6, all of these issues pertain to all perspectives. I will aim to underline the multi-perspective nature of these issues by returning to some ideas as I consider other emerging experiences. I am not trying to respond to every issue that I have raised in earlier chapters though (issues of certainty or those that lead to negative participatory experiences). I do not have the space to do this and even if I did, I am not looking to provide answers to everything, just to show that we are in many ways closer than we think to a better possible way of doing things.

Carrying on from here?   a/f?

Interweaving with systems

Let's start with an example of high-level decisions, which have been going in the right direction towards reducing marginalising pressures, and consider what is getting in their way.

Finland is not the only system to engage with socio-cultural ideas at a policy level. For example, Indonesia introduced thematic-based learning in primary schools in 2013 as did Turkey in 2006. However, it is also common to read that teachers struggle to work in these new ways, struggling to enrich and connect resources and assessments (Dewantara, 2020). Policy makers can struggle too. At the end of the 20th century, Norway introduced the Laerplan 97, which combined a core of centrally determined knowledge while allowing teachers flexibility to plan and teach topical issues with learners' interests, the local environment and resources in mind. Teacher decision-making, thematic work, active investigation and peer cooperation were at its core (Broadhead, 2001). While it was widely understood that Laerplan 97 would require considerable changes to teachers' and students' ways of working, in practice the approach was never really given time to bed down. Colleagues in Norway inform me that within a few years, the concern had shifted to the PISA league tables and concerns about how to improve national standings, with a subsequent focus upon school outcomes rather than pedagogic processes. Consequently, there was a shift in 2006 to a competency-oriented approach (with 198 competences to be achieved), following calls from the Organisation for Economic Cooperation and Development. This was further undermined by an ongoing reliance upon established textbooks (Sundby & Karseth, 2022).

A fundamental challenge, then, is that despite best intentions and research evidence new top-down policies frequently fail to change people's beliefs and/or find themselves in competition with other drivers. Lightbown and Spada (2020) describe, for example, how proposed policy changes to enable intensive second-language instruction in Quebec schools kept being put back with changes in government, so that the conversation just kept starting again.

They also describe presenting research evidence to practitioners and the Ministry of Education in a Latin American (unnamed) country. But having been told about the ineffectiveness of drip-feeding language instruction early in the school curriculum, the Ministry went ahead and introduced a policy that did just that. On a smaller scale, in the Netherlands, for more than 30 years, a community of over 300 primary schools has been involved in the development and implementation of a cultural–historical theory approach. They have been giving agency to teachers and pupils to shape a half-open curriculum, while thematically organising study and using texts as sources for exploration (Oudes-Slob et al., 2022). However, even though this has been shown to be an effective approach, the external rules and regulations of the national system (e.g. standardised tests in assessing children's development, predefined curricula and learning outcomes) have stopped its roll-out more widely (van der Veen et al., 2016).

It is easy to dismiss the possibility that the external rules and regulations of our national systems will be changed, retreating to the position that our governmental policy makers are expected (by voters and other vested interests) to provide certainty of this kind. But there is extensive pushback from these same sources. In countries that maintain end-of-school high-stake examinations, it is not uncommon to hear calls from advisory and representative bodies, as well as think tanks for changes to the system. For example, there are calls in England for a system of multiple, forms of continuous assessment between 16 and 18 (Coulter et al., 2022). Similar suggestions emerge whenever business leaders are asked about what it is that their companies need. Their top priorities are interpersonal and intercultural competencies, and they would like methods of assessment to evidence these relational skills. They are still seeking some certainty, but they are concerned with such things as:

- life experience and attitudes.
- team working skills.
- communication skills.
- business and customer awareness.
- customer handling skills.
- foreign language skills.
- international cultural awareness.

(Rix, 2015)

For example, the global professional services group, Arup, has called for a curriculum that encourages adaptability and dealing with the unknown, with children taking control of their own learning and sourcing their own knowledge. This curriculum should recognise that children have different interests, learn at different speeds and respond to different learning opportunities.

Similarly, Arup calls for new ways to evaluate abilities such as creativity, innovation and problem-solving, moving away from the traditional assessment methods (Kovachevich et al., 2018).

What is evident is that we have top-down processes which have set in place flexible learning opportunities, which have been constrained by established processes, in particular the assessment mechanisms, but at the same time we have extensive calls for these assessment mechanisms to be changed.

Just another perspective...?   b/f?

Interweaving with strategies

So now let's consider some examples of fairly commonplace strategies for support that can challenge and disrupt the embrace of certainty and enhance our experiences of participation.

Globally, many schools still focus on the one-sided transmission of knowledge and skills and dismiss strategies based upon cultural–historical/sociocultural understandings as being 'children doing whatever they please' (van der Veen & Wolbert, 2014). However, there are a variety of socio-cultural approaches that are part of mainstream practice, for example, in the early years (e.g. the Mosaic approach and In-the-Picture) or with marginalised groups (e.g. Photovoice); key concepts such as 'the zone of proximal development', 'play-based curriculum', 'scaffolding' and 'meaningful learning' have also become a part of the language of the wider educational community. New Zealand has introduced Te Whariki, their Early childhood curriculum, which comes with a statement of intent:

> He whāriki hei whakamana i te mokopuna, hei kawe i ngā wawata
> (A whāriki that empowers the child and carries our aspirations)
> *(Te Kete Ipurangi, 2023)*

As well as citing socio-cultural and critical theories, Te Whariki also makes strong links to the local; for example, recognising the differences between, and within, Pacific Islander cultural groups and the need to engage with Pacific values, languages, and worldviews.

In the United States, the National Research Council created the Framework for K–12 Science Education, not only outlining core practices, ideas and crosscutting concepts but also arguing for the broader participation of emergent bilingual learners. It also cited a good deal of socio-cultural literature, while suggesting that learning can be assessed through participation in multicomponent and collaborative tasks, evaluating how people practically engage with concepts. Fine and Furtak (2020) explore how this framework can support translanguaging, drawing on perspectives from across the community, and creating multiple entry points for assessment. They point to the use of interpersonal, intrapersonal and external material resources, offering opportunities to undertake authentic tasks where learners can show what they know and use their entire linguistic repertoire.

Engaging with and valuing the voice of the learner has become a widely touted strategy too. For instance, in the Irish system it is embedded in the inspection regime. Teachers and school leaders do not always respond to this positively of course. In the context of the Irish system, the voice of students and parents is variously viewed by staff as being divisive, threatening and idealistic. As a consequence, these student and parent voices have little impact upon everyday decision-making, but they are valued by management and administration when identifying their agendas. It also shows there can be a shift towards greater involvement, even if it is still only at the level of being consulted and being better informed (Brown et al., 2020). The pressure on broadening voice has also received a fresh impetus with campaigns to decolonise the curriculum and to enhance diversity within schools and across the curriculum. For example, a study of the Greek curriculum shows how readily the work of disabled artists can be utilised across ages and subject areas (Symeonidou, 2019). Similarly, counter-narratives have been used in various countries (e.g. United States, Norway, Poland, Turkey and Greece) to bridge cultural, racial and linguistic gaps. This has been utilised at the very start of the education process, as well as between young people and teachers and between the young people themselves (e.g., Golombek et al., 2022; Kim, 2019).

Another strategy that has been in evidence in different parts of the world for a great many years is co-teaching or team teaching. This does not mean that its use has not been problematic. In Ireland, for example, team teaching has been mandated for many years but is still practised less than the withdrawal of students. The types of challenges teachers refer to are planning time, different teaching personalities and styles and a belief that they lack the necessary knowledge (e.g., Casserly & Padden, 2018). This (unnecessary?) lack of self-belief is evident in the Greek context too where co-teaching has been promoted in legislation since 2000. This mismatch between policy and practice is not that surprising though, since Greek special education teachers are likely to have explored this approach in their initial training unlike the classroom teachers with whom they will work (Strogilos & Stefanidis, 2015). The development of team teaching in Finland has tried to grapple with this. Policymakers and funders have recognised that teachers had to be increasingly flexible in their ways of working and trust each other. At a structural level, school leaders had to support open communication across the setting, while also allocating time and resources for collective planning. Working in these new spaces called for the development of organisation of and adoption of novel practices and roles, valuing and accepting other's priorities and contributions (Niemi, 2021).

Across the literature it is evident that if leaders and facilitators want to enable collaboration of any kind, they should not focus their attention on one aspect or level. They need to consider factors across the six perspectives, related to the people involved, the processes, guidance, organisation and structure. This includes giving consideration to such things as the administrative support and priorities in school, as well as the personal characteristics of all those involved (de Jong et al., 2022).

Just another perspective...?   c/f?

Interweaving with support

Let's now consider some examples about how the nature of the support we provide can build upon a diverse range of skills and capacities.

When reading the discussion of voice above, some of you may have felt that schools are not always great at opening up to their wider community. A direct challenge to this statement is evident in various forms of community service, with specific national and regional programmes in countries such as Germany, Italy, Australia and the United States, often with a long history and involving a great many schools (e.g. Skinner & Chapman, 1999). Though not unproblematic in its delivery (e.g., in encouraging a deficit view of need), it demonstrates how the in-school focus can be turned outward. Service-learning, for instance, generally mixes community service with classroom instruction, being linked to the curriculum, with clear learning objectives while meeting community needs and involving reflection and critical engagement with the activities. There is a tendency for service-learning projects involving disabled students to be about helping them; however, programmes can and do challenge this. Perhaps unsurprisingly, they are more impactful if the disabled people are active participants with an opportunity to apply the wide range of skills associated with community service (Garwood et al., 2023).

There are also programmes which focus upon children of all ages as social activists working on grassroots campaigns, so that they became knowledgeable about issues and the kinds of skills to engage in social change. Above and beyond the sense of personal achievement they experience, it appears that the children come to focus upon understanding the issues and can critically engage with the causes of social problems, particularly when allied to a supportive school ethos and curriculum. Achieving this requires a supportive environment, which provides time and resources, but the communities involved can benefit greatly from the children's engagement (Torres-Harding et al., 2018).

Another idea which has emerged from the United States and spread globally (including Australia, New Zealand, the Netherlands, Israel, Italy, Kenya, Canada and India) is Big Picture schools (Hogan & Down, 2015). Their aim is to build a collaborative, rigorous educational experience based upon the learners' priorities and interests. This approach not only speaks to how schools can engage with the wider community, but it also offers alternative ways for people to demonstrate learning that could/should satisfy policymakers and bureaucracies. As part of the 12 key components of Big Picture schools is the notion of authentic assessment. This involves individuals producing a portfolio of work that shows how they have progressed against agreed learning goals and how they have reflected on the process. They share this with a group made up of teachers, family, peers, mentors and other community members (Hogan et al., 2020).

Our support can also build upon the skills and capacities of learners and teachers by recognising the diversity of opportunities to utilise those skills and develop them further. Approaches such as content-based language teaching (CBLT), where a second language is taught across the curriculum has been adopted in many places around the world (Lightbown & Spada, 2020). This is not the same as straightforward emersion, where students struggle to develop the necessary academic language to do well in the system, but involves receiving a significant part of the curriculum in the target language. For instance, in Hong Kong, Malaysia, Thailand, Taiwan and China, it is not unusual to find subjects such as Maths and Science being taught in English. We can also explore ways in which the study of a subject can help us to explore cultural and personal values. For example, the teaching of music can engage with the established canons of work but situate these within their historical and social context (Bate, 2020).

Another key idea for socio-culturalism, echoing those within new materialism, is that our experiences are actively mediated through artefacts and tools, as well as social–communicative processes. Considering the thingness of the materials with which we engage opens us a great many educational opportunities in schools and other learning contexts (e.g. Hood and Kraehe, 2017). For example, on a visit I made to one of Ruskin Mill's colleges in the UK, they talked about the importance of experiencing resistance. This emerges from the learner's relationship with materials and is seen as of far more importance to their understanding than the production of a final product. Exploring the situated nature of artefacts and tools can also create opportunities for learners to explore the nature of their support. For example, in focusing upon the materiality of objects and our entanglement with them, we can explore the capacity of textbooks to provide authority (Nelson et al., 2021). Going back to the Norwegian continued use of textbooks, for example, teachers and learners can still use the resource but consider how they:

- freeze understanding through their representations of the physical and social.
- exemplify issues of absence in relation to voice and outlook.

Much of what has been suggested above can feed into the idea of delivering our support <u>across</u> the traditional subjects of the curriculum. Thematic curricula have a long history, for instance, being (briefly) popular in the UK in the 1960s. More recently, the curriculum for Wales (established in 2020) has followed other countries by introducing areas of Learning and Experience with a range of cross-curricular skills. The curriculum guidance emphasises learner centredness, active pedagogy and 21st-century skills with teachers as the facilitators of learning. This shift away from a focus upon predetermined content has its critics of course. For many, learning outcomes of the sort being adopted in Wales blur the well-established boundaries between disciplinary and everyday knowledge. The fear is that they overemphasise how learning is to be supported rather focusing upon what is to be learned (Sinnema et al., 2020). However, this cross-curricular approach is increasingly encouraged around the globe. The ethos of the Finnish curriculum, for example, is that study is more inspiring and meaningful if students take an active role in planning their work, particularly in multidisciplinary projects.

Just another perspective…?   d/f?

Interweaving with staffing

Let's now consider some examples of people's roles in supporting learning and how we can encourage a broad involvement from all practitioners.

As the cautionary comments in the section above suggest, changing expectations about the nature of support does not guarantee the expected shift in practice. Teachers identify a range of barriers when asked to contextualise the curriculum (including the length and complexity of the national curriculum – Leite et al., 2018). In discussing such challenges in Indonesia, Trinidad, Tobago and Uganda, Ghunu (2022) notes the ongoing dominance of teacher-centred practices as well as challenges ranging from training and motivation to class size and lack of resources. In Finland, teachers have at times struggled with the vagueness of goals (making it harder to plan for and assess learning) and having to negotiate between the vision of the school leaders and their own practice (Braskén et al., 2020). In the Welsh context, it is evident that schools' bureaucracies need to provide considerable support for teachers to deliver resources and activities, as well as allowing them to have the time to develop the understandings and skills to work in these new ways, particularly for students on the margins of the system (Power et al., 2020). At the point at which the new Welsh curriculum was introduced, teachers recognised that they were moving from an assessment-driven system, governed by external accountability, which encouraged performative pedagogic practices. But the teachers struggled to envisage an alternative system which relies upon creativity and teacher agency when the focus towards the end of compulsory education was still on the outcome of assessments. They feared the changes to the curriculum would be (ostensibly) compromised (Titley et al., 2020).

An effective means of dealing with many of these challenges is for practitioners to explore their own practice, particularly alongside colleagues and learners, so that they can take ownership of the development of that practice. Globally, this reflective approach has been allied with the ubiquitous interest in (mainly qualitative) action research. This relatively simple process is a non-threatening, enjoyable and rewarding way to get people to ask questions and explore possibilities. Teachers exploring their own practice, for example, are able to see how cross-curricular learning modules (linked to Forests) enhanced social interaction, peer group autonomy and sense of being competent and capable participants (Niemi & Kiilakoski, 2020). It also helped them identify difficulties in group working and the challenge some learners faced in focusing on the task at hand. As part of this, the teachers had to devise innovative approaches to evaluation, involving students producing learning narratives, engaging in peer evaluation, producing picture books with images taken by the teachers and being interviewed about the experience. Action research projects also demonstrate how teachers can apply theoretical ideas to their work in order to develop their practice. For example, McNeill (2020) talks about working with the pedagogy of accompaniments. She explores how to create the space for students to speak about the knowledge and interests they bring to the classroom, building relationships through learning, by doing things together, encouraging her to strive to continue to develop their ways of working beyond that research.

Engaging with outside voices also enables teachers to come to understand and develop their ways of working. A socio-cultural understanding of knowledge helps in this context too. A key part of collaboration is identifying professional boundaries and when they are being crossed. In this context, it important to recognise how different knowledge and resources are prioritised in different situations and how this in turn effects the relationships between the practitioners (Vesterinen et al., 2017). A valuable starting point for developing practice would be, for example, to recognise that even though early years teachers view speech and language therapists as useful, many of them do not actually understand what they do (Fernandes et al., 2017).

Our systems also need to be better at recognising who can make a contribution to the learning context. Above we talked about the knowledge that people in families bring with them, but so too does the wider community. In the United States, last time I looked, 2.5 million children and adolescents were paired each year with adults through mentoring programs (though primarily as a low-cost intervention for people identified as being at psychosocial and academic risk (Raposa et al., 2019)). Cross-age peer mentoring programs for youth are also widely used in the United States, with similar levels of (quantitative) effectiveness (Burton et al., 2022). Perhaps unsurprisingly, though, having a strong relation with any older or more experienced individual (a natural mentor), regardless of whether a person is deemed at risk and without being part of a formal programme, will also produce positive outcomes against the same kinds of measures. This is particularly the case if they have a high-quality relationship, spending time to get to know each other (Van Dam et al., 2018). This is probably why peer-to-peer support approaches are so effective.

Just another perspective...? e/f?

Interweaving with space

Let's now turn to how our notions of space can be reimagined to enhance our capacity to innovate and understand what is additional.

Open learning classrooms had their first wave of interest in the late 1960s and 1970s, and in the 2000s have been making a comeback in countries such as Australia, New Zealand, the United Kingdom, Germany, Finland and Spain. These are seen as a way of responding to 21st-century learning needs, while also creating the opportunity to increase student's physical activity (Hartikainen et al., 2021). They create multipurpose, adaptable spaces. They would typically have moveable furniture and the means to vary the nature of spaces, integrating physical and virtual space, with a view to providing greater student learning interaction and autonomy. Some have been specifically designed and built, others have been repurposed. Invariably, these new spaces present challenges in relation to issues such as shared space and resources, variable student responses and staff–student ratios. To align with policy shifts to a 21st-century /multidisciplinary/learner-centred curriculum, the creation of these spaces needs to be done in such a way that recognises that learning involves participation in the learning environment. This includes its material artefacts, verbal and embodied social interactions and the interaction between the collective and individualised mind.

However, the development of these spaces is not a binary situation where traditional schools invariably provide passive, teacher-led practices and open spaces lead to student-centred, interactive and creative learning. Just as old space can be used in new ways, innovative spaces are frequently inhibited by the realities of everyday schooling grammars (Byers et al., 2018). This is not just a result of us as teachers either. It is imbued with our understanding of the student–teacher relationship. I often reflect on this truth as I deliver lectures to ranks of university students about the value of socio-cultural approaches. In a traditional lecture hall with fixed banks of seating, it is nearly impossible to encourage meaningful activity. But even in the classroom where the chairs and tables can be moved around, it is tempting to stick with the predictable, particularly since a collective understanding is that the main focus is on the assessment at the end. Even though I often try to disrupt the sessions by encouraging peer-to-peer activity, students often resist being involved. It is easy to dismiss their struggles as being a consequence of their prior educational experience, but much of it must be down to the fear of myself and colleagues to offer real alternatives. We stick with the desks, the whiteboard, the PowerPoint, the lecture hall, the expert at the front. We show a few videos. We ask for a few student presentations. We don't really feel able to reimagine our ways of working and what that might mean for our workload management systems. The students are mostly okay with that too as long as they get the grade at the end. All of which takes us back to the issues above about opening up our assessments the collective exploration of our practices and our relationship with risk.

Perhaps predictably, given the ongoing dominance of top-down processes, the focus seems to have been more on the design of these spaces and less on their implementation as a space for learning. For example, in Finland (where all new or totally renovated schools have incorporated open and flexible designs and principles since 2016), teachers report that they have not participated in the design phase and have even found their ideas being dismissed. They have felt, for instance, frustrated in their need to maintain quiet, enclosed, undisturbed spaces where they could engage in dialogue (sometimes confidential) and scaffold learning without distractions (Niemi, 2021). Saltmarsh et al. (2015) report that having less structured timetables, routines and practices allows for more spatially responsive pedagogies, but they also underline the importance of teachers and students learning together about how to best make use of the space. In creating and working in these spaces, it is essential to work with the access and learning preferences of those who will be using them. As with the discussion about teachers and action research above, it seems essential that the development of these spaces is seen as a learning opportunity/need of itself. For instance, in Australia a carefully managed transition that shifted across a year from a traditional to an innovative learning environment allowed for such a process of learning. Not only did it lead to statistically significant improvements in attitudes, use of technology, behaviour and engagement but also academic outcomes. This involved a pedagogical shift to greater collaborative learning, critical thinking, creativity and learner communication, reducing the time spent in teacher-centric whole-class instruction (Byers et al., 2018).

The principles of open learning are also evident in many of the established alternative forms of schooling around the world, from Free schools to Democratic schools, Montessori to Pupil Referral Units, Flexi-schools to Forest schools. So, for example, the priority within Australian flexi-schools is to reengage with learning through the development of relationships with staff, fellow students and their wider community (Brunker & Lombardo, 2021). Riele (2007) positions such provision within a framework of the locus of change (young person or provision) and stability of provision. Similarly,

I developed a typology of educational programmes with a colleague which identified provision by its length, educational approach, learner choice, opportunities of access, age range, regulation and location (Rix & Twining, 2007). Often this alternative provision will be contrasted to the mainstream around it, providing greater flexibility around attendance, behaviour, dress, curriculum and teacher–learner relationships. Often in these spaces, children and young people have a greater say in what they do, how they do it and how the setting is organised. It is not unusual for researchers to suggest that much can be learned from this alternative provision (e.g. McGregor & Mills, 2012). For instance, students often report positive experiences in these settings, despite often having trouble in mainstream contexts. They tend to report positive staff–student relationships, with people taking time to listen, being disposed to caring and being flexible (Malcolm, 2020).

Often these learning opportunities are provided in non-school-like spaces too. Schools have a long tradition of engaging with 'informal' learning opportunities. Above we discussed community learning, but other spaces include museums, field trips, theatre visits and home. Another such space (and another global movement) are Forest schools. These began in Denmark before moving through Scandinavia, into the United Kingdom and United States and now can be found all around the world, including in South Korea, Japan, Germany, Australia and New Zealand (Dean, 2019). The tendency is to position Forest schools on the periphery of the core activities of the education system, where it is associated with well-being. Often activities in Forest schools need to fit in with classroom-based discourses, ignoring the opportunities they provide children to negotiate interactions in a range of contexts which are fundamental to their education (Garden & Downes, 2021). By engaging with learning in a relationship with forests, van Groll & Fraser (2022) suggest we are working with pedagogy that troubles ideas, our sense of time and space; it is unpredictable and requires us to think with uncertainty, paying attention to everyday encounters. This takes me back to the earlier point about the value of experiencing the nature of resistance.

Just another perspective...? f/f?

Interweaving with students

Let's now consider examples of how our focus of support can open up our capacity to respond to a wider range of need and opportunities within schools.

Globally, I have found (to my disappointment) little evidence of teacher's planning for children's social relationships. There are calls for practitioners to encourage interactions and take a strategic overview of learner relationships (Blatchford et al., 2003) as well as an extensive tradition which seeks to examine and enhance social interactions for specific disabled groupings and to a lesser degree to enhance their social relationships (e.g., Rosa & Menezes, 2019; Batchelor & Taylor, 2005). But there are so many other ways and places where teachers could focus upon these relationships [for instance, in devising tasks to undertake at home, creating sporting activities, monitoring break times, organising out-of-school activities, delivering interventions, evaluating learning, providing support, meeting with other practitioners, overseeing organisational routines, devising school assemblies, devolving school duties, running school clubs and so on.] The value of these social relationships is not just what it brings to the learning context but also to the children's subjective sense of well-being (Goswami, 2012). There is a range of well-researched strategies which can be used to develop social interactions in the classroom as well; for instance:

- working in groups.
- encouraging everyone to contribute verbally.
- using open questions.
- seeking extended contributions.
- allowing for people to voice and explore differences of opinion.
- explicitly linking to people's ideas and aiming to develop a metacognitive overview.

(Howe et al., 2019)

Of course, some children will struggle with collaboration or group work. Some may feel excluded by a focus upon the spoken word or use of a particular language or by types of group work. But these are everyday challenges which go to the heart of participation. They are opportunities for creative thinking just as much as they are barriers. I would suggest that we need to go further than simply asking practitioners to be more active in facilitating social interactions for pupils identified with special educational needs (e.g. Mamas & Avramidis, 2013). Across the globe, teachers are used to engaging in everyday planning and assessment. It seems a small step for this planning and assessment to include consideration of social interactions within the class and beyond. For example, peer interactions will be directly impacted by the ways in which the physical spaces (such as play areas) are organised and used (Fernelius, 2018) or by keeping some children apart from others at lunchtime or by providing support activities at the start of break sessions (Woolley et al., 2006). The promotion of cross-group friendships in such contexts (and others) is likely to foster inclusive and accepting school environments, providing further opportunities for collaboration and out-of-class contact (Grütter et al., 2018).

A fundamental aspect in engaging with the community of students is our understanding of who they are. For example, a group of Dutch teachers demonstrated how engaging with the students' funds of knowledge increased peer respect and understanding in their classes (and also positively influenced classroom engagement, attitudes, behaviour and well-being alongside)

(Volman, 2021). In recent years, there has been a movement from a paradigm focused on children's needs to one focused upon their interests. This sees children as independent from adults, able to recognise their interests and pursue them within a given context. This movement is associated with many of the shifts in policy, strategies and approaches discussed above. By promoting the voice of the learner and in engaging affective interpersonal relationships, teachers are taking a risk with personal trust and agency (Farini & Scollan, 2021). This need not be seen as an age-related issue either. For instance, two Irish national consultations in 2015 and 2016 involved a great many young people aged 5 to 17. This involved using a variety of strengths-based consultative approaches, allowing them to identify and explore issues in relation to their everyday experiences (Horgan, 2017). This approach does not require the wholehearted curriculum changes described above either. For example, it is evident in a small way through changes to the curriculum in China, in relation to career studies (Lee, 2017).

This view of the able child, based upon their strengths and interests, can also be seen to link back to the notion of access preferences mentioned above and discussed in Chapter 5. Within the participatory research project participants identified categories ranging from Blue badge parking to Sign Language, Induction loops to Magnifying glasses, One-to-one support to Gallery stools. Such categories of access preferences were specific to the museum context in which they were collected, but they far more effectively enable people working in museums (and elsewhere) to consider possibilities and solutions for visitors, rather than having to make presumptions based upon a generalised diagnostic label (Rix, 2023). It would not be hard to identify similar, locally relevant access preferences in schools and utilise them in planning and assessment. As the participants were quick to point out, many of these access options would also have benefits across a range of users too, not just a particular group to whom they might be typically supplied.

Yeah but I'm not as bad as the statistics might suggest...

FIGURE 7.2 About average.

While in the community

As I was writing the sections above, I kept wanting to make links across to the *while* of participation. I was aware for example that:

- the introduction of open-plan schooling was about creating a space that was adaptable and flexible, which opened up relationships.
- in discussing how these spaces were designed and managed, we touched upon issues of teacher's power, voice and support.
- by situating these innovative classrooms as the means to deliver the learner-centred curriculum, we were talking about being open to moments of learning, which were of value to the learner and enabled them to represent their lived experiences (which could in turn lead to a consideration of being adaptable and flexible, opening up relationships, touching upon issues of learner's power, voice and support).
- all of which required people having time to listen, having access to the languages of the learner and being willing to change their roles.
- and throughout I have touched upon different people's beliefs.

I was tempted to unpack such observations as I went along, but in the end it did not seem helpful. I was already selectively presenting examples through the six overlapping perspectives. I had already asked you to reflect upon how each issue I raised needed to be considered through these other lenses.

Engaging with these open representations of complex interactions is not a tick-box exercise. In the moment of experience, there is too much going on to think through all aspects of the *while* and the six community perspectives. This is a fundamental risk we need to accept in opening up to the uncertainty at the heart of socio-cultural approaches. Being open to the collective learning experience means there will always be the unexpected. Surprises (pleasant and unpleasant) will be. Tying something to singular points of reference will rarely be possible. Reflection in the moment is possible, but it is always retrospective and benefits from time.

If we wish to bring ourselves closer to the aspirational community of provision (see Figure 7.3), we need to accept this risk which is at the heart of the process. Each aspect of the community is entwined with the *while*, which is both a collective and individualised experience, and therefore always out of our control (see Figure 7.4).

Exploring the complexity of our situation through the models of the community of provision and the *while* of participation cannot explain our experiences. They can open up points of reference to help us consider the dimensions of what we are/have been doing and our participation with/in it. They are intended to serve as a means to consider the uncertain – as points of

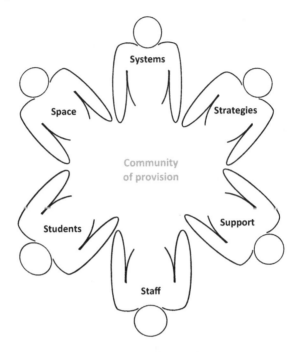

FIGURE 7.3 An aspirational community of provision.

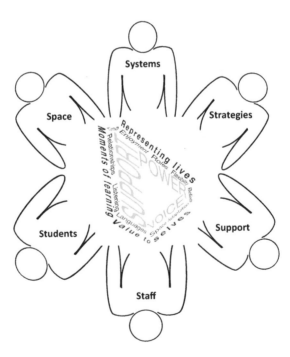

FIGURE 7.4 Participation within an aspirational community.

reflection – as conversation starters. They can help us explore. It is when we are planning and evaluating a particular experience that they can serve their purpose.

This is I believe the most powerful tool at our disposal. It is about finding ways to engage with our collective understanding. The knowledge we share, if we give ourselves the time and space (and all the other component parts of the *while*), is the best means to focus our community.

Measuring us?

As I have been writing this chapter, I have kept wanting to make links across to ideas I have, which will resolve the challenges I was identifying. Some of the issues I have raised as I have gone along; for example, in relation to the nature of the curriculum, the creation of learning spaces, the involvement of people and how we think about the learners. There are some barriers which arise from current power structures or traditions, which are only overcome if we can take a risk and trust teachers, learners and administrators. But one issue stands out and comes up repeatedly, assessment. Clearly, our assessment systems create a block on opening up our curriculum and our pedagogy.

In the section on systems, I mentioned how advisory groups and businesses are calling for new forms to assess what might be called 21st-century skills. Calls for this kind of change have emerged from academic bodies too as a result of imbalances in the assessment system. For example, a dominant narrative at the end of schooling in Australia is a person's Australian Tertiary Admissions Rank score, even though a great many enter higher education through bridging courses or vocational study or work and life experience (Twining, 2020). In response, there are increasing calls for portfolio outputs from education, such as Education Passports (e.g. Education Services Australia, 2020). Like the standard CV, we are all expected to have when we apply for a new job, the portfolio can record the person's capabilities, skills, various types of courses and professional development opportunities at school and beyond. Of course, there is a long history of people using similar assessment tools, but as part of a curriculum rather than as the end point for an education system.

An approach I developed with colleagues (Twining et al., 2016) was an attempt to design a socio-cultural assessment system, using swipe cards and card readers based on a system being used with thousands of teachers in Egypt. This approach to evidencing learning went beyond setting personal targets or individual goals. People within the community of provision created bottom-up collectively owned aspirations, which could be verified by anyone and everyone in that context. These could be short-term and long-term aspirations, and people could give feedback on how they and others worked towards these aspirations. The intention behind these was not monitoring or accountability but specifically to inform personal and collective identity, agency and participation.

This collective ownership helps confront the increasing complexity which practitioners face too, and the pressure to engage in data-informed instruction. Just as it has always been for teachers, it is unclear how assessment effects the motivation and self-esteem of many students and their relationship to learning and the school (Ryan et al., 2020). Lots of people do not like being assessed as part of a collective, of course. Some people respond badly to peer evaluation. Unfairness is bound to emerge along the way. But this should not stop us from opening up the possibility in order to allow the space for the kinds of changes discussed above. After all, it really cannot be that hard to come up with an alternative that can satisfy policy makers, bureaucrats and other end users of the school system. It cannot be that hard to come up with systems that create a far more accessible space for those on the margins of our current systems nor for those who do not use the dominant communication systems nor for those who will be entering an adult life with more support than others.

Other ways

A key challenge in moving to a socio-cultural evaluation of learners is how we maintain what is useful about our current ways of working – that it helps us share our ideas and acts as a record of intentions and actions, while at the same time overcoming the barriers it creates around:

- learner and teacher identities.
- excessive workload.
- being of limited value to classroom practice.
- using highly knowledgeable individuals to do paperwork when they could be working in the learning context instead.

These challenges seem particularly evident in relation to the other form of assessment which drives so much inequality and is currently firmly rooted in notions of certainty, identifying those who need additional support.

I have three simple solutions.

Firstly

We move away from individual (education) plans and towards plans for the classroom community. We aim to encapsulate the rich knowledge that emerges in discussions about collective teaching and learning situations in which diverse individuals are situated (Rix & Matthews, 2014). The paperwork that evidences and plans for this would therefore be a record of discussion about current priorities in a class situation. It would more closely resemble a set of minutes from a committee meeting, reflecting topics of discussion with action points. The key would be what is on the agenda. The possible questions might be as varied as the contexts which need to be drawn upon, but the discussion would recognise that people can only develop as part of a developing context which itself develops as the people do. The discussion would need to consider all aspects of the community of provision, the space, support, staffing, students, strategies and systems. This would include availability of resources at all levels of the system, as well as personal and professional experiences across the setting – what people feel they cannot do, as well as what they might be able to do, and why. Such an approach also lends itself to more regular discussions. It is not required once a year; it can include individual points of focus, but it is not about singular children; it does not take place after numerous reports are written. It can happen once a week. Process can still be recorded. Responsibility can be allotted. But the paperwork can respond to the shifting reality of the uncertain classroom.

Secondly

We move away from medically defined labels within our planning to labels of opportunity (Rix, 2007). If we have to provide a label, school staff need one that encourages them to think about how they can best work with a child – that would support teaching, learning and social interaction. Labels such as Autism, D/deaf, Down syndrome may be useful in a medical context and as a matter of personal and collective pride but within an education/social care/ everyday situation it fails to open up a huge range of possibilities. Even if a teacher knows all the characteristics associated with this label, the child they are teaching will only have some of those characteristics. Depending upon this child's circumstances and the resources available in the setting, they may be more usefully described as '*a person who benefits from support to build social relations*' or '*a person who will use the break out space*', or they might be linked to their access preferences, such as '*a person who uses a Note-taker*'. Such a label would not cover everything, but it would be a start and would help both the person who used the label and the person it was applied to. They are far simpler to share, to comprehend and to hold yourself to account for. They can be locally relevant, easier to assess and less prone to the postcode lottery. It is a label about how to do something – situated in the social, creating relational opportunities and provocations. They can also change in ways that reflect the priorities of the people they are describing and the people involved in their lives. Labels of opportunity are not who you are forever. They are who you are at the moment. They are simpler, more manageable, don't call for more training and are more likely to make teachers feel capable.

Thirdly

We move away from the individualised element of additional support funding, to a class-based funding model (Rix, 2009). This model would not be a conglomeration of individual assessments, each with a score that can be totted up to produce a banding total. It would be based on the evaluation of needs of that community of learners. As I have mentioned in previous work:

- the head of a commune education service in Norway told us that their intention was to focus funding more on the class than on the individuals within it.
- a principal of a cluster of schools in Italy told us how they allocated resources taking into consideration not just classified individuals but also staff time, staff experience and the wider class context, including the number and diversity of pupils in a class.
- in Italy, class councils are made up of all the teachers and support staff who worked with a particular class and parent representatives for that class. The council focuses upon the educational activities and teaching approaches for the class, evaluating its progress as a unit as well as the progress of individual pupils.

Drawing upon such ideas, this funding evaluation would begin with the collective context. It would identify not only the individuals and their access preferences but also the support that was available and what was required to deliver collectively agreed goals for the whole class. It would still acknowledge the individual, but it would place them in the collective context of the other individuals around them, taking into account the skills and experiences of not just the pupils but the adults working alongside them. It could encourage possible learning opportunities when people are together. A class model could be flexible, with long-term and short-term budgetary processes. It would have local direction but could still be controlled by traditional mechanisms of governance. Importantly for the established professions, allying class-based funding models to collectively focused paperwork would not remove expertise from the frame. It is not about saying that there is no place for speech and language therapists or educational psychologists and so forth, but it reduces the need for them to be churning out the paperwork, to be making final decisions and allows them to be part of a team, critical friends and/or active participants. It respects that they have wisdom to contribute to the benefit of all. It reduces the need for training because the trainers are in the room.

(Can) I have a dream (?)

There are lots of ideas I would have liked to have talked about in this chapter but have left out. I love the idea of slow pedagogy, for example, allowing children to take time to reflect, find out and go deeper. I am delighted to see schools in Spain that have adopted this approach and that the Froebel Trust in the UK is supporting its usage. We could open up our schools too by engaging children in philosophy, which I can believe makes many children happier, making classes and school communities more open and understanding (Love, 2018). I think the call for more creativity within the class, across the setting is also essential and recognise that much of what is understood as creative speaks to socio-cultural understandings of learning (Cremin & Chappell, 2021). I recognise too the potential in multi-age approaches, even if this can be constrained by the practitioner's own understandings (Teszenyi, 2023) and that people are calling for a shift to evidence-informed practice (Ainscow, 2020). I don't doubt the importance of voluntariness which is at the heart of the Golden Key programme based upon Vygotskian cultural-historical notions, which sees the children and teachers in a family relationship (Kravtsov & Kravtsova, 2011). And of course, there are so many other locally situated practices which speak to notions of uncertainty, for instance, the pedagogy of Aloha which (among other things) sees the teacher as a researcher, guide and co-learner (Kahakalau, 2020).

I would also like to tell stories of my son – of how he learned to ride a bike, to ski, to take photographs and to use his phone. How my relationship with someone who is a total failure by most educational standards has shown me what is possible when people learn together, convinces me of the potential benefit of so much that has been discussed over the last few pages; makes me believe that this can be achieved without making the curriculum less challenging for anyone nor making our processes less reliable. I would also like to have spent more time thinking about how change is possible, both slowly (across the ages) and rapidly (in ways we do not expect). As Kozleski (2020) notes (in outlining her views on what are required to enable inclusive practice), during the COVID pandemic in the early 2020s, there was a dramatic and fluid mobilisation of knowledge. In just a few weeks, nations changed where and how children were taught, shifting the roles and identities of teacher and learners. This allowed us to show that we can rapidly transform our approach to assessment, our culture of learning, our understanding of the possible, by inspiring our imagination.

Just as the current systems marginalise huge swathes of the school population through the dominant teaching and assessment systems, the alternatives discussed in this chapter are going to be problematic. There will be children and young people who struggle with collective, open space, who need considerable support to benefit from having greater control over their learning. There will be difficulties in creating processes that are considered reliable by outside bodies. There will still be falling outs and disagreements and political shiftings. But the aim of such a system is that it is better able to move with these challenges, to respond to them in ways that enable more to do better through our schools.

The ideas in this chapter are not that radical.

They have been tried somewhere in the world
(well nearly all of them).

They have just not all been put together
in one system bundle.

References

Ainscow, M. (2020). Promoting inclusion and equity in education: Lessons from international experiences, *Nordic Journal of Studies in Educational Policy, 6*(1), 7–16.

Batchelor, D., & Taylor, H. (2005). Social inclusion—The next step: User-friendly strategies to promote social interaction and peer acceptance of children with disabilities. *Australasian Journal of Early Childhood, 30*(4), 10–18.

Bate, E. (2020). Justifying music in the national curriculum: The habit concept and the question of social justice and academic rigour. *British Journal of Music Education, 37*(1), 3–15.

Blatchford, P., Kutnick, P., Baines, E., & Galton, M. (2003). Toward a social pedagogy of classroom group work. *International journal of educational research, 39*(1–2), 153–172.

Braskén, M., Hemmi, K., & Kurtén, B. (2020). Implementing a multidisciplinary curriculum in a Finnish lower secondary school – The perspective of science and mathematics. *Scandinavian Journal of Educational Research, 64*(6), 852–868.

Broadhead, P. (2001). Curriculum change in Norway: Thematic approaches, active learning and pupil cooperation-from curriculum design to classroom implementation. *Scandinavian Journal of Educational Research, 45*(1), 19–36.

Brown, M., McNamara, G., O'Brien, S., Skerritt, C., O'Hara, J., Faddar, J., Cinqir, S., Vanhoof, J., Figueiredo, M., & Kurum, G. (2020). Parent and student voice in evaluation and planning in schools. *Improving Schools, 23*(1), 85–102.

Brunker, N., & Lombardo, M. (2021). Ripples of hope: Learning to support student behaviour from the pedagogical practice of a flexi-school for marginalised youth. *Journal of Peace Education, 18*(1), 27–47.

Burton, S., Raposa, E., Poon, C., Stams, G., & Rhodes, J. (2022). Cross-age peer mentoring for youth: A meta-analysis. *American Journal of Community Psychology, 70*(1–2), 211–227.

Byers, T., Imms, W., & Hartnell-Young, E. (2018). Evaluating teacher and student spatial transition from a traditional classroom to an innovative learning environment. *Studies in Educational Evaluation, 58*, 156–166.

Casserly, A., & Padden, A. (2018). Teachers' views of co-teaching approaches in addressing pupils with special educational needs (SEN) in multi-grade classrooms. *European Journal of Special Needs Education, 33*(4), 555–571.

Coulter, S., Iosad, A., & Scales, J. (2022). *Ending the big squeeze on skills: How to futureproof education in England.* Tony Blair Institute for Global Change

Cremin, T., & Chappell, K. (2021). Creative pedagogies: A systematic review. *Research Papers in Education, 36*(3), 299–331.

de Jong, L., Meirink, J., & Admiraal, W. (2022). School-based collaboration as a learning context for teachers: A systematic review. *International Journal of Educational Research*, *112*, 101927.

Dean, S. (2019). Seeing the forest and the trees: A historical and conceptual look at Danish forest schools. *International Journal of Early Childhood Environmental Education*, *6*(3), 53–63.

Defever, E., Randall, V., & Jones, M. (2021). A realist case study inquiry of English primary school physical activity initiatives. *Sport, Education and Society*, *28*(1), 30–43.

Dewantara, P. (2020). Curriculum changes in Indonesia: Teacher constraints and students of prospective teachers' readiness in the implementation of thematic learning at low grade primary school. *Ilkogretim Online*, *19*(2), 1047–1060.

Education Services Australia. (2020). Looking to the future – Report of the review of senior secondary pathways into work, further education and training. Retrieved December 16, 2022, from https://uploadstorage.blob.core.windows.net/public-assets/education-au/pathways/Final%20report%20-%2018%20June.pdf

Farini, F., & Scollan, A. (2021). Between marginalisation and agency. Primary school teachers' narratives in London and the position of children with migrant backgrounds. *Migration Studies Review of Polish Diaspora*, *182*(4), 79–96.

Fernandes, D., Lima, M., & Silva, I. (2017). The perception of kindergarten teachers about the speech therapist work at school. *Distúrb Comun*, *29*(1), 86–96.

Fernelius, C. (2018). Evidence-based practices for the design of inclusive playgrounds that support peer interactions among children with all abilities, Doctoral dissertation, Utah State University.

Fine, C., & Furtak, E. (2020). A framework for science classroom assessment task design for emergent bilingual learners. *Science Education*, *104*(3), 393–420.

Garden, A., & Downes, G. (2021). A systematic review of forest schools literature in England. *Education*, *3–13*, 1–17.

Garwood, J., Peltier, C., Ciullo, S., Wissinger, D., McKenna, J., Giangreco, M., & Kervick, C. (2023). The experiences of students with disabilities actually doing service learning: A systematic review. *Journal of Experiential Education*, *46*(1), 5–31.

Ghunu, N. (2022). The challenges of remote area elementary schools in thematic curriculum implementation. *International Journal of Instruction*, *15*(2), 19–36.

Golombek, P., Olszewska, A. I., & Coady, M. (2022). Humanizing power of counter-stories: Teachers' understandings of emergent bilinguals in rural settings. *Teaching and Teacher Education*, *113*, 103655.

Goswami, H. (2012). Social relationships and children's subjective well-being. *Social Indicators Research*, *107*(3), 575–588.

Grütter, J., Gasser, L., Zuffianò, A., & Meyer, B. (2018). Promoting inclusion via cross-group friendship: The mediating role of change in trust and sympathy. *Child Development*, *89*(4), e414–e430.

Halinen, I. (2018). The new educational curriculum in Finland. *Improving the Quality of Childhood in Europe*, *7*, 75–89.

Hartikainen, J., Haapala, E. A., Poikkeus, A. M., Lapinkero, E., Pesola, A. J., Rantalainen, T., & Finni, T. (2021). Comparison of classroom-based sedentary time and physical activity in conventional classrooms and open learning spaces among elementary school students. *Frontiers in Sports and Active Living*, *3*, 168.

Hogan, J., Carr, D, & Down, B. (2020). *Transforming schools: All of the design, all of the time, all of the way through… The implementation of Big Picture Education in five schools*. Big Picture Education Australia (BPEA), Murdoch University.

Hogan, J., & Down, B. (2015). A STEAM school using the big picture education (BPE) design for learning and school – What an innovative STEM Education might look like. *International Journal of Innovation in Science and Mathematics Education, 23*(3), 47–60.

Hood, E., & Kraehe, A. (2017). Creative matter: New materialism in art education research, teaching, and learning. *Art Education, 70*(2), 32–38.

Horgan, D. (2017). Consultations with children and young people and their impact on policy in Ireland. *Social Inclusion, 5*(3), 104–112.

Howe, C., Hennessy, S., Mercer, N., Vrikki, M., & Wheatley, L. (2019). Teacher–student dialogue during classroom teaching: Does it really impact on student outcomes?. *Journal of the Learning Sciences, 28*(4–5), 462–512.

Kahakalau, K. (2020). Pedagogy of Aloha. *Encyclopedia of teacher education. Springer*.

Kim, S. (2019). Counter-storytelling: Preschool children as creative authors. *Kappa Delta Pi Record, 55*(2), 72–77.

Kovachevich, A., Roberts, J., Northey, M., Darcy, L., & Macke, J. (2018) Future of schools, Arup. Retrieved December 15, 2022, from https://www.arup.com/perspectives/publications/research/section/future-of-schools

Kozleski, E. B. (2020, August). Disrupting what passes as inclusive education: Predicating educational equity on schools designed for all. *The Educational Forum, 84*(4), 340–355.

Kravtsov, G., & Kravtsova, E. (2011) The cultural-historical basis of the 'Golden Key' program. *International Journal of Early Years Education, 19*(1), 27–34.

Lave, J., & Wenger, E. (1991). *Situated learning*. Cambridge University Press.

Lee, J. (2017). Curriculum reform and supporting structures at schools: Challenges for life skills planning for secondary school students in China (with particular reference to Hong Kong). *Educational Research for Policy and Practice, 16*(1), 61–75.

Leite, C., Fernandes, P., & Figueiredo, C. (2018). Challenges of curricular contextualisation: teachers' perspectives. *The Australian Educational Researcher, 45*(4), 435–453.

Lightbown, P., & Spada, N. (2020). Teaching and learning L2 in the classroom: It's about time. *Language Teaching, 53*(4), 422–432.

Love, R. (2018). Taking it slow: Enhancing wellbeing through philosophy for children. In E. Duthie, F. G. Moriyón, & R. R. Loro (Eds.), *Parecidos de familia. Propuestas actuales en Filosofía para Niños. Family resemblances. Current trends in philosophy for children* (pp. 105–117). Anaya.

Malcolm, A. (2020). Heads of alternative provision: Committed to realising young peoples' potential in an unregulated market. *International Journal of Inclusive Education, 24*(5), 513–526.

Mamas, C., & Avramidis, E. (2013). Promoting social interaction in the inclusive classroom: Lessons from inclusive schools in England and Cyprus. *Learning, Culture and Social Interaction, 2*(4), 217–226.

McGregor, G., & Mills, M. (2012). Alternative education sites and marginalised young people: 'I wish there were more schools like this one'. *International Journal of Inclusive Education, 16*(8), 843–862.

Mcneill, E. (2020). Immigration stories in the emergent bilingual classroom: Revealing funds of knowledge and brave spaces through literacy curriculum, Doctoral dissertation at Indiana University.

Morgan, H. (2014). Review of research: The education system in Finland: A success story other countries can emulate. *Childhood Education*, *90*(6), 453–457.

Nelson, P., Segall, A., & Durham, B. (2021). Between aspiration and reality: New materialism and social studies education. *Theory & Research in Social Education*, *49*(3), 449–476.

Niemi, K. (2021). 'The best guess for the future?' Teachers' adaptation to open and flexible learning environments in Finland. *Education Inquiry*, *12*(3), 282–300.

Niemi, R., & Kiilakoski, T. (2020). "I learned to cooperate with my friends and there were no quarrels": Pupils' experiences of participation in a multidisciplinary learning module. *Scandinavian Journal of Educational Research*, *64*(7), 984–998.

Oudes-Slob, L., Dobber, M., van der Veen, C., & van Oers, B. (2022). Developmental Education in Dutch primary schools: Review of research outcomes from a CHAT-based teaching approach. *Learning, Culture and Social Interaction*, *32*, 100596.

Power, S., Newton, N., & Taylor, C. (2020). 'Successful futures' for all in Wales? The challenges of curriculum reform for addressing educational inequalities. *The Curriculum Journal*, *31*(2), 317–333.

Raposa, E., Rhodes, J., Stams, G., Card, N., Burton, S., Schwartz, S., Sykes, L, Kanchewa, S., Kupersmidt, J., & Hussain, S. (2019). The effects of youth mentoring programs: A meta-analysis of outcome studies. *Journal of Youth and Adolescence*, *48*(3), 423–443.

Riele, K. (2007). Educational alternatives for marginalised youth. *The Australian Educational Researcher*, *34*(3), 53–68.

Rix, J (2007). Labels of opportunity – A response to Carson and Rowley, *Ethical Space: The International Journal of Communication Ethics*, *4*(3), 25–27.

Rix, J. (2009). Statutory assessment of the class? Supporting the additional needs of the learning context. *International Journal of Inclusive Education*, *13*(3), 253 – 272.

Rix, J. (2015). *Must inclusion be special? Rethinking educational support within a community of provision*. Routledge.

Rix, J. (2023). Re-examining special needs – What could be better? In R. J. Tierney, F. Rizvi, & K. Erkican (Eds.), *International encyclopedia of education* (Vol. 9). Elsevier.

Rix, J., & Matthews, A. (2014). Viewing the child as a participant within context, *Disability and Society*, *29*(9), 1428–1442.

Rix, J., & Twining, P. (2007). Exploring education systems: Towards a typology for future learning?. *Educational Research*, *49*(4), 329–341.

Rogoff, B., Matusov, E., & White, C. (1998). Models of teaching and learning: Participation in a community of learners. In D. Olson & N. Torrance (Eds.), *The handbook of education and human development: New models of learning, teaching and schooling* (pp. 373–398). Blackwell.

Rosa, L., & Menezes, A. (2019). Educational inclusion and social interaction: A literature review. *Trends in Psychology*, *27*, 385–400.

Ryan, A., Tocci, C., & Moon, S. (2020). How Do We Know What Students Have Learned?. In A. Ryan, C. Tocci, & S. Moon (Eds.), *The Curriculum Foundations Reader* (pp. 143–162). Palgrave Macmillan.

Saltmarsh, S., Chapman, A., Campbell, M., & Drew, C. (2015). Putting "structure within the space": Spatially un/responsive pedagogic practices in open-plan learning environments. *Educational Review*, *67*(3), 315–327.

Sinnema, C., Nieveen, N., & Priestley, M. (2020). Successful futures, successful curriculum: What can Wales learn from international curriculum reforms?. *The Curriculum Journal, 31*(2), 181–201.

Skinner, R., & Chapman, C. (1999). *Service-learning and community service in K-12 public schools.* National Center for Education Statistics.

Strogilos, V., & Stefanidis, A. (2015). Contextual antecedents of co-teaching efficacy: Their influence on students with disabilities' learning progress, social participation and behaviour improvement. *Teaching and Teacher Education, 47,* 218–229.

Sundby, A., & Karseth, B. (2022). 'The knowledge question' in the Norwegian curriculum. *The Curriculum Journal, 33*(3), 427–442.

Symeonidou, S. (2019). Disability, the arts and the curriculum: Is there common ground? *European Journal of Special Needs Education, 34*(1), 50–65.

Te Kete Ipurangi. (2023) Te Whariki Online, accessed from https://tewhariki.tki.org.nz/en/early-childhood-curriculum/ on April 20, 2023.

Teszenyi, E. (2023). Exploring features of multi-age practice and adult-child interactions: A case study from Hungary, Doctoral dIssertation, the Open University.

Titley, E., Davies, A., & Atherton, S. (2020). '[It] isn't designed to be assessed how we assess': Rethinking assessment for qualification in the context of the implementation of the curriculum for Wales. *The Curriculum Journal, 31*(2), 303–316.

Torres-Harding, S., Baber, A., Hilvers, J., Hobbs, N., & Maly, M. (2018). Children as agents of social and community change: Enhancing youth empowerment through participation in a school-based social activism project. *Education, citizenship and social justice, 13*(1), 3–18.

Twining, P. (2020). Do you need an ATAR to get into Uni? halfbaked.education blog, November 13, 2020. https://halfbaked.education/do-you-need-an-atar/

Twining, P., Rix, J., & Sheehy, K. (2016). *Developing point of learning: An innovative approach to enhancing professional learning.* Imagine Education.

Van Dam, L., Smit, D., Wildschut, B., Branje, S., Rhodes, J., Assink, M., & Stams, G. (2018). Does natural mentoring matter? A multilevel meta-analysis on the association between natural mentoring and youth outcomes. *American journal of community psychology, 62*(1–2), 203–220.

van der Veen, C., Dobber, M., & van Oers, B. (2016). Implementing dynamic assessment of vocabulary development as a trialogical learning process: A practice of teacher support in primary education schools. *Language Assessment Quarterly, 13*(4), 329–340.

van der Veen, C., & Wolbert, L. (2014). Human flourishing in developmental education schools: A collaborative project perspective. *Collaborative Projects: An Interdisciplinary Study* (p. 336). Brill

van Groll, N., & Fraser, H. (2022). "Watch out for their home!": Disrupting extractive forest pedagogies in early childhood education. *Journal of Childhood Studies, 47*(3), 47–53.

Vesterinen, O., Kangas, M., Krokfors, L., Kopisto, K., & Salo, L. (2017). Interprofessional pedagogical collaboration between teachers and their out-of-school partners. *Educational Studies, 43*(2), 231–242.

Volman, M. (2021). The effects of using students' funds of knowledge on educational outcomes in the social and personal domain. *Learning, Culture and Social Interaction, 28,* 100472.

Woolley, H., Armitage, M., Bishop, J., Curtis, M., & Ginsborg, J. (2006). Going outside together: Good practice with respect to the inclusion of disabled children in primary school playgrounds. *Children's Geographies, 4*(3), 303–318.

8

WHAT DOES IT TAKE TO EMBRACE? PART 2 – BEING A-PART

You know I am right (?)

A few years ago, I was observing practice in a primary classroom. After the lesson I passed on the following observation to the teacher:

At the end of the whiteboard session, you asked which of the sentence components – Nouns, Adverbs and Verbs – are connected together. A young lad said: "They all are" and you said to him quite abruptly, "If you are not going to give sensible answers, I am not going to want to ask you." and he went puce with embarrassment. Of course his answer was right ... it was just not the answer you were looking for.

The teacher concerned never responded to my feedback. Perhaps she did not feel the need to. She was highly regarded by the school community. She exuded confidence and reassurance. This high regard for her pedagogic knowledge was evident in her leading the way in the school's use of assessment for learning. However, the certainty she felt for this process created a profound barrier of which she was not (apparently) aware.

I feel I can say this because of the way she made use of an accessible PowerPoint version of *The Iron Woman* by Ted Hughes, across a six-week period of study. I had created this (following her enthusiastic agreement) with my son (a non-verbal child) and other struggling readers in mind, because the story was otherwise only available in its dense text form. Every page of the PowerPoint had a series of pictures, a few key words from the text and sometimes a bit of animation or audio. All you had to do was click and explore. However, even though this teacher made this PowerPoint

DOI: 10.4324/9781003281405-8

available to the whole class (and told me how much a group of young boys loved it), she would not let the non-verbal child (my son) use it. This was because she did not believe he would understand it. So, following (her interpretation of) assessment for learning and understanding of development she had simplified the story to a printed-out sequencing exercise and would only let him use the accessible PowerPoint when he could sequence the first six slides. Needless to say, he was not interested in this activity and by the time he had done it to her satisfaction, the class had moved on to something else. As a consequence, her need to assess for learning and her certainty in her knowledge about development had served to discourage that learning and left one very bored and isolated child at the (metaphorical) back of the class.

[Actually, the bank of computers were are the back of the class, so that was where the enthusiastic group of boys were engaging with the in/accessible PowerPoint.]

In this book, I have been trying to show how so much of what we seek is based upon our embrace with a yearning for and belief in something which is unattainable, CERTAINTY. Of course, there are plenty of (wise?) people who are in such an embrace who recognise that it is unattainable. They recognise that they are simply getting as close to the certain as possible, but our systems are full of people whose wisdom is in other arenas. They frequently accept the expressed views/policies/practices of knowledgeable others, views/policies/practices which have the appearance of being based upon an underlying 'truth'.

This is an embrace in which we find (and recreate) ourselves.

It is the space in which we (currently?) identify:

what we value

      what it is to educate

           our teaching/learning/support.

FIGURE 8.1 It must make sense.

I have also tried to show that there is another embrace. In the multiple worlds of education, we are not only in (an) embrac/e/ed/ing with certainty but also with uncertainty. We are enclosed and enfolded by the things that will not work and will not be done.

We cannot change how everyone thinks; we cannot get everyone to agree; we cannot force people to change their practice; we cannot deliver training that meets everyone's priorities; we cannot make people learn what we want them to learn; we cannot create a curriculum that covers all that people might want us to teach; we cannot assess and group people consistently and equitably; we cannot have an evidence base for every eventuality; we cannot expect any approach we devise to be delivered with fidelity. We cannot rely on relying on anything.

There is perhaps only one (fairly obvious?) certainty. We are in (uncertain) socio-cultural-environmental relationships.

However, this means there are some things we can control to a greater degree than others. We can create rules about all kinds of things; we can create requirements about measurable aspects of our systems; we can change what we fund; we can change the resources we provide; we can change what we ask people to do with their time. We can alter our structures and means of support.

Seeking an uncertain future?

Throughout the previous chapters, I have made links to a variety of theoretical positions which I recognise as being ontologically and epistemologically rooted in uncertainty. I have made mention of critical theories, indigenous theories, post-humanist/materialist theories, trans- theories and socio-cultural theories as well as ideas such as inclusion, decolonisation, participation, 21st-century skills, collaboration, all of which are generally framed around fundamental uncertainty within our relational existence. There are bound to be other approaches I could mention in this list (or which I failed to incorporate into the overall text), but I have endeavoured to show the weight of thinking which should push us towards creating systems that work with this uncertainty rather than against it.

As I suggested in Chapter 7, there are many practices which are evident in countries around the world that draw upon the relational nature of learning. However, all systems maintain an (unhealthy?) tension with certainty. For example, in 2020 in Finland, in a system which claims to be comprehensive and advocates a learning community model, 9% of children were identified for special support, over 40% of whom received all education either in a special school (there are more than 60) or in one of the many special groups or classes in the general system (Statistics Finland, 2021). The Czech Republic is a recent convert to inclusion, but only 67% of pupils officially identified with special educational needs are educated in 'inclusive' settings (EASNIE, 2020). England is a system with a complex educational market place, with Free Schools and Academies unchained from the national curriculum but where special school numbers have grown by over 20% since 2011 (Selfe & Richmond, 2020). The number of special schools in Ireland has grown in recent years too (over 140 when I last looked) and nearly 25% of the school population have been identified with special educational needs, many of whom are in special classes despite a range of policies advocating for inclusion (Kenny et al., 2020); while Italy may have shut the vast majority of their special schools, but it maintained a strong diagnostic approach, with over 26% of disabled children spending more than 50% of their time out of the mainstream class (Anastasiou et al., 2015) and when I last looked more than 5% were out all the time (Rix, 2015).

Everywhere I have read about, visited or researched separates learners into mainstream and additional support groupings based around an evaluation of the childrens' abilities. Similarly, everywhere would seem to have graded school leaving qualifications, based around defined subject areas. The vast majority also have exams and assessments at various intervals in a student's life, while more than 90 countries undertake regular testing as part of the Programme for International Student Assessment (PISA), which measures 15-year-olds' reading, mathematics and science knowledge and skills. This is before we reach all those other locally defined traditional school constructs (around such things as dress, behaviour, language, hierarchy, school inspection and so forth) that are endemic and hugely variable across (and within) nations.

These are however practices that policymakers and administrators can control and so can do something about. They involve rules, requirements and resources; they are connected to our structures and means of support. If they look around the globe, as is evident from Chapter 7, the models are there to frame alternative ways of doing things. It is only in the area of assessing and funding support that is deemed additional that we need to try new ways of doing things. And if we wish to do this, we seem to have a couple of options:

(Not an) Option 1

We could establish two systems, one still seeking certainty and the other working with notions of uncertainty. This would require us to embrace such a two-stream approach, placing equal systemic value upon the outputs of both systems, so that it is not a hierarchical two-tier option between 'traditional' and 'innovative'. This would seem a possible solution, both as a model for funding and for curricula. However, from the outset there would need to be buy-in from the users of the current certainty outcomes (e.g., employers and universities). This would be necessary to ensure equivalent access to employment and education and to ensure people coming out of systems premised upon (probably) certainty were not automatically valued/rewarded more highly. Otherwise, such a dual system would still venerate the traditional above the innovative and replicate the current dualities of mainstream/special, academic/vocational, regular/alternative or private/public. Perhaps, I should have more confidence, but I am doubtful that such a two-track system would deliver equivalence in life opportunities any time soon. More likely it would perpetuate existing social divisions. It would leave in place what already is and continue to rely upon all those things we cannot rely upon.

Option 2

We seek a shift in emphasis within the current system. One that embraces ideas of uncertainty but is premised upon relatively simple reconfigurations alongside an acceptance that the voice of certainty is not going to go away. It does require two fundamental points of agreement, though. They are:

- a recognition that the current emphasis upon certainty is at the heart of much inequality in our school system,
- a recognition that we are not taking best advantage of the challenges and opportunities of uncertainty.

Consequently, to create new possibilities, we must find ways to rebalance structures and practices based upon certainty with those based upon uncertainty.

Figure 8.2 is my attempt to show how/why this might work.

The left-hand side of the picture (and/or stage right to fans of uncertainty) shows the system as it currently is. The model of uncertainty has plenty of advocates, but their ideas meet the inherent resistance of a fixed position within the model of certainty. As has been discussed in earlier chapters, this is major contributor to profoundly unequal educational experiences and outcomes. If we wish to move towards a more equitable/socially just/effective education system, however, we can recognise the primacy of uncertainty and that the model of certainty can act as a powerful influence in the asking of questions and seeking perspectives. Such a shift would allow the model of certainty to be a key, prioritised perspective within the overall 'model of uncertainty'. It would be acknowledged as a valued and reliable perspective, but the 'model of uncertainty' would no longer be marginalised. Our systems would be open to emergent, often bottom-up, processes and practices and (hopefully) more relevant to their context.

In previous chapters, I have suggested processes such as labels of opportunity, class-funding models, a focus upon social interactions and education passports alongside communities of learners, open learning spaces, peer support, community service, action research, thematic working, co-teaching, mentoring and funds of knowledge. If these are allied to an open curriculum

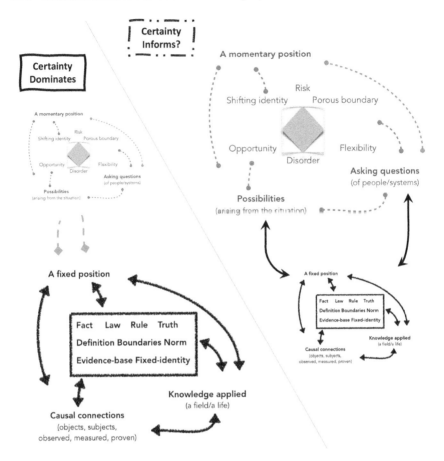

FIGURE 8.2 Seeking a rebalance.

and emergent assessment, many might fear that the system would be unbounded and chaotic, without goals to motivate and guide learning and behaviour. This is missing the point, however. The key trigger to this shift would not be about delivering the things we cannot control but rather the things we can. It would be about changing the required outcomes at the end of education and changing how we identify and fund support needs. All the rest can stay in place. We still need all those subject experts, specialists and therapists (for example), but the systems (rules and requirements) are not asking them to focus upon predetermined outputs but to be part of the processes which are outcomes in themselves. They can focus far less upon material for a particular exam or assessment or the formal recording of needs. They will need to have the time and space to be part of the conversations from which collective agreement can occur. Our system will need to recognise the primacy of enabling such resources (as well as using others such as people's knowledge and experience, our surrounding environment and available technologies).

I am sure to some readers, what I am suggesting is tantamount to a complete system transformation of the kind that inclusionists have been advocating for many years. I am less sure about this though. I think it just requires us to encourage a movement which is already underway. It is in many ways, about embracing the (obvious?) next steps. In some systems – which have perhaps already taken a step away from a predetermined curriculum or moved towards one which is competence based – the next step may seem smaller than for others. But maybe not. Different cultures come with different resources, priorities and experiences, and will have to deal with different vested interests. But when we begin with where people are, we need to start with the things we can influence. It is very likely that there will be many practitioners, parents, learners and administrators in many communities who will be drawn back to the traditional grammars. However, if we make those changes to the rules and regulations, it will not be required of them. The possibility will be there. The chances of another way will be close at hand and in evidence. More importantly (perhaps), entry into adulthood will not be dependent upon them in the same way.

Participating in uncertainty

In Chapter 7, I suggested that the *while* of participation is entwined with every aspect of a community of provision. If we are to embrace uncertainty in the ways I have mentioned, we need to consider how this challenge manifests itself in practice. For example, if we are to introduce a learning passport system (for want of a better term):

> We will need to reflect upon how this will be governed. We will need explore how we oversee the maintenance of quality and the support of their delivery, as well as where responsibility lies for their production, how this is organised, where they will be used and who will use them. We will need to ensure that we engage with young people, teachers, administrators, employers, universities and other potential end users in responding to these challenges, providing support to ensure that any particular view is not allowed to overly dominate when deciding the function and management of the procedures. This will require that the processes involved in organising, producing, and using these passports ensures they are of value to these participants, representing them in ways they recognise and are accessible to other users, enabling learning moments to be clearly evidenced and further supported. We will need to consider the nature of the languages we use in defining their form and function, how these effects the ways in which passports may represent lives. We will have

to also explore how our overarching functions can constrain and enable the role of people in using and supporting others to use these documents. We will need to explore how our practices of governance and the spaces they utilise enable relationships between the participants, as well as considering to what degree these systems allow for flexibility or constrain people as result of issues of time or tedium.

Such a complex weave is bound to create conflicts between the different priorities of those involved. They are sure, too, to produce compromise decisions which are unsatisfactory to many of those involved. We will also need to be considering the development of the learning passports from the other five perspectives of the community of provision. We will (at the least?) need to consider how we use the passports to enable participation in learning, how we support their use, the roles of those involved, their understandings and values, as well the nature of the spaces in which all these relationships emerge, and we will need to have conversations about all these while recognising that they too are operating within the *while* of participation.

All of this may feel as unwieldy as the most complex paperwork processes designed by certainty. But such a process is not one which is being constantly started anew. It is about establishing a process which is open to change, which is not fixed but allows for flexible usage, so that it suits: a person who needs a great deal of intensive support, as well as a highly academic scholar or a lover of craft or a person who wants to work in social support, an 8-year-old, a 16-year-old, a 45-year-old and so on and on. It needs to encourage learning experiences that will help that individual build, maintain and share their lives, as well as for others to support and shape those experiences. It will also need to be accessible to the person who produces it and the people who want to use it, to give others the best opportunity to understand the person, their strengths and possibilities in as equitable way as possible. Yet, this does not seem that tall an order. If you have ever sat down with a national curriculum document, it is quite clear we can take a hugely complex range of ideas and goals and weave them together. Coming up with a way to represent a life in a way that feels right to the person at the centre of that life is relatively straightforward in comparison, particularly if that representation is understood to be our momentary position.

Take a chance on we?

Of course, at the heart of all this are risks. By participating within the community of provision, we are involved in relational interactions involving space, materials, beings and institutions, the tangible and intangible, concepts and feelings, cultures and identities. It is in the now, from before now and feeding into after now. It is slippery and full of hope; it is about disappointment and feelings of ambivalence; it is about establishing things which need constant re-attending. To work (together) in such a situation requires us to trust. This is what the search for certainty feels like it is delivering. It feels as if we can rely upon the boundaried things with which we are working. However, to participate in the recognition of uncertainty requires that we trust in a different way; we take the risk of trusting less in the past and more in the moment we are in. We are putting this trust in the relationships much more than on the traditions of institutions and our predetermined notions of what is required.

This presents challenges to the perspectives of (arising from) (giving rise to) our communities of provision and many of the established/dominant ways of doing things. All/most countries will have established government departments with relevant legislation, funding mechanisms, inspection regimes, codes of practice, national curriculum, teacher training mechanisms, local administrations and so forth. There will also be well-established structures such as exam boards, assessment centres, home visiting and support services as well as policies around issues such as collaboration, leadership, ownership and oversight which reflect local values and ways of doing things. By their nature, these are institutionalised, serving as regular functions that reduce the need to reorganise or explain to others. These institutions are not only in the embrace of certainty, but it is from them that so much of the certainty permeates throughout the rest of the community. [As we have discussed earlier, many countries have made changes from this perspective, embracing uncertainty to some degree, in particular by having a more open curriculum. However, they have also maintained controls that have undermined this].

To make the most of the opportunities which an open curriculum offers, people within the community of provision need to take risks from the perspectives of support and strategies; in particular, what this support involves, when, where and how it takes place. From a staffing perspective, though this requires people to step into the territory which we cannot control. Many members of the community will be eager to open up their practice, but many will feel constrained by their beliefs and established ways of being. Telling people to deliver evidence-based practice and build up their knowledge base is not going to deliver this openness. As with so much in this book, this is not a huge step into the unknown, though. This requires a more trusting embrace with such things as action research, communities of practice and cultures of enquiry. We need to risk allowing teachers and the whole community of provision to explore their own practice, to develop the strategies and support that learners benefit from.

Basing our strategies and support upon a community's exploration of practice (obviously?) requires not only a shift in expectations from a system perspective but will also be facilitated by the shift in opening up our assessment processes. From a staffing perspective, we should have greater access to a range of professionals who currently sit on the edge of the system evaluating struggling learners or delivering training courses. To engage effectively with each other, we do not need to adopt highly funded teacher education models (such as Finland) or seek to replicate the rigour of (gold standard?) highly funded researchers (though we could be proactive and work more closely with university researchers and other community networks, if we wanted to). This is about taking a risk on conversation. It is about believing people are best placed to understand what is possible in the contexts in which they find themselves, drawing upon collective understandings. Such conversations are harder of course, in smaller communities or if we are faced with a very unusual situation, but this is an issue of people as resources. This is something which we can do something about, particularly given the ongoing development of communication technologies.

Another risk goes to the centre of our ideas of special, and the need for additional time and space for particular learners. In many systems, there is already a move (back) towards more open-plan learning spaces, to allow for more flexible approaches from the perspectives of staffing, systems and strategies. The risk is not about investing in building such spaces, however; it is about how we see the spaces we have. This is about the space between people and between groups; it is about our boundaries and it is about how we create and police them. Of course, I am now entering a realm we cannot control. We cannot rely on changing the ways in which people view others. The best we can hope for (perhaps) is that they:

- see what is possible in the actions of those around them.
- are willing to risk new ways of doing things because they see that the constraints of certainty have been lifted (and they don't need to hold onto them quite so tightly?).

However, even without an expectation of change, by bringing together this open approach to spaces with the open curriculum + bottom-up assessment + conversations about practice, we create new opportunities, not only about the nature of support but also about how to understand the learners within those spaces. It is within this space that we can take the risk to reimagine the nature of additionality.

An act of imagination

I often wonder how it would have been for my son in a system like the one I have been discussing. My belief is that he could have had more power in this space, with the possibility of having his ideas, priorities and interests better supported. I reckon he could have learned more about the world, our cultures and our everyday lives, he could have had more opportunities to relate to those around him, express his ideas and identity and could have found the experience more directly relevant to who he was *becoming*. I think there could have been far more opportunity for people to adapt to his communication needs and preferences. I reckon these people could have had more time to be flexible, to develop practices and to use spaces that allowed for a great many more commonalities to emerge between him and his peers, as well as opportunities for collaboration. I imagine that his participation could have been a far more positive experience (in a system like the one I have been discussing). I imagine it could have been for his sister too. And me. And the vast swathes I have mentioned in this book who experience marginalisation in systems seeking certainty.

Of course, could is not would.

It is a risk we'd have to take.

Coming to an uncertain end

I don't know how to finish this book.

My thoughts have found nowhere to settle.

Writing is like that (I find).

This moment is situated

In a whole bevvy of cultural, social, political, economic and environmental considerations.

In this moment

FIGURE 8.3   Making sense.

> I find myself embraced by the need to complete this work,
> having sat here for 42 minutes (or more),
> prevaricating.
> I have played with my notes.
> I have cut, I have pasted.
> I have typed.
> I have deleted.
> Then I got up
> I made tea. I ate chocolate.
> I ate nuts.
> (Even reflecting briefly on some of their cultural, social, political, economic and environmental considerations).
> I could not embrace the moment, but it held me.
> And then I decided to begin no matter what.
> I took a risk on a line that was going nowhere.
> And now I am here and this feels right.
> This is a moment of everyday learning.

Like it or not we are in the embrace of what is expected of us. But that does not mean we always embrace it back. A great deal of the time I hated being a child at school. I much preferred being a teacher. What does this say about the underlying tensions inherent in my participation? I only ever had the power to disrupt when I was a young one. My voice was silenced. I was supported to be what someone else wanted me to be. As a teacher, I was supported to support others. I was listened to (when I said I wanted to hear the young people I was supporting).

I felt included (in school) far more as an adult than I ever did as a child.

Which brings me to the poem – which I decided to leave for quite a few reasons. Mainly:

- Because I can.
- Because it is a risk.
- Because I want the reader to see themselves in the moment.
- Because it feels free not to follow the plan.
- Because so often we value the outputs of our learning for the wrong reasons.
- Because it made me remember this story.

When I was on teaching practice in 1981 (in a Coventry comprehensive), I asked the boys (no girls in that school) to write a poem for homework. The next lesson they all brought their pieces of writing in and (some) enthusiastically handed them to me. I handed them back. There was some tension in the air. 'They are for you', I said. The next week I gave them the same homework, and most of them did not bother. But I kept on giving them this homework at least once a week. I was at the school for two and a half months. By the end of my time there, a good many of the young people had (quietly) informed me that they had read a poem (or more) (that they had written) to friends or family.

Learning is a different embrace to education (and to school?).

Learning is dynamic and fluid. It is fundamental to being alive. It is about exploring and understanding within relationships, through relationships and about (...well, probably, metaphorically at least?) relationships. It is a space for not knowing, for knowing a bit and knowing a bit more. Learning is about opening up and being vulnerable to the risk of what may come your way. It is not linear. It is never quite as expected. It is about finding out something new or afresh. Otherwise, it is not learning.

Teaching is the support of this process of learning. It is to be The catalyst. The mediator. The provocateur. The guide. The questioner. The answerer. The sounding board. The fellow traveller. It is the partner of learning. To teach is an attempt to offer something that requires an act of receiving.

To teach and to be taught is to open ourselves up to possibility.

This learning/teaching partnership can be very mundane, almost at the level of observation. But at its peak it is about a shared embrace. We are together; we are apart; we are part of a moment together – participants in the *while*.

This is what (I believe) our communities of provision should be trying to enable. We are looking for dynamic, fluid processes, structures and practices. We are looking to create boundaries that can constantly shift. We are seeking to allow people to use their imagination and creativity, but allowing for not everyone being able to or wishing to. We are recognising that to achieve such things we have to open up the space to share what we have and what we can do, so that our support can be much more than the sum of our parts. We need to focus upon social relationships, to understand the importance of supporting the vulnerable, and accept that we are enacting our ethics of being.

Yet, school is education. It is an institution. It serves a sorting function and social control role. It is full of the tradition. School is as it is, not a simple matter of learning and teaching. It lives right here, right now. This is why it is hard to argue with people who fight for separate space when the universal provision does not provide the kind of experience they feel is necessary for themselves or their child. It is no good telling them that it can improve or that statistics show that their choice is not as good. A person's inclusion (should that be their experience) is a by-product of their participation. It is a type of participation. (*Inclusion is being a part but not being apart? Inclusion is being a part because you can be apart?*). It is what it is when it is. Yet it is where we are, together.

Making our school experience(s) better (more equitable?) requires taking a bigger risk together, where relationships can guide us.

All of which brings us around in a circle.

It has us staring at the screen/space/person/material-being/emptiness wondering what comes next. I have shown how the dominant discourses about educational practices are framed around notions of certainty, while numerous research examples suggest that it is uncertainty that arises. I have tried to lay out the nature of participation and how this is a constant ebb and flow between those involved and between its tensions, outcomes and practicalities. I have suggested ways in which these issues of participation, when allied either to the search for certainty or an acceptance of uncertainty, can play out across the perspectives of the communities of provision (which work together to provide learning and support for all children and young people within their locality). I have tried to explain the need to take a step into the unknown, to be open to the risk of failure (can you risk success?) across all these perspectives.

I feel the embrace, the being embraced, the embracing of these ideas. I recognise that I want you to feel this triadic moment too. I want us to do this together. I want us to confront the boundaries and borders we create/recreate in our search for educational certainty. These both define and contain us, keeping us in separation, holding us back from embracing the disorganisation of our everyday *becomings*. In seeking a better education (one in which people have a greater sense of participation, out of which their inclusion can arise), we can (or is it should?) focus upon creating greater possibilities for learning. Up until now, we have ensured our failure by keeping the voices of uncertainty in the background. If we wish to create the new, to create a space which is both open to the universal and the additional, which is better suited to the endless diversity of being, then it is time to trust ourselves more.

References

Anastasiou, D., Kauffman, J., & Di Nuovo, S. (2015). Inclusive education in Italy: Description and reflections on full inclusion. *European Journal of Special Needs Education*, 30(4), 429–443.

European Agency for Special Needs and Inclusive Education (EASNIE) (2020). Czech Republic Data. https://www.european-agency.org/data/czech-republic/datatable-overview#tab-official_decision_on_sen_v3

Kenny, N., McCoy, S., & Mihut, G. (2020). Special education reforms in Ireland: Changing systems, changing schools. *International Journal of Inclusive Education*, 1–20.

Rix, J. (2015). *Must inclusion be special?: Rethinking educational support within a community of provision*. Routledge.

Selfe, L., & Richmond, R. (2020). *A review of policy in the field of special needs and inclusive education since the 1990s*. SEN Policy Forum, Department for Education.

Statistics Finland. (2021). https://www.stat.fi/til/erop/2020/erop_2020_2021-06-08_tie_001_en.html

INDEX

194 Index

Printed and bound by CPI Group (UK) Ltd, Croydon, CR0 4YY

27/09/2024

01038769-0001